W. E. Biederwolf

History of the One Hundred and sixty-first Regiment

Indiana Volunteer Infantry

W. E. Biederwolf

History of the One hundred and sixty-first Regiment
Indiana Volunteer Infantry

ISBN/EAN: 9783337059798

Printed in Europe, USA, Canada, Australia, Japan

Cover: Foto ©ninafisch / pixelio.de

More available books at **www.hansebooks.com**

HISTORY

OF THE

One Hundred and Sixty-first

REGIMENT

INDIANA VOLUNTEER INFANTRY

By

W. E. BIEDERWOLF

CHAPLAIN OF THE REGIMENT

1899:
WILSON, HUMPHREYS & CO.
LOGANSPORT, IND.

Dedication.

To the
Men who Carried the Guns
this Work
is Sincerely Dedicated
by their friend,
The Chaplain.

PREFACE.

A preface is not an apology; a book that needs an apology ought never be written. Every man of a regiment is a part of its life, and to be a soldier is an experience that comes to most men but once and makes an important chapter in the history of every man thus privileged. Who, that was there, can ever forget the life we led together; our camps, our marches, our reviews, the life of a day and the evening till taps! These will be remembered without a written history, but there are offices which only a written record can fulfill; that of acquainting the regiment's friends with the history so familiar to its members and of furnishing exact historical and numerical data, the value of which increases with time, and the perusal of which, when memory is less distinct, will make it all happen again as it did in '98 and '99. The preparation of such a work is no easy task, and all the more difficult when the author has kept no diary or chronicle of events. The information herein contained has been gathered from every available source, but every detail fully verified before giving it place in these pages. For the hearty co-operation of his fellow officers the fullest appreciation is here expressed by him who has undertaken this work. Some have rendered a material aid without which the present value of the book would have been impossible. Special acknowledgment is due to Lieutenant Goodrich for his share in the preparation of the Savannah chapter, and to Dr. George B. Jones for like service in the section devoted to the medical department. Special thanks are also due to Captain

W. T. Stott and to Lieutenants Patton, Welch and Owens, and also to Private E. M. Blake of Company K.

In producing the company roster such as adhered to the form given them will show first the original roster in so far as promotions would allow, it being equally desirable to present in due form the roll of officers as they appeared at the date of mustering out. Where cuts are missing, it is simply because parties failed to furnish them after repeated solicitation, or because they were not to be had, which was the case with several among the dead. A few photos were poor, but the best possible was done with them. With the hope that this volume will bring pleasant reminders to all it is sent to press.

       W. E. BIEDERWOLF,
         Chaplain 161st I. V. I.
Monticello, Indiana, June 1, 1899.

INDEX.

Chapter I—Organization	17
Chapter II—Camp Mount	23
Chapter III—En Route to Jacksonville	48
Chapter IV—Camp Cuba Libre, August 14, '98–September 30, '98	60
Chapter V—Camp Cuba Libre, October 1-23, '98	78
Chapter VI—Camp Onward	91
Chapter VII—Havana to Camp Columbia	115
Chapter VIII—Camp Columbia, December 17, '98–January 31, '99	125
Chapter IX—Camp Columbia, February 1, '99–March 31, '99	151
Chapter X—The Departure, Voyage and Arrival	182
Chapter XI—Mustering Out Month, Camp Homeward	193
First Battalion—K, M, A, E	231
Second Battalion—B, I, F, D	287
Third Battalion—C, G, H, L	345
Medical Department	405
History of the Medical Department	410
Regimental Band	425
Roster of Regimental Band	428
Organization of Regimental Band	429
Bugle and Drum Corps	431
Roster of Bugle and Drum Corps	431
Roll of Honor	435
History of Company A	263
Roster of Company A	267
History of Company B	294
Roster of Company B	298
History of Company C	353
Roster of Company C	360
History of Company D	333
Roster of Company D	339
History of Company E	275
Roster of Company E	281
History of Company F	320
Roster of Company F	324
History of Company G	369
Roster of Company G	375
History of Company H	383
Roster of Company H	385

History of Company I... 306
Roster of Company I... 311
History of Company K.. 239
Roster of Company K... 241
History of Company L.. 396
Roster of Company L... 398
History of Company M.. 250
Roster of Company M... 255

PORTRAITS AND ILLUSTRATIONS.

Anderson, James L... 393
Anheire, Anthony A.. 304
Backus, Victor M.. 232
Biederwolf, William E... 225
Brown, Denver... 444
Brunt, John R... 222
Buchanan, Richard W... 331
Caldwell, George H.. 383
Crooker, William W.. 273
Comstock, Paul.. 317
Cosby, Charles E.. 335
Dexter, Jacob W... 447
Dority, Charles E... 395
Drapier, William H.. 319
Durbin, Winfield T.. 216
Durbin, Fletcher M.. 262
Durbin, W. T., and Staff.. 21
Espey, James E.. 417
Everson, Charles.. 447
Fitch, George W... 249
Fortune, James W.. 272
Gerrish, Millard F.. 408
Goodrich, George E.. 350
Gould, Andrew... 450
Graham, Alonzo M.. 449
Guthrie, William.. 303
Gwinn, James M.. 380
Hudgins, Thomas J... 349
Jackson, Cyrus A.. 332
Johnson, August H. W.. 261

Kepperling, George... 443
Kimmel, Elmer E... 318
Kuns, Clarence D... 441
Lewis, John J.. 440
Megrew, Harold C.. 288
Menzies, Winston.. 290
Meyers, James I... 368
Mount, James A.. 44
McCauley, Edward A... 274
Ogborn, Albert D.. 366
Olds, Lee M... 346
Owens, Temple H.. 238
Parkhurst, Layton M... 333
Patton, Henry B... 381
Peterson, Eli W.. 394
Pittman, Charles M.. 369
Puhlman, Ernest R... 439
Reynolds, Ivy L.. 352
Saltzgaber, Baird G.. 19
Silverthorne, George M...................................... 260
Smith, Charles C.. 237
Smith, Will M... 322
Smith, Wickliff.. 406
Starr, W. Thompson... 19
Stille, Henry.. 443
Stivers, Wallace D... 442
Stott, Wilfred T... 236
Tichenor, Oliver M.. 220
Trimble, Charles.. 448
Turner, Joseph F.. 446
Ward, John R... 305
Weaver, William G.. 445
Welch, Percy.. 293
West, George A... 248
Williams, Asa E... 292
Williams, Ernest S... 426
Wilson, James... 410

Company A.. 264
    Non-Commissioned Officers.............................. 266

Company B.. 295
    Non-Commissioned Officers.............................. 297

Company C.. 355
    Non-Commissioned Officers.............................. 357

INDEX.

Company D	334
Sergeants	336
Corporals	338
Company E	276
Sergeants	278
Corporals	280
Company F	321
Sergeants	323
Corporals	325
Company G	370
Sergeants	372
Corporals	374
Company H	384
Sergeants	386
Corporals	388
Company I	307
Non-Commissioned Officers	309
Company K	239
Sergeants	242
Corporals	244
Company L	397
Sergeants	399
Corporals	401
Company M	251
Non-Commissioned Officers	253
A Cuban Camp	122
A Mixed Race	146
Backus Garbage Burner	73
Barb Wire Defense	123
Barn—Camp Cuba Libre	65
Bastile—Camp Cuba Libre	229
Block House	124
Bonaventure	104
Bugle and Drum Corps	432
Camp Airing	172
Camp Columbia	139
Company G Street by Moonlight	175
Company Street in Camp Cuba Libre	61
Commissary—Camp Cuba Libre	62
Cuban Plowman	147

INDEX.

Fatigue Duty—Camp Mount	24
Fumigated Gloves	191
Going Aboard Transport "Mobile"	108
Going on Board the "Logan"	185
Government Warehouse at Quemados	169
Graves	437
Guard Mount—Camp Columbia	39
Hangman's Tree	178
Headquarters—Camp Onward	92
Human Bone Yard	160
Kangaroo Court	198
Live Curios	184
"Logan"	186
Medical Officers and Helpers	420
Midway	170
"Mobile"—Off for Cuba	109
Monument	143
Morro Castle	111
Next	176
Off for the Mail	171
Packing Up—Camp Onward	106
Passing in Review—New Year's Day	135
Post Exchange at Camp Onward	83
Prisoners Cleaning Camp	138
Regimental Band	427
Regimental Hospital at Camp Columbia	141
Relieving the Guard—Camp Mount	27
Ruined Estate	148
San Jose Espigon (Wharf)	183
Sea-Sickness on the "Logan"	187
Second Battalion, Skirmish Drill—Camp Cuba Libre	85
Sentinel on Duty—Camp Cuba Libre	71
Soupee! Soupee! Soup! Soup!	136
Storm Scene at Third Division Hospital	79
The Maine Graves	158
The Way Mother Used to Do	137
Vento Springs	167
Wagon Train on its Way to Camp	113
Waiting for the Train—Camp-Breaking at Camp Cuba Libre	89
Wreck of the "Maine"	156

CHAPTER I.

ORGANIZATION.

The war with Spain was on in earnest; Manilla had fallen, several Spanish prizes had been taken at sea, and every preparation was being made for pushing a vigorous campaign into Cuba. Already two hundred thousand troops were in the service of the United States, when President McKinley, on the 25th day of May, 1898, issued a second call for seventy-five thousand more volunteers. Indiana could have furnished them all, but after her other regiments, with companies averaging eighty-six men each, had been recruited to their full quota of one hundred and six men it was her further privilege to furnish one full regiment and an additional two companies of colored men. There was at once the greatest competition and the greatest diligence on the part of influential friends to secure one of the twelve coveted places in the new regiment which, in order, was to be the One Hundred and Sixty-first Indiana Volunteer Infantry. Letters poured in upon the governor from every corner of the state telling of companies formed and ready to move at notice, but desiring to give the congressional districts a somewhat equal representation in this matter the twelve companies now composing the regiment were selected. Of this selection the companies were notified by the governor on the 24th day of June. The original intention of bringing them to the capital, a company at a time, for examination was abandoned as the urgency of the hour demanded that all should come as soon as possible. Accordingly all companies were ordered to repair at once to the state fair-grounds at Indianapolis. The first company, " H," reported at 12:40 June 30. The others in quick order, Company " I" entering the grounds last at 4:30, July 5th.

The man whom Governor Mount had chosen to be colonel was Winfield T. Durbin, of Anderson. He was sitting in the factory of the Diamond Paper Company, of which he was at that time general manager, when he was 'phoned from Indianapolis by Colonel Charles E. Wilson, military secretary to Governor Mount, asking him to come at once to the capital. Upon his arrival he was informed by Secretary Wilson of the governor's desire. It was his first intimation of such a decision and the following day (Sunday) he called at the governor's home and there gave his promise to lead the One Hundred and Sixty-first Indiana to its destiny in the conflict then on.

Doctor Wickliff Smith, of Delphi, was called to the position of surgeon, and Drs. Milliard F. Gerrish, of Seymour, and James Wilson, of Wabash, were chosen assistant surgeons. The surgeons were examined by the State Board of Medical Examinations, Friday, 24th, and were the first of the officers to be mustered into the service (June 25th) as it was essential to begin at once the physical examination of the men. Every man had been required to pass one, and the majority two, similar examinations at the place of his enlistment, but the final and more severe test of acceptance was to be made by the regimental surgeons themselves. The examinations began Tuesday, July 5th, and lasted eleven days, the highest number of men examined in any one day being two hundred and eighty-six. This examination resulted in a further rejection of fourteen per cent. of the men, and gave to the state as sound and as healthy a body of soldiers as ever volunteered their service. The following statistics, taken toward the close of their period of service and read in their presence by the colonel at regimental review, will be of interest and may be appropriately inserted here as the regimental makeup was in general the same throughout its period of service.

The average age was twenty-six. The average height was five feet eight inches. The average weight was one hundred and forty-nine pounds. Two hundred and ninety-six were farmers, one hundred and eighteen were clerks, three hundred and sixty-two were common laborers, four hundred and thirteen were skilled laborers, forty-seven were professional men, twenty-five were merchants; twelve hundred and sixty-five were American born, fifty-four foreign; one hundred and twenty-eight were married and eleven hundred and ninety-one were single.

On June 28th Baird G. Saltzgaber, of Lebanon, Indiana, a recent graduate of Wabash College and former

W. THOMPSON STARR.   BAIRD G. SALTZGABER.

graduate of Kenyon Military Academy, was mustered as quartermaster sergeant, and on July 5th W. Thompson Starr, of Richmond, Indiana, class of '98, Michigan Military Academy, Orchard Lake, Michigan, was mustered as regimental sergeant major.

On July 11th, at 4:30 P. M., four companies, A, B, C, D, each member of whom had signed the muster-in roll, were mustered. On the same date Harold C. Megrew, of Indianapolis, was mustered as major and Oliver M. Tichenor, of Princeton, as first lieutenant and regimental adjutant. The following day, July 12th, four other companies, E, F, G, H, were mustered and the remaining companies, I, K, L, M, on the succeeding day, July 13th.

There was some unavoidable delay in the appointment of Matt R. Peterson as major. The position had been tendered Lieutenant Bundy, of the Third Infantry, who was at that time with his regiment at Santiago, Cuba. Being impossible to await his reply, owing to the destruction of the cables, it became necessary to make another appointment, which was given to First Lieutenant M. R. Peterson, of the Sixth United States Infantry, who was at that time on duty in the quartermaster department at Indianapolis. Lieutenant Waterman, of the Eighth United States Cavalry, who was the United States mustering officer, refused to muster the regiment as a whole until such appointment was made. Accordingly, on July 15th, in the evening about 6:30 o'clock, the whole regiment was massed to the east of the Administration Hall and in the presence of numerous friends and visitors who were there to witness the ceremony, Colonel Durbin and such of his staff as had not yet taken the oath were mustered into the service of the United States. Besides the colonel there was Victor M. Backus, of Indianapolis, who was mustered as lieutenant-colonel, and William E. Biederwolf, of Logansport, who was mustered as chaplain. This completed the roll of staff officers with the exception of John R. Brunt, of Anderson, who had been mustered as first lieutenant and

Colonel Durbin and Staff.

quartermaster on June 30th, in order that he might begin officially the administration of his required and urgent duties.

It will not be out of place to have here said by one who came in closest daily contact with the men and who learned to know their individual history and character, that the quality of the regiment was exceptionally fine. The men occupying the most responsible positions were men of experience and of the best caliber, and the official body as a whole may be safely characterized as one of exceptional character and capacity. Among the enlisted men were hundreds belonging to Indiana's best families; young men of learning, of profession, of wealth and of social standing, and while in any and every such body of twelve hundred men there is much and much-to-be-regretted immoral conduct, yet the record of the One Hundred and Sixty-first Indiana during the time of its service shows it to be a regiment of unusual high moral character for a military organization.

CHAPTER II.

CAMP MOUNT.

June 30, '98—August 11, '98.

The State Fair ground was admirably adapted as a place for holding the regiment during the completion of its organization and preparation to report for duty wherever sent. Headquarters and the dispensary were established in the administration hall and here for many days was a rush of business of a character such as the place had never seen before. The fine art building was used as the commissary and quartermaster department and one of the pavilions near by as a shelter for the guard.

To each company as it reported was assigned one of the large stock buildings. The two colored companies, A and B, commanded by Captains Jacob M. Porter and John J. Buckner, who, by the way, were the first colored captains ever commissioned, were sheltered in the barns nearest the main entrance to the grounds.

The companies were, for convenience at the first, lettered according to the order of their arrival; they were met at the entrance by Lieutenant-Colonel Backus, who escorted them to their quarters, and at once, or as soon as possible thereafter, they were in line at the quartermaster's department for some of the articles such as would be immediately necessary for the new mode of life into which they were then to be initiated.

They were given axes and spades and picks and rakes and wondered what it meant; then to each company were also issued one hundred and six blankets, meat-cans, knives, forks, spoons, tin-cups, two Meyers cooking ranges with

FATIGUE DUTY.

utensils complete, one cord of wood, and one day's rations. Some of the companies had a little of camp experience at home, sleeping in barns taking a few meals picnic style, and more from the well loaded tables of their towns people, but when they opened those marvelous double-sided, self-sealing meat-cans to receive their first army cooked food and looked into the depths of those delicate quart coffee cups, washed their own tin-dishes, made up their own beds of boards and straw, then they knew they were soldiers; and so for twenty-six days they lived together, twelve large families in twelve large barns. Here were formed the first impressions of something, but only something, of what army life really was. Here the rich and poor, the college graduate, the mechanic, the laborer and the fellow who was "doin' nothin" touched elbows at night and here were formed many of those friendships such as hallow the memory of every war. The work of the hour was the examination of the men. Each company was sent to the creek for a bath and then in squads of twenty reported up stairs in the administration building for the ordeal. Every one knew pretty well his chances from the previous like experience, and many a one stood before the scrutiny of the merciless surgeons and forgot their nakedness for the fear and trembling that was in them. And the ordeal was severe. The surgeons looked right into them. A man must be all there: of course there are always exceptions; the fellow with one toe *did* get in; they said "you can't run, suppose we have to retreat what will become of you"? "Run," he said, "you ought to see me; me and some more stirred a hornet's nest yesterday, and I beat the hull of them out of the woods." And the fellow who could'nt read got in: he said "———," and he forgot himself when he said it for he said it in an awful way, "I did'nt come here to teach school, I came here to fight." However the fellow in the regiment with a glass eye—but we promised not to mention it for you know science is very perfect these days, and a fellow can see through a glass eye about as well as he can through a good one. Most companies came with more than the required number of men, and after one out of seven had been rejected the average strength of the companies was ninety-six. New recruits came in from time to time and the companies left Camp Mount with an average strength of one hundred and four.

As fast as the men were examined attention was turned to the preparation of the rolls for "muster in;" a herculean task, to do it correctly and neatly, as the best and most careful penman from each company will most certainly testify.

While such steps were being taken preparatory to the complete regimental organization, the men were not idle;

they spent one-half hour each morning and evening doing the setting-up exercise and marched out of their barns every day at 7:30 A. M., 11 A. M. and 4 P. M., and spent one hour in the evolutions of squad and company drill. The colonel, however, at once ordered all drills to be confined exclusively to squad drill; in those early executions one would hardly have recognized the crack steppers of the Seventh Army Corps. To their last day the boys will hear the "left, right; one, two; hepp, hepp; unc, anc," and although the drill leaders had not as yet learned to spell "March" with an initial " h," nor to put the Spanish on the last syllable of "Attention," they did their best in pure English and the men did their best and it was this doing their best and the excellent *Esprit de corps* of the entire body that brought them to the enviable position they later enjoyed in the Seventh Army Corps.

They were only "boys in blue" in name for the uniforms were not yet issued and the single outfit they brought along soon had the appearance of a "Weary Willie" costume, and on July 10 many of the boys had a most excellent excuse for not coming to church to hear the Chaplain preach his first sermon in the great grandstand by the race track. But this could scarcely be called their hardest trial; it was rather when *she* came down on the Sunday excursions to see him once more before he left. He hoped she would excuse his appearance and tried to explain to her something about the "channels" through which the new suits had to come. He never turned his back upon her then and when he said good-bye he backed away; anyhow those were happy Sundays with their home friends and their heavy baskets; the soldiers remember them; the surgeons remember the Monday mornings sick call.

On the 1st day of July, when five companies only had arrived, the first guard was posted by Lieutenant Crooker.

There were five posts and three reliefs, and the men were armed with hickory clubs. Later the guard was increased and were armed with the old-time guns of the National Guard brought from the state house, and each company,

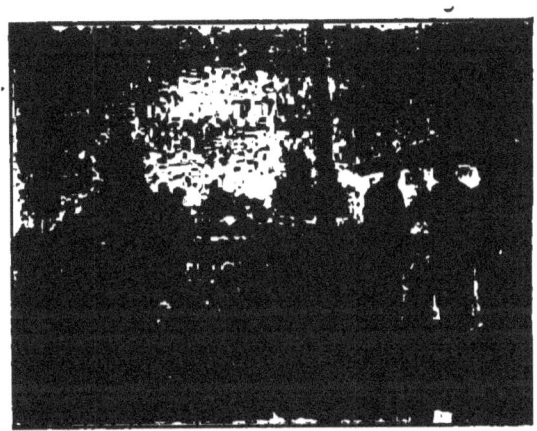

RELIEVING THE GUARD.

commencing with Company B, took its turn in doing guard duty, the chief service of which was to keep at bay the venders of sweetmeats and pies, the arrest of whisky smugglers and guard-line runners.

It's an old saying that whisky is easy to get. Well, it was. It was captured, quart after quart, and turned over to the surgeons *for use in the medical department.* One scoundrel was brought in——yes, he did have a bottle for a friend who ordered it. Lieutenant-Colonel Backus found it difficult to locate that particular bottle, for, in searching the fellow, he found eight others——nine bottles on one man. The Colonel was indignant; he would show the fellow some military discipline; forthwith he and his three pals were lodged in the guard-house for the night, where they stayed—until they took a notion to climb out.

Of course the guards had to be tested; they must learn never to surrender their gun, not even to the colonel; but it was just as one poor crestfallen darkey guard, who had surrendered his gun, said to the officer of the guard: "He done won my confidence, sah," and it was a rather underhanded and merciless way to do; but it isn't generally known that the colonel was held up one night till the next relief came on; the calls did not work that night; neither corporal, sergeant nor officer of the guard came, and the colonel—well, he waited. The men were there for a purpose and they knew it, although there were some things they all as yet could not be expected to know, for instance:

Stranger approaching—"Are you a sentinel, sir?"

Company A man on guard—"No, I am a Swede."

Such was life amid the busy scenes of those first days of Camp Mount until the regiment was ready for muster, July 15.

The following day, July 16, Colonel Durbin issued the first general order of the regiment, a copy of which is here inserted. An important document to the compliance with the admirable tone of which is greatly due the standard afterward attained by the regiment under his command, and which contains regimental data of special interest for officers and men.

HEADQUARTERS 161ST REG. IND. VOL. INF.
CAMP MOUNT, INDIANAPOLIS,
July 16, 1898.

GENERAL ORDER NO. 1.

Congratulating the officers and men of the One Hundred and Sixty-first Regiment Indiana Volunteer Infantry upon having passed and received the approval of the Examining Board and mustering officer, and imposing the fullest confidence in the officers and men, the following is published for the information and guidance of all concerned:

Obedience and proper respect to the superior officers are the first requirements of a soldier. An officer in any grade in command should and must receive the same obedience and respect as though he be of the highest grade. Fidelity to duty, with zeal and energy, is none the less a requisite.

In the present war, to create armies and make soldiers of men in the shortest time is the aim of those in control. Therefore, in order that the highest state of efficiency may be attained, it will be expected of you that you should at once and at all times call forth your best energies, and let it be the effort of each and every one, of whatever station, to have it said of him, "duty well done."

All authority should be exercised with firmness, decorum and, above all, impartiality, and authority should be respected by implicit obedience and loyal support from subordinates. Let it be the aim of each and every one to labor earnestly to perfect himself in military drill, instructions and discipline.

It will be necessary, and one of the first cares, to preserve health, and as your commanding officer I enjoin upon officers and men to look well to preserving your present physical condition, which is evidenced to be good by reason of your acceptance by the surgeons and mustering officer. Going into a hot climate, as we doubtless will, it will be necessary to the preservation of health to abstain from the use of intoxicating drinks.

Let your aim be at all times to be prepared for duty by presenting yourself in your best physical condition, without impairment of body or intellect produced by any article that will weaken or impair. Let your stimulants be a pride in the perfectness of your bodies, and a zeal and energy to become the best regiment not only from our own state, but any other state.

It is expected of you, and is due the government which you serve, that we will do nothing that will interfere with all the requirements demanded of us.

    2. The letter designations of companies is as follows:

Captain Lee M. Olds, Company A.
Captain Winston Menzies, Company B.
Captain Thomas J. Hudgins, Company C.
Captain Charles E. Crosby, Company D.
Captain Louis C. Baird, Company E.
Captain William M. Smith, Company F.
Captain Albert D. Ogborn, Company G.
Captain James M. Gwinn, Company H.
Captain William Guthrie, Company I.
Captain Wilford T. Stott, Company K.
Captain James L. Anderson, Company L.
Captain George A. West, Company M.

The relative rank of all commissioned officers of the same grade corresponds to the designation by letter of their companies, those of Company A being senior, and through regular gradation by letter to Company M, its officers being junior. For instance, the captain, first and second lieutenants of Company A will be the seniors in rank in their grade in the regiment, and those of Company M the juniors.

Precedence of non-commissioned officers of the same grade and the same relative positions in a grade will, likewise, be determined.

For instance, the first, second, third, etc., sergeants of Company A will be senior in rank to the first, second, third, etc., of other companies, but the third sergeant of Company A will not be senior in rank to the second sergeant of any other company.

3. The following assignment of companies to battalions is hereby announced:

First Battalion, Companies A, E, K, M.
Second Battalion, Companies B, D, F, I.
Third Battalion, Companies C, G, H, L.

Lieutenant-Colonel Victor M. Backus, Major Harold C. Megrew and Major Matt. R. Peterson, One Hundred and Sixty-first Indiana Volunteer Infantry, are assigned to the command of the First, Second and Third Battalions respectively. They will be obeyed and respected accordingly.

Battalion commanders are authorized to appoint their commissioned and non-commissioned staff officers, with the approval of the regimental commander.

4. On and after the 17th inst., officers' school will be established and held daily, Saturdays and Sundays excepted, from 3:15 P. M. to 4:15 P. M. Officers' call will be sounded at 3:05 P. M., at which time all officers not excused by regimental commander will repair to regimental headquarters.

5. On and after the 17th inst. non-commissioned officers' school will be held daily from 8:45 A. M. to 9:45 A. M., at such places as company commanders may designate. The instruction of each company will be under the supervision of company commanders, and all company officers and non-commissioned officers not excused by the regimental commander will be required to attend. School call will be sounded at 8:35 A. M.

6. All drills, until further orders, will be squad drills. Battalion commanders will see that this order is strictly enforced.

7. The verbal appointment of John R. Brunt, first lieutenant and quartermaster One Hundred and Sixty-first

Indiana Volunteer Infantry, to be acting ordnance officer of the regiment is hereby made of record.

By order of Colonel Durbin.

OLIVER M. TICHENOR,
1st Lieut. and Adjutant 161st Ind. Vol. Inf.

It will be noticed by the order of companies herein mentioned that the company from Hammond, commanded by Lee M. Olds, was made the ranking company of the regiment. No body of men worked harder than did the boys and officers of Company A. They were at it early and late and attained very speedily to the degree of excellency that characterized their work. Other companies as well were doing most excellent work, but the Mount Vernon company was perhaps the one that made the Hammond boys work hardest for their distinction, and the earnest and pleasant rivalry resulted in a hard choice between them. The four company commanders first mustered were called into the presence of Colonel Durbin and the battalion commanders. They were given the preference of choosing the ranking company themselves or leaving the decision to the committee before them. They prefered to abide by the decision of the latter, and the choice was accordingly made. At a meeting of all officers the following evening a like method was determined upon for fixing the rank of companies mustered on the 12th and 13th.

The first meeting of officers was held July 13th in the dispensary room of the headquarters building where Major Megrew, Captains Smith and Guthrie were appointed a committee to suggest some out-fitter's establishment for uniforms, etc. There was only one man in those days and his name was Pettibone. Accordingly Mr. Pettibone's agent was busy for weeks fitting (?) the officers out. Patience is a most excellent virture and the officers now had the most excellent opportunity for its display. They waited many weary weeks after those gilded coats and striped pants were due, and when they came,—to see those fits! The officers had to do something and not being profane men, they had to laugh; they had a perfect fit of this. To see John R. Brunt poke his long arms through a Kaki that would quicker fit a Lilliputian—short sleeves perhaps intended for evening dress;—to see Victor M. Backus color up with blood as he tugged to squeeze himself on the inside of his—to see W. T. Durbin lose himself in his—and every one else look ridiculous—to see this would have made Pettibone himself laugh. In fact those were marvelous suits, self-fitting, warranted to fit anybody and lest any one who is in the distance heard the hilarious proceedings that lasted so long into the night of July 25th should form an unfavorable impression of our sobriety let it here be chronicled that the officers of the One Hundred and Sixty-first Indiana Volunteer Infantry were simply trying on the Pettibone suits.

At a similiar meeting of officers the next day the colonel announced the first officers' school, which met on Monday, 18th, in the upstairs of the headquarters building. A few remarks were made by Colonel Durbin in which he designated Major Peterson as instructor. A typical school in which "Tactics" were explained, for which a man was supposed to study his lessons, at which the roll was called and which no officer could absent himself without a legitimate excuse. The officers always knew how to execute the movement in question with their men but could not tell in school just what command they would use to do it with. This was the one peculiar and mysterious feature.

On Tuesday, July 19th, the first issue of clothing was made by the quartermaster and as fast as possible thereafter the men were supplied from United States clothing department. One can easily imagine the change that such change of garments made. The boys did really look taller, but it is doubtful if they looked as much taller as it seemed to them they were. On Wednesday, 20th, the first battalion formation was made by Major Megrew, commanding the Second Battalion.

In the evening of the 21st the friends of Lieutenat-Colonel Backus presented him with a sword. Concerning that occasion the following is from the Indianapolis Sentinel, of the 22nd of July:

The porch of the headquarters at Camp Mount was the scene of a very pleasant gathering last evening on the occasion of the presentation of a sword to Lieutenant-Colonel Backus by a number of his friends in this city. It was filled with the officers of the regiment, and a number of ladies and gentlemen and a crowd of soldiers of the camp were gathered before it.

Mr. Ben Webb and Mr. E. M. Johnson were the chief managers of the ceremony. The presentation speech was made by Mr. J. P. Dunn, who spoke as follows:

"LIEUTENANT-COLONEL BACKUS—We are come to tender to you a token of esteem for the past and a confidence for the future. A third of a century has passed away since the gloomy cloud of civil war lifted from our country, but time has not dimmed the memory of the glorious deeds that were done in that gigantic struggle. With us of Indiana and Illinois there is no part in the achievements of that war that is looked upon with higher pride than that borne by Wilder's brigade. The rest of the country does not know as we know the story of that flying swarm of the pioneers of battle. We have listened with eager earnestness to the account of its brilliant victory at Hoover's gap. We have heard with breathless interest the story of its daring destruction of the supply depot at Decker, and its escape over the hills from the overwhelming Confederate force that came just too late for its protection. We have thrilled with excitement over the description of the unlooked-for attack on Chattanooga when Lilly's guns wakened the enemy from a sense of security. We have heard with quickened pulse the account of its stubborn fighting at Chickamauga, at Selma and at Macon. It is a wonderful story of wild raids and desperate chances taken—of riding by night and fighting by day—for there was little rest where John T. Wilder commanded. And we may well wish it were all recorded in permanent form that those who come after us may know it as we know it. Those who can recount it are swiftly passing from our sight. It is but a few weeks since they laid to rest that true and tried soldier, John Fleming. But a little later this whole community bowed in sorrow at the announcement of the death of that peerless man—that knight errant in war and peace— Colonel Eli Lilly. Only this week you buried gallant Bill Bray—as brave a man as ever carried a musket in our army. And I can but think that there must have been great satisfaction to that grizzled veteran in his last days, when he heard how you, his youthful protege, the youngest soldier of the brigade, had given to Indiana the unprecedented honor of tendering the services of a full regiment of volunteers before the president's call was received.

"But while we treasure these memories of the past, we rejoice that we have reached new times and new conditions. We glory in the knowledge of an united country, and we know that the blood now shed in battle against a foreign foe shall cement the hearts of all sections so that we shall be disunited no more forever. Surely our soldiers shall march with quickened step and lighter heart because America is all on one side and under one flag. We are one nation and one people.

"Lieutenant-Colonel Backus, I address you in behalf of your fellow-citizens, your neighbors, your friends. We offer you this sword with unbounded confidence that it will never know dishonor. We know that if its blade shall be reddened it will be with the blood of the enemies of your country, shed in fair and honorable combat. We know that when it flashes in the charge it will be before the eyes of your men. We wish that when you grasp its hilt it shall bear the message to you that our hopes, our kindliest wishes and our prayers are with you and all your comrades who go to uphold the nation's honor. Some of you may not return. The enemy's arms or dread disease may leave you lifeless in the foreign lands. Some of you may return broken with sickness or with wounds. We hope for the best. We trust that God may deal kindly with you. We wish this sword to be with you in remembrance that whatever may befall you, and all of you, shall be held by us in honor, in esteem and in affection, while we shall live."

Lieutenant-Colonel Backus received the sword with evident emotion and briefly returned thanks to the donors. He said that he was certain that the regiment was the best one that had been sent out to the war. It had the best colonel, the best majors, the best captains and the best men. He was certain that good reports would come from it when it got to the front. When he returned from the the Civil war thirty-three years ago, he carried a Spencer rifle and he only hoped that this sword would come back with as good a record as that rifle. He would promise one thing, and that was that it should not come back dishonored in any event.

On Saturday, July 23d, occurred the first wedding. The Second Batallion, of which the bridegroom was a member, formed in hollow square in an open space of the grove. Two other companies were also present, and here in the presence of comrades and friends, on nature's soft carpet, and under her beautiful skies, after Colonel Backus had said "I give this woman to be the soldier's bride," the regimental chaplain performed the ceremony that made Sergeant Robert L. Cromer, of Company I, and Miss Pink Allen, of Logansport, man and wife, and the soldiers gave three rousing cheers for the happy couple. On Sunday, July 24, the first regimental parade took place. Visitors were in abundance that day and from the grand stand and from the windows and balcony of the Administration building they watched eleven hundred boys form in one long line of companies that stretched through the oval race track from end to end; it was a big crowd of soldiers and and as Lieutenant-Colonel Backus looked upon it, it seemed to grow bigger with every second; finally he shouted: "Right forward! fours right!" and after a remarkable maneuver got them to pass in review before Colonel Durbin. It was on this day that the adjutant's remarkable riding furnished material for such favorable newspaper comment.

In the meantime international concerns were progressing exceeding slow, and while the men were speculating as to the when and where of our departure, public opinion was forming itself into the impression that we were on our first and only camping ground. As soon, however, as tentage was received the regiment was to change quarters, to leave the old barns and pitch a more model camp in the eastern portion of the grounds. This savored of a longer stay but was simply the purpose to improve the time and camp and give the men a little more military experience, even though the tents should stand only for a day, but who knew? Accordingly the camp was laid out, thirteen wells were driven, tents were issued, and on July 29 and 30 the boys took up their beds and walked to the little village of tents and in the evening at taps laid themselves down by fives in the little white houses.

The ground was the same as that occupied by the other Indiana regiments, but so orderly and in such system was this camp laid out that favorable comparisons and comments were heard by all who visited the regiment while there. It was the idea which later perfected made the One Hundred and Sixty-first camp a "revelation."

On July 31st (Sunday) occurred the first muster for pay. "Of all the signing of rolls that was the best one yet," said one man as he finished. On the 2d day of August the 45-caliber, 1884 pattern, Springfield rifles with bayonets were issued. They made the men appear very formidable, and they began at once the practice of the manual of arms; and for several days the boys drilled and speculated on the future, and posed for Treadwell-Shane, who hung the "Father of his Country" out to smile upon the boys, while he made mounted heroes out of them on a card 14 x 20, all for the small sum of $1.50 each.

Saturday, August 6, at 5:30, the first guard was mounted, in a military fashion, Major Peterson acting as regimental adjutant; Captain Olds was officer of the day, and Lieutenant Reynolds was officer of the guard. The band was in formation, but instrumentless, and two of them accompanied the ceremony with bugles. This has always been an attractive feature; it was interesting that evening because it was new, but later, when executed with such spirited precision, the inspiring music, the inspection of guns, the entire ceremony, from the marching up of each detail to the passing in review before its officers, the act, although somewhat dramatic, was attractive and interesting, and impressed thoughtful minds with a world of meaning. In that ceremony one could see the whole history of a war; so much have sentinels to do with battles.

GUARD MOUNT, CAMP COLUMBIA.

Boys, do you remember the brave deed of August 5? History would be incomplete without it. It was 2:30 P. M. when you formed yourselves and with determination deeply stamped upon your brows you advanced on headquarters. Lieutenant-Colonel Backus was not the man you was looking for, and when he asked your purpose you demanded that he bring the colonel out, and the colonel came out of his tent; you remember when came and looked right at you—you know how the colonel could look—and when he said: "What does this mean?" your leader swallowed the lump that rose like lightning in his throat and managed to say: "We want more privileges?" and the colonel said: "Every man of you to your tents, at once!" In a minute not a man was in sight. You always were obedient.

On August 7 (Sunday) the regiment was called out for parade; Lieutenant-Colonel Backus passed the regiment in review and rode to his place by the side of Colonel Durbin. The colonel asked him to form the regiment in line of masses, as he had something to say to them. After complimenting them on their appearance as a regiment he told them of the following order he that day received.

WASHINGTON, D. C., August 7, 1898.
Col. Winfield T. Durbin, commanding One Hundred and Sixty-first United States Volunteer Infantry, Camp Mount, Indianapolis, Indiana:

By direction of the secretary of war, you will proceed as soon as practicable with your regiment to Jacksonville, Florida, and report to the commanding general there. Upon receipt of this order you will at once communicate with the chief quartermaster, Chicago, for the necessary transportation, and with the chief commissary, Chicago, for ten-days' field rations, the necessary travel rations and coffee money. The quartermaster general and commissary general have instructed the chief quartermaster and chief commissary as above to provide the transportation rations, and coffee money. Telegraph day of departure to commanding general of Seventh Corps, also to this office, specifying amount of tentage, kind and calibre of arms and ammunition taken with you. Acknowledge receipt.

By order of the secretary of war.

H. C. CORBIN,
12:38 P. M. *Adjutant General.*

No one present will forget the demonstration which followed the reading of this order. It meant that the One Hundred and Sixty-first Indiana was not to go home, but was to share in whatever there was yet to do to accomplish the end for which war was declared. And didn't the boys shout, and didn't they yell, and didn't every hat go up in the air, and didn't the officers do their share of noise-making, and how the people in the grand stand did wonder what the Colonel had said that threw the boys into such a commotion, and then when they were given "fall out" after reaching the company streets, how each company vied with every other in seeing which could make the most noise. After supper breaking the news to mother and other friends was the order until taps, and immediately next morning all loose articles were carefully packed away and preparations made for an immediate departure. Tents were searched and all side arms demanded. The boys had enlisted to fight and couldn't understand this seeming hardship, but experience calls it a wise precaution.

Tuesday, the 9th, the paymaster squared every man with the Government, and on Wednesday we would have been marching to the cars had transportation been furnished as per expectation, but all was in readiness the following day, and 1 P. M., August 11, found the One Hundred and Sixty-first Indiana marching toward the North street depot, from which point, by contract, the Big Four was to carry us all to Jacksonville. Concerning this day's events the following is taken, in part, from the Indianapolis Journal of the 12th instant:

"The One Hundred and Sixty-first Regiment has gone to Jacksonville, leaving Camp Mount deserted except for the two colored companies. There were no drills in camp in the morning, but every soldier was intense with excitement in anticipation of the move to the south, even though none of the troops may ever see the smoke of battle. The officers were instructed to have a man at each corner of every tent at nine o'clock promptly, and at bugle call to draw the ropes and pack tents and equipment at once. As soon as the bugle blew the blast every tent fell over to the north just as if a cyclone had struck camp and swept the field clean. In twenty minutes the tents were down, packed and loaded into wagons to be hauled to the cars near by.

"An early noon mess was ordered, and at one o'clock the ride to Sixteenth street began. The colored companies, which acted as escort to the regiment, came first and were followed by the First Battalion. These were followed by the Second and Third Battalions. The soldiers left the cars at Sixteenth street and marched across to Meridian, where they halted, waiting for Colonel Durbin and staff, who came up a few minutes before three. Governor Mount, his secretary and the When Band were in waiting. At three o'clock the order to 'fall in' was given and the line of march began, the colored men in front, then Governor Mount, Colonel Durbin and staff. The First, Second and Third Battalions followed in the order given. Company F carried the flag in the middle of the regiment. The length of the line was six blocks, four abreast. Hundreds of people lined the way along the line of march, shouting 'good-bye' to the soldiers. When the flag was carried along the crowd went wild with applause and hats were lifted until it had passed.

In front of the state house the troops were drawn up and passed in review before the governor."

We have always thought of the governor as our friend, and every officer and private felt something of the debt to him for its magnificent beginning under his care and supervision. Every regiment claimed and received his interest and his attention, and he dealt fairly and impartially with them all, out of concern for the credit they were to reflect upon the State that sent them forth, but the One Hundred and Sixty-first, being the only volunteer regiment, he necessarily came into closer touch with its organization. His notable wisdom in the selection of officers and the justice characterizing his every dealing with the regiment, won the admiration of every soldier. Its welfare received his attention in every possible way and the good reputation it afterward sustained was to him a source of deep pleasure. It is a pleasure to here insert the governor's speech which was made to the regiment drawn up before him and which so many of the men far down the narrow street could not hear.

THE GOVERNOR'S SPEECH.

"Soldiers of the One Hundred and Sixty-first Indiana Volunteers—You are to-day bidding good-bye to friends, to home and to your native state. In behalf of this commonwealth I desire to bid you good-bye and godspeed on your journey. In common with thousands of brave men, you tendered your service upon the first call of the President of the United States for volunteers. You pleaded earnestly and with importunity that your service might be accepted. You reflect but the patriotism of tens of thousands of other brave men in Indiana who tendered their

Governor James A. Mount.

services and who have importuned earnestly that their service might be accepted. (Applause.) It has been your patriotism and the patriotism of the brave men of Indiana that enabled the state to take her proud position at the front of the states in furnishing her quota of soldiers. (Applause.) It was this patriotism that enabled Indiana to report her quota ready first of all the states. It was this patriotism that enabled Indiana to have her soldiers first mustered into the service. It will not, soldiers, militate against your patriotism or your honor that you may not engage in battle. You have made personal sacrifice—no one knows but a soldier and a soldier's family the personal sacrifice he makes when he enlists in his country's service. He goes forth to meet the dangers of battle and the disease of the camp. He goes forth perhaps not to return to those who are dear to him. He enlists and is ready for whatever service the government may accept of him. He sacrifices his home, he leaves loved ones, and only a mother can tell what sacrifices she makes when she bids farewell to her darling boy, and only that boy knows the sacrifice of leaving home when he bids farewell to his mother and his friends. Some of you have bade good-bye to a loving wife, some of you to a mother and a father, some to brothers and sisters, but you are all bidding good-bye to friends who are as dear to you as your own life. Not only this sacrifice, but many of you are sacrificing your business. You have allowed nothing to come between you and your country. I may truthfully say of Indiana that the five regiments that have gone forth from this state, and are now going, and the two independent companies, and the two batteries, are as grand men as ever enlisted in any cause. (Applause.) And they are all of them as brave men as ever entered an army for the defense of the country. (Renewed applause.) And if opportunity offers Indiana soldiers will reflect credit upon the government and upon this great commonwealth. (Applause.)

"It looks at this time as though the war might be near its termination, and in the dawn of peace we all rejoice. These brave men have been willing to give their lives, but God spare their lives and permit them to return.

all of them, to this state. (Great applause.) But, soldiers of the One Hundred and Sixty-first, I am not a prophet, but I predict that you will tread on Cuban soil before you are welcomed back to the state of Indiana. (Tremendous applause.) I believe that the gallant Fitzhugh Lee, if he does not go to Cuba as conqueror, will go there with an army of occupation (applause), and I believe this regiment, with General Lee, will be on Cuban soil next winter. And, comrade soldiers, there will be battles for you to fight, though they may not be against the enemy. The insidious temptations that follow camp life require courage to meet and maintain your honor and your dignity. I would counsel you, meet these temptations of camp life like heroes. There is no schooling, in my judgment, that is grander than the schooling a soldier receives in camp and in battle. The mask will be thrown aside. You will see men in their true character. In the army some men will do that which they would scorn to do in society. But the true soldier will maintain his dignity, his gentlemanly demeanor, in camp and in battle, as well as in society. (Applause.) And those soldiers that meet the dangers and temptations of camp and return with their characters unsullied, dignified, temperate, gentlemanly at the close of war will be men who have learned lessons that will be of incalculable benefit to them through life. So my parting words would be to these brave men, be diligent, be active, be brave, be temperate, be contented, maintain a cheerful disposition. We are told that a cheerful spirit doeth good as a medicine. The soldier that becomes disheartened and discouraged in camp is in danger of inviting disease and of meeting death. So, soldiers of the One Hundred and Sixty-first, acquit yourselves like men, so that when you return to your friends and to your state you will return bringing back that nobility of character and manhood as well as a brave record as a soldier. I have no fear the good name of Indiana will be vindicated in the camp or in the furnace of battle. (Applause.) Go forth, brave men of Indiana, and may God's blessing and God's protecting power go with you, and in his good providence may you be permitted to return and receive that welcome that patriotic soldiers deserve from their friends and from their native state." (Tremendous applause.)

Colonel Durbin made a few happy remarks and then, dismounting from his horse, shook hands with the governor. Colonel Backus followed Colonel Durbin's example. Cheer after cheer was given by the soldiers for the flag and officers. The march then continued to the North street depot, where cars were in readiness.

At 8:30 o'clock the first section, bearing the Third Battalion, left the depot; a few minutes intervened between the starting of the other two sections, the first of which carried the First Battalion and the second the Second Battalion. The arrangements were complete and were carried out with precision in every detail.

The One Hundred and Sixty-first Indiana Volunteer Infantry was on its way to join the army of Fitz Hugh Lee.

CHAPTER III.

EN ROUTE TO JACKSONVILLE.

The three trains left North street station a few moments apart and passed in close succession through the Union depot at 9:10 P. M., and a few moments later the lights of Indianapolis were shining far behind us as the well-loaded coaches sped away to the south.

The entire train save the baggage and freight accommodations was composed of sleeping cars and the troops were transported with every possible convenience and comfort. The brief run of each section is better described by one who was there.

THE FIRST SECTION.

While the big guns were belching at Santiago the One Hundred and Sixty-first Regiment, just mustered into service, was listening with bated breath and wondering if ever it would be theirs "to do or die." The wiseacres knowingly shook their heads and said "you fellows will never leave Camp Mount until you are mustered out," so it was a great relief to all when the orders came to report at Jacksonville. The Third Battalion was designated as the first section, carrying besides its four companies, Colonel Durbin, with Major Smith and Adjutant Tichenor of the staff and Lieutenant-Colonel Crooker, commissary officer, and the usual amount of impedimenta including the regimental horses. It was 8:50 P. M. before we were loaded on Pullmans at the North street station and started on our mission for humanity's sake over the Big Four by way of Louisville, Kentucky. Our first stop was at Shelbyville at 11 o'clock, where a large number of people were waiting with a farewell for the boys of Company C; but little time was given them, however, and we were soon speeding on our way, arriving at Louisville about 3 A. M., where we were transferred to the L. & N. Railroad; a few hours more and we were passing through some battle fields of old upon which there is a monument to the memory of the boys in blue who had fallen there long before the majority of us were born.

At Bowling Green trouble began with a native selling whisky to the men and who had no intention of respecting the order of Lieutenant Dority, who had been appointed provost marshal for the section, and when the bystanders interfered in behalf of their fellow townsman trouble of a very serious character began to brew, until Colonel Durbin and the adjutant came to the marshal's assistance; the liquor was confiscated, the soldiers ordered to the train, and the offending party allowed his freedom for lack of time to punish him. The train went flying away, making Nashville about noon, where coffee was served for the first time since leaving Camp Mount. We were soon on our way again, reaching Birmingham, Alabama, shortly before midnight, where we passed General Carpenter and staff of the Fourth Army Corps on their way to Huntsville, where that corps had been ordered from Tampa. At Birmingham several colored men boarded the train and began to go through some of the clothing of the men whose fathers had made them free. They were, however, soon promptly fired from the train, and, after a few shots fired in the air by the daring lieutenant appointed for that purpose, the train was ready to proceed. The next morning papers at Decatur told us that the protocol had been signed and that the war was virtually at an end; but on we went, arriving at 2:45 P. M. at Thomasville, known as the "garden city of the south," and one of its best known and most popular health resorts. Late in the afternoon we came to Waycross; here we had an hour's stop. The colonel ordered the battalion off and instructed company commanders to give their men the setting-up exercise and some of the foot movements. A heavy rain interfered even before Company G could complete its roll call, yet it was finished despite the fact that every man got soaked through; the other companies broke for shelter at the first sign and were soon scattered over town, some looking for a bite to eat, others for a drink, the former getting the best of the deal, for Waycross is a sure enough "dry town," despite the fact that the streets were flooded with water and the mud ankle deep. At Waycross an old darkey brother came to us with the query "is you all gwine down to jine Sherman?" Assuring him that we were, we again boarded the train and soon finished our journey, arriving at Jacksonville at 9:30 P. M. of the 13th, where we were run into the yards and there awaited the coming of the other sections, which were said to be somewhere in our rear. The trip was devoid of any incident further than the excitement, to some of the favored ones riding on the engine while passing through Georgia, caused by running over an occasional steer.

SECOND SECTION.

This section followed closely after the first. It carried the First Battalion with Lieutenant-Colonel Backus in command and with Lieutenant Gerrish and Chaplain Biederwolf of the staff.

The men were comfortably fixed, two in a lower berth and one in an upper and with every one in highest spirits we chased away in hot pursuit of the section in advance. Captain Baird was made officer of the day and Lieutenant Fitch officer of the guard.

For every coach end there was a guard who stood without in the day and sat within at night. We knew the good example the first section would set us in sobriety and it was desirable to set the same example to the section following us and one of the works of chief importance was preventing liquor being passed to the men through the windows by those who were dwarfed in character enough to do it.

One son of darkness was caught in the act just before we started; he was brought into the presence of Lieutenant-colonel Backus who ordered him turned over to civil authorities; how he did beg and promise and finally when the Colonel asked him how quick he would get out if allowed to run he said "Now boss, foh God! if you give dis chile three seconds you can shoot at him." The colonel gave it to him and he was out of sight in less time than he had bargained for. At every stop along the way guards were placed outside along the cars who did double duty of keeping the men in and every thing undesirable out. In this regard the section is indebted to Lieutenant Gerrish for admirable service rendered. The train reached the smoky city of Louisville early on the morning of the 12th where it had the misfortune of starting up before some of the men got on board. Billy Woods, of Company A, and a few others had only met some friends but they turned up in Jacksonville as good as new a few minutes after the regiment was on the ground.

The boys didn't do a thing to the big juicy watermelons that were waiting all along the way to meet the train. They were dessert to the corn-beef and beans and hard-tack that fed the boys, and revenue to the sleepy old farmer who was fortunate enough to have his crop in the right market at the right time.

Everywhere we were greeted with characteristic southern cordiality, especially generous under circumstances fast obliterating the last bit of sectional feeling and calling us together in the common struggle then on. There were cheers and there were waving handkerchiefs, there were hand-shakings and expressive good-byes though they had met but for a moment. Beautiful bouquets, roses and loose flowers were laid in our hands at every stop and on every side expressions of universal good feeling and best wishes to cheer us as we went, made the run an interesting and delightful one.

From an occasional inquiry as to when the preceding section had passed we learned that either they were gaining time or we were losing it; our frequent stops to repair couplings suggested the latter; the platforms were pulling off and in order to arrive with the same number of cars with which we started it became necessary to stop at Decatur, Alabama, and throw three cars to the rear. The train then rolled on to Montgomery, Alabama's capital, and for a brief period capital of the Confederate States; here the men who cared to wake up got coffee at 2 A. M. The first section seemed to be uneasy about the tardiness and sent us the following telegram, received about one hundred and fifty miles out of Montgomery.

"Lieut.-Col. Backus:

"Why is second section so far behind; report condition of your command, including chaplain.

"COL. W. T. DURBIN."

The following reply was wired at once.

"Col. W. T. Durbin:

"Making best possible time, three couplings broke; all sober except chaplain."   "V. M. BACKUS."

That was an ingenious stroke, but a few hours later when information was received that beer was substituted for coffee at Thomasville the chaplain had a fit of genuine sobriety. Could any one think that a hungry man would prefer beer to a quart of delicious hot coffee; were the men who did not drink beer to have nothing? No. A canvass was made. "Boys remember those who take beer get no coffee." Be it to their credit that three-fourths chose coffee, which they got; the guzzler gulped his beer and then begged for coffee which he didn't get and the train rolled on to Waycross. More than a century ago General Oglethorpe, then governor of the colony of Georgia, had his headquarters in Waycross; it is to-day one of the most attractive places in the state, its temperature and its environs making it a rendezvous for many a winter visitor. After a short stay for supper the train pulled out for the last part of the long run to Jacksonville just as the third section came up at 9 P. M. Arriving at Jacksonville at 2:30 A. M., we found the first section a few hours in advance of us and after waiting until 6:30 A. M. the men had an opportunity for breakfast, and were ready to leave for the campsite, six miles out of the city.

THE THIRD SECTION.

After a long, weary wait on the transportation department there came a scramble for berths in the train which was to convey the third section to Jacksonville, Florida; then another one of those unexplained delays which seemed to be intended for those who had mothers, wives and sweethearts to bid goodbye, and we steamed slowly away from anxious friends and relatives, from our native state and from the scene of our regimental birth. Our trip was to be a long one, uneventful in most part, but in fact made up of numerous modest incidents which become more interesting with retrospection.

Besides the battalion commander and his companies this section was accompanied by Quartermaster Brunt and Dr. Wilson of the staff. Officers of the day and guard were appointed, the train was carefully searched, all lockers and other places of possible concealment opened and every discovered drop of intoxicants thrown away and every precaution taken to bring the section through in an orderly and commendable way.

Sleep and sociability were scarce that night; in subdued wakefulness the boys lay quiet and thought of the past and the unknown future. Of course the coffee did not turn up at the breakfast hour, but it came later. The first meeting with the preceding section occurred at Bowling Green, Kentucky, where, after a short breathing space, we separated for another run. At Nashville it was late coffee again. We were fast leaving our beloved North behind us as was plainly noticed by the increase of colored people and by the increase of R's in the speech of the whites. We stopped for a short time at the historic town of Pulaski, made historic by its association with the Army of Tennessee in the last great war. We stayed in Pulaski too long, all on account of a dog; just a shepherd dog, nameless so far as we knew, but he left Pulaski with our train, it is presumed, and soon the wires were hot with messages which were being continually poked at us in regard to that dog; the militia was not ordered out by Governor Taylor, nor was the military force of Alabama called upon to restore the much desired canine, but many a self-important marshal of many a sleepy southern town was forced to stop whittling his favorite store-box and inquire for the lost pet. In the meantime the dog's conscience troubled him for leaving home and we kindly put him in a condition to return, and when we were next approached by a diplomatic representative of the Montgomery police force in reference to the dog he was given *carte blanche* to search the train, but in vain, for if the dog wasn't on his way home, who could be blamed? Surely not the policeman.

The short stops at the small stations, such as Ashford in Alabama, Bainbridge, Thomasville and Naylor in Georgia, gave us an opportunity to observe the strangers among whom fate had thrown us. At Bainbridge and Naylor our coaches were strewn with beautiful southern roses; at the former of these places a charming little southern beauty gave to Major Megrew a sweet smile, accompanied with a beautiful bouquet of roses, on the inside of which was a little note which read: "If you want to make the Spaniards run, just give the rebel yell," and signed "A Little Rebel." The extreme cordiality which was shown to us all through the south was too strong to be misunderstood; it was a feeling of friendship and good will. We reached Jacksonville about 3:30 A. M., August 14, and in six hours with the rest of the regiment we were disembarked at Panama Park, and the pine and palm thickets were being razed in a most unceremonious manner, and palm trees that were sold for dollars in our own states were being chopped down like thistles, and in their stead arose the square white houses of the new comers—the tall hoosiers of the One Hundred and Sixty-first Indiana Volunteer Infantry.

FIRST IMPRESSIONS.

First impressions are not always reliable, but the men were scarcely ever relieved of the unfavorable impression which Florida first made upon them. No doubt they were expecting too much; their imagination had been fired by glowing accounts and exaggerated pictures of her luxuriant vegetation and they were going

" Way down in the South where gulf breezes blow,
  Where tall, stately pines and the live oaks grow,
Where soft summer nights are cooled by the dew,
  And a summer sun shines the winter months through."

They were bound for the "sunny South," where luxurious fruits of untold variety would be theirs for the trouble of gathering them; they were expecting monkeys to threw cocoanuts at them out of the tops of beautiful palms. But it is true that the Seventh Army Corps did not locate in the best part of this reputed land of flowers and although recent winters have been too severe for much of its fruitage yet there are many portions of the great peninsula that are veritable garden spots. But there was an abundance of some things; for instance, there were darkies enough; there were pine trees enough and there was sand enough; enough for a whole Sahara if you made up in depth what it lacked in breadth; there was also sun enough; the boys always had trouble about noon in finding their shadows and the direct and intense heat made one dull and stupid; and there was Florida moss enough dressing all those live oaks in mourning so prophetic with their drapery of the spirit that was so soon to take hold of the men.

When the several trains arrived at the camping site the regimental effects were at once unloaded and the men began to carry them to their proper places where the company streets had been laid out. An elevated piece of ground already cleared for drilling purposes by the Third Nebraska, who were immediately on our right, had been reserved for us and immediately the busy scenes incident to arranging camp commenced; by late evening all tents were up and the camp in such shape as a day's work of a regiment will usually put it, but all the men were tired; the tramping over sand and scorched by a hot August sun that cooked the vitality out of a fellow and the hard work after a hard ride went a good ways for the strongest man who was not accustomed to such depressing environment and when the evening came with its cool blessing the boys laid down to sleep and in a few moments might have been for all they knew back in the Hoosier state where so many soon wished they were.

Immediately to our right was the Third Nebraska, beyond them the Second Mississippi and behind us a little to the left the Third Division Hospital. Upon our arrival Colonel Durbin was notified that his regiment had been assigned to the First Brigade, Third Division of the Seventh Army Corps. The Seventh Army Corps had at that time the following composition:

Major-General Fitzhugh Lee, Commanding.

FIRST DIVISION.

Major-General J. Warren Keifer, Commanding.

FIRST BRIGADE.

Brigadier-General Lloyd Wheaton, Commanding.

First Texas Volunteer Infantry.
First Louisiana Volunteer Infantry.
First Alabama Volunteer Infantry.

SECOND BRIGADE.

Brigadier General W. W. Gordon, Commanding.

Second Texas Volunteer Infantry.
Second Louisiana Volunteer Infantry.
Second Alabama Volunteer Infantry.

THIRD BRIGADE.

Colonel C. B. Hunt, First Ohio Vol. Inf., Commanding.
Fourth United States Volunteer Infantry.
First Ohio Volunteer Infantry.

SECOND DIVISION.

Brigadier-General Abraham K. Arnold, Commanding.

FIRST BRIGADE.

Brigadier-General Andrew S. Burt, Commanding.
Second Illinois Volunteer Infantry.
First North Carolina Volunteer Infantry.
Second New Jersey Volunteer Infantry.

SECOND BRIGADE.

Colonel D. V. Jackson, Fiftieth Iowa Volunteer Infantry, Commanding.
Fiftieth Iowa Volunteer Infantry.
First Wisconsin Volunteer Infantry.
Ninth Illinois Volunteer Infantry.

THIRD BRIGADE.

Brigadier-General H. C. Hasbrouck, Commanding.
Second Virginia Volunteer Infantry.
Fourth Virginia Volunteer Infantry.
Forty-ninth Iowa Volunteer Infantry.

THIRD DIVISION.

Brigadier-General Lucius F. Hubbard, Commanding.

FIRST BRIGADE.

Brigadier-General Lucius F. Hubbard, Commanding.
Second Mississippi Volunteer Infantry.

Third Nebraska Volunteer Infantry.
One Hundred and Sixty-first Indiana Volunteer Infantry.

SECOND BRIGADE.

Brigadier-General James H. Barklay, Commanding.

Fourth Illinois Volunteer Infantry.
First South Carolina Volunteer Infantry.
Sixth Missouri Volunteer Infantry.

THE SECOND UNITED STATES VOLUNTEER CAVALRY.

Colonel Jay L. Torrey, Commanding.

SIGNAL CORPS BATTALION.

Captain H. C. Giddings, Commanding.

The Seventh Army Corps on September 1st consisted, therefore, of three infantry divisions, one cavalry regiment, one signal corps battalion, three hospital and four ambulance companies. A total of twelve hundred and fifty-two commissioned officers and thirty thousand one hundred and nineteen enlisted men.

CHAPTER IV.

CAMP CUBA LIBRE.

August 14, '98–September 30, '98.

The following day was like the first and with the coming of the next came also the news that on that day, August 16, there would be held a brigade review in honor of the governor of Nebraska; Governor Holcomb had arrived in the city, Saturday evening, the 13th, and had come as a visitor of Colonel Bryan, of the Third Nebraska, to Camp Cuba Libre on Sunday, and after spending the night in camp witnessed the review on Monday. Being the first review with which the regiment was connected the officers had naturally a little solicitude about the part it was to play in the parade and did not return in the highest elatement over its deportment, but the fault lay elsewhere than in the regiment.

On the 17th occurred the first regimental formation in the South, regimental parade being held late in the afternoon; the following few days were spent as usual under such circumstances; there were tents to be floored, sinks and shacks to be built and land to be cleared; the temperature was 103° and the drilling necessarily very light, one and one-half hours only being devoted to those military gyrations which some of the men have dubbed "The Soldier's delight;" now Florida was a part of our country and still is, although some of the men were of the impression that one of the peace conditions should be that Spain should take it back, yet being of their native land, like true patriots whose sole purpose it is to sacrifice themselves for their country, the men all became members of "The Florida Land Improvement Company" and spent their spare time in grubbing stumps and roots and underbrush, thereby enhancing the value of the land so that an acre wholly worthless when we came might under pressing circumstances be sold for a few farthings when we left. On the banks of the St. Johns, not far away, was situated the famous Cummer Lumber mills, one of the largest establishments for the sawing and shipping of yellow pine in the United States and with its genial proprietor arrangements were made for furnishing the regiment with lumber. All told two hundred

COMPANY STREET IN CAMP CUBA LIBRE.

and forty thousand feet of lumber were there used by the One Hundred and Sixty-first Indiana; as fast as it could be hauled to the regiment it was made up into floors and needful structures and by the 19th every tent in the regiment had its floor that was to guard its sleeping inmates from those sneaking malarial microbes that came up out of the ground like a thief in the night to fill the men with poison fever and to steal away their color and their spirits.

By the end of the first week the carpenters detailed for the purpose had erected all the company cook shacks; back of headquarters the battalion and noncommissioned mess tents arose and finally after the colonel and all his staff had more sand in their craws than ever before or since a kitchen and breeze catching dining room covered a spot on the sand where they could humour their stomachs in comfort when there was any thing else besides fish to eat. Among the first regimental buildings to be erected was the

COMMISSARY. CAMP CUBA LIBRE.

structure to be used for the purpose of the commissary. Here the meat was handled and the bread baked and the rations issued and in this building the Exchange had its birth the following month.

The commissary business at Camp Mount had been in the hands of M. R. Peterson, assisted by Lieutenant Meston and rations were issued from the Fine Arts building. Upon the regiment's departure for Jacksonville First Lieutenant Crooker was appointed regimental commissary officer, which position he held until sickness made necessary a leave of absence and Second Lieutenant Freeman was appointed to succeed him on the 5th of September and served till the service closed except during the time between February 23 and March 23, when sick in the Second Division hospital at Camp Columbia, during which time Lieutenant Brunt acted in his stead. Lieutenant Freeman has been ably assisted by the valuable clerkship of Sergeant Charles E. Wolf, acting regimental commissary sergeant.

This department draws and issues all rations for the regiment and besides the one thousand three hundred to one thousand five hundred loves of bread baked each day, practically a loaf a day for each man, the following figures will show at what cost to the Government a month's rations are issued to a regiment of men. These figures are furnished by Lieutenant Freeman.

Fresh beef, 31,500 lbs. at 6c.............	$1,890.00
Beef roasted, one-pound cans, 3,900 lbs. at 14c	195.00
Flour, 30,400 lbs. at 2c.................	608.00
Hard bread, 11,700 lbs. at 6c.............	702.00
Beans, 3,000 lbs. at 2c.................	60.00
Rice, 2,000 lbs. at 6c.................	120.00
Potatoes, 208 bush. at $1................	208.00
Onions, 52 bush. at $1.................	52.00

Tomatoes, 3,480 lbs. at 8½c	$295.80
Coffee, green, 2,000 lbs. at 8¾c	175.00
Coffee roasted, 1,440 lbs. at 12¾c	183.00
Sugar, 5,900 lbs. at 4½c	265.50
Vinegar, 400 gals. at 12c	48.00
Salt, 1,600 lbs. at ⅞c	14.00
Pepper, 100 lbs. at 15½c	15.50
Soap, 1,560 lbs. at 3c	46.80
Salmon, 3,936 lbs. at 9c	354.24
Bacon, 8,775 lbs. at 7c	614.25
Total	$5,847.09

On the 19th another review was ordered, and the brigade was passed in review before its commanding officer, Colonel Montgomery, of the Second Mississippi. On this occasion, as on the previous one, there was no band to furnish music for the regiment, but after a long wait a very inferior set of brass band instruments came on the morning of the 22d. All around us from other regiments had been heard the music of their bands, but now the boys were fixed and that day there was music down the lines. "Tich" beat the bass-drum, and the band marched down by the companies, while all the men fell in to cheer; the next morning at "can't get 'em up" time they were aroused in the same way. It was only two weeks until the instruments in question were laid aside and replaced by the high-class ones of the Second Mississippi, who were bound for home.

There was another review held on this day, this time it being the division which was passed in review on the usual parade place at 4 o'clock P. M. before Brigadier-General Hubbard. On the 24th the chaplain's assembly tent arose, a cool and commodious affair, where the officer in charge could always look for his detail when they turned up missing, and where the men licked the ice when there was no water in the barrel and the hot sun made it dangerous for them to venture after a bucketfull.

On the same day the barn, with its sixteen stalls, the best the horses ever saw since leaving Hoosierdom, was ready for them, previous to which they had stood about making the best of it. At Camp Mount they were sheltered in the comfortable stock barns, in Savannah in a rented affair that passed for a barn, save a few that were given free stalls by a kind friend across the way, while the accommodations in Cuba are shown in the accompanying cut.

BARN—CAMP CUBA LIBRE.

The 25th saw the colonel start on his flying trip to Washington; no one could swear to the purpose for which he went but every private in the ranks knew. Already some of the men wanted to go home but the colonel was in for "On to Cuba," to which place when he returned the following Sunday he told them they had the brightest prospects of going; it was Sunday evening just time for the chaplain's service when the colonel decided by reason of the exigence of the occasion to hold a little service of his own; he always drew a bigger crowd than the chaplain and that night the men being particularly anxious about their future state he got the whole regiment and when he told them of their probable going to Cuba the same fellows who had just before preferred home-going broke loose in uncontrollable enthusiam upon the expenditure of which the chaplain had to wait for his service.

During the colonel's absence the division was reviewed on the 26th by its commander, and a few days later was passed in review before General Lee. This was the first time the corps commander had reviewed the Third Division, and it brought to the men their first opportunity of seeing the general, of whom they had heard so much. The men were in heavy marching order, and the formation was in masses, on three sides of a hollow square, in the clear space by the side of Panama park. It was the most elaborate affair the boys had yet attended, and they did themselves proud; their excellent training was beginning to show, and the regiment received the unqualified recommendation of the general. This review was closely followed by another on the last day of the month. This was, however, to be a review, and the first one, of the entire Seventh Army Corps, and was to be held in the city of Jacksonville before the commander of the corps.

The regiment left camp at 12:30 and marched into the city, taking its place in the Third Division, which was reviewed first after Torrey's Cavalry and the Signal Corps had passed the reviewing stand. Twenty-three regiments and more than twenty-eight thousand men were in line. The entire police force of the city went before the procession, and General Lee and staff headed the column until the reviewing stand was reached. Every inch of available space was crowded with a mass of white and black humanity, while from the piazzas of the Windsor the more favored looked down and pitied(?) the less fortunate. It took two hours for the corps to pass the reviewers, and the men were greeted with long and continued shouts of approval, although, from a military standpoint, the review could not begin to compare with those put up by the same corps, though reorganized, in later months. Among the remarks of the press it was said "Colonel Durbin's command won much praise by its fine marching, full companies and straight lines." Not more than a dozen men from the One Hundred and Sixty-first fell out from exhaustion, but it was a noticeable and notable fact that the men of the southern regiments could not stand the ordeal as well as those from the north, but with drooping heads, laid down in every spot, as the sturdy Hoosiers showed them how to endure their own climate. The companies returned at leisure, marching slowly and resting at will, until they arrived at camp, from 6 to 7:30 P. M., glad the day was over and ready for the night.

With the corps review closed the month and its events; much of the men's spare time was spent in exploring the country adjacent to the camp, many whiled away the hours between drills along the shell road that led to Jacksonville, that fine driveway that came into existence when northern generosity sent the suffering south more money than she needed or knew what to do with; others sought the shade under the solemn live oaks in Panama park and glanced in upon the concrete oval where some of the world's bicycle records have been made. The chief amusement was fishing in the placid St. Johns at Cummers mill or at the railroad bridge at Trout Creek. Saturdays and Sundays found many disciples of Izaak Walton with line and net angling for drum and bass or devoting all energy to catching crabs, for it took two men to haul in a crab and then they generally missed him. There was so much sameness to the scenery and the men saw it always before them so they will never forget it were there nothing else but impressions of idle moments to fix it before them.

For sixteen days now the regiment had been sweltering in awful heat; the burning sun was above and the burning sand beneath, filling all space with direct and reflected rays of intensest heat that drove the men moping to their tents. A small breeze about 10 o'clock that came blowing its way so gently up from St. John's direction, as if it felt uncertain of its welcome, was all that made the day endurable. Between the hours of 11 and 2 wisdom drove every man into the shade and regimental work had to wait for cooler hours. The chief blessing of that climate is in the cool nights; all that yellow pine grows in the night time; the humidity of the atmosphere is so dense that a man must either roll his clothes up and hide them or wring them out in the morning before dressing. Unaccustomed to such conditions, the men soon showed the effects of the change; acclimation was an impossibility; not for a citizen with home comforts, but for northern army men, yes. The number at sick call was gradually increasing and the eyes of some of the men were touched with a tinge of beautiful yellow. Then came the fever in terrific force, but it was a sickness the German calls "Heimweh," known in Camp Cuba Libre as "Home sick fever." It was *not* unmanly; going to Cuba was not a certainty; when it was the men cheered, although false reports of its heat still more intense and of its yellow plague were not alluring. Let them fight, let them move—anything rather than an indefinite stay where they were, and the reason was legitimate, gainsay it he who will, and the same ground that justified the resignation of some of the army's highest officers and men of soundest judgment; and the funny part of it all was the farce played by the line officers before the colonel on the 3d of September, when each reported in turn a possible half dozen who were anxious to go home, and one a probable three or four who might go if the way was clear, while a regimental vote would have revealed eighty-five per cent. of the men with their hearts in Hoosierdom; in fact, a quiet ballot by the first sergeants resulted in ninety-five per cent., and a telegram of the information sent the governor. The next day was Sunday, and the time for the chaplain's evening service had come, and the pulpit was to be occupied by the colonel. The regiment was there, and it was a great and notable event. The colonel only asked for five minutes, and when urged to use the hour modestly replied that such a thing would be an impossibility, but when he got started, like all men who really have anything to say, he forget himself in the interest of his subject and what he said was a plenty. No one doubts to-day that he said the right thing; it was a searching speech, with plenty of sarcasm, plenty of encouragement and plenty of good advice, and the men went to their tents thoughtful and hopeful for the future.

On the 3d of the month the inspector-general of the corps, Lieutenant-Colonel Curtis Guild, Jr., came to the regiment on a tour of inspection. He was a genial officer, and the men liked him. The tents were all in order for his inspecting eye and the men were in company front in the streets. Their guns and clothing and military knowledge were inspected. A beautiful face on an enamel button was pinned to one man's coat. "Your sweetheart, I suppose," said the colonel. "Yes, sir," was the polite answer. "I suppose you think a great deal of her," remarked the colonel. "Yes, sir," said the soldier. "Well," said the colonel, with a twinkle in his eye, "put her under the lapel where she can't be seen; it's not military."

To another: "Well, young man, what would you do if you were a sentinel and an enemy should attempt to cross your line in the night?" "Present arms," was the prompt reply. "And you, my young man, what would you do if in the night time you discovered a fire in your captain's tent?" "Report it to headquarters, sir, through channels."

Headquarters tents were then visited, and the staff lined up for inspection, a favorable report was rendered, and the *inspector retired to Major Smith's tent.*

During the next few days some of the companies indulged in the beginnings of skirmish drill, and on the 6th the regiment was once more in line for a division review on the parade ground by the park at 5 P. M.

On the morning of the 9th, Colonel Durbin was, by General Order No. 15, made commander of the First Brigade, in which capacity he served until October 14.

This same day saw the departure of the Third Nebraska. Colonel Bryan had gone some time before on a sick leave and his regiment was now going to Pablo Beach. The regiment did not move as a whole and as the men passed through our camp on the way to the train a portion of the band before the colonel's tent played them a parting march as they moved through in a drenching rain, and the next day found the One Hundred and Sixty-first with a supply of sentry boxes that had been put together by Nebraska labor.

On the 12th about fifty men were sent to the Recuperative Station at Pablo Beach. Lucky men! every one but one got a furlough home within fifteen days, and that

NUMBER NINE—RELIEF.

one preferred to grin and bear it out in the regiment, and accordingly returned. The same morning saw the departure of the Second Mississippi Regiment, which left a brigade of one regiment only in the camp. It was the privilege of the One Hundred and Sixty-first to clean up the camping site of the departing regiment, and after gathering out any lumber that could be advantageously used all else was burned, the city authorities took up the water pipes and the ground was left clean but forsaken. The Third Nebraska sent a detail back from Pablo to do this work on the ground they left, but of all camps that needed cleaning the one left by the First South Carolina needed it most; the condition of men and camp on the day of departure was a fit matter of report to General Barclay by Major Megrew, field officer of the day; that some had more sickness than the One Hundred and Sixty-first is not strange in view of the contrast between their camp conditions; it was a matter of self protection that took a detail from the Indiana regiment into the filth and foul smelling odor left behind by these Carolina troops, and set fire to everything that would burn and filled all their sinks with sand.

There is no question but that the idea of burning garbage instead of burying it is an excellent health preservative, and the "Backus Garbage Burner" will always invariably connect itself with the health status of the regiment. It is generally supposed that water will extinguish fire, but the lieutenant-colonel declared that the only thing science revealed was that when water and fire came together, one of the two would be consumed, from which he deduced the idea that if he had enough fire he could burn water. A little search revealed an old engine boiler made of heavy iron and lying rejected in the yards of Merrill Steven's Engineering Company in the city.

The necessary purchase was made and the mammoth concern hauled to the rear of camp and there set up as shown by the accompanying illustration. A mighty fire that would have put the old time infernal regions to shame was there created and the colonel said "Bring on your garbage." Every thing that goes to make up slop was then brought, potato peeling, bread refuse, hardtack, tin cans, coffee leavings, dish water and all its other wet ingredients and into the fiery furnace it went; the flames licked up the water, then consumed the dry stuff and ended by burning up the ashes, while its designer looked on with a complacent smile. The garbage was dumped in above, the machine operated twice a day and consumed a half load of

Backus Garbage Burner.

wood at each operation. The institution was presented to the Third Division Hospital on the regiment's departure and a somewhat smaller one procured at Savannah which did service throughout the stay in Cuba, where the locomotive was fired by Harry Rider, of Company F.

For ten days after the 12th nothing of note occurred save the faithful work of the men at drill. Every morning from 7 till 9 battalion drills were on, and a regimental parade for every afternoon at 4:30. In looking back upon the work of these early days and upon the continual marching in review at "port arms" before the colonel one may discover the chief reason for that degree of excellence afterwards attained. It was not meant to pass in silence the narrow escape of our old friend Newton Burke, the wagonmaster; may he live long and prosper; his laugh was a cross betweeen a bantum cackle, a horse neigh and a sheep bleat; you can tell him in the next world if you're near him and he takes a notion to laugh. Others had escapes; Goodrich just missed a cork leg; the chaplain a swampy grave and Stott a humiliating death in the presence of the command, all on account of a horse—the first two from inferior horsemanship, but to manage the steed that Stott rode took skill and strength that few possess. Every one has seen the picture of Sheridan in his daring ride so highly tragic as he dashed along the line of his command, but Phil wasn't in it with Stott. He was mounted on "Kaki." Everyone knows Kaki and knows that if he could speak he could tell some ancient tales, but the way he flew up and down the lines that day was most surprising to Stott and made him think seriously of resigning his commission and joining the Rough Riders. But Newton Burke's experience beat them all. You see, Newton was the new wagonmaster, and, before the corral equipments came, had a few days of leisure and would see the wonderful country into which he had come. Now, Newton should have known better than to get on Pete (pronounced as two syllables) for Pete would do anything for Sam Kahn and knew that Sam and Newton didn't get along very well, and consequently had it in for Newton; he couldn't dump the old man outright, for his purpose would have been too apparent, and so waited an occasion which came when a neighboring regimental band began playing as Pete and Newton were going along a ditch by the railroad. Now, Pete didn't do a thing to Newton but roll down the ditch and light on Newton with enough force to break his rib, and the latest is, that Newton got even with Pete by applying for a pension for being kicked by a government mule.

September was a month of noted camp improvement. The latter part of the first week's work was begun on the guard-house and ended by erecting a veritable prison, which the men called the bastile, and a cut of which is on another page. Prior to its construction the men were lodged in the assembly tent, and called it a snap; but when put in the bastile the thing was different, and yet how seemingly strange that some men were willing to spend much of their time there rather than make an effort to be a good soldier.

About the middle of the month the bath-houses were built, one for each battalion, and a little later, one for headquarters; then the mess-shacks were built, and the necessary work of this character at an end; provision for comfort, cleanliness and sanitary conditions had been made, but work did not stop here. Improvements continued; early in the month two poles were spliced, making one of enormous length, and raised before headquarters to bear the regimental flag, and at reveille and retreat the stars and stripes were raised and lowered as long as Camp Cuba Libre lasted. This ceremony is at once beautiful and impressive, the flag going up to the music of "My Country, 'tis of Thee," and dropping slowly to the soft strains of the "Star Spangled Banner," as every man uncovers and lays his hat over the place of his heart. Witness it once and you will know the American loves his flag. Around the base of this pole was a seven-pointed star-shaped frame, filled with fresh sawdust from the mill, which, when the new pole was raised after the storm had broken the first one, was replaced by a mortar star, covered over with a pure white coat, imprinted with the name of the regiment's brigade and division. Later in the month, on the 19th, was begun the rustic fence running to the right of the regiment and bearing in letters, made from limbs, the regimental and battalion designations; the tall pines standing in the camp were dressed in a coat of whitewash; the walks along the officers' quarters were covered with sawdust, every visible root was grubbed up and the utmost pains taken in policing the ground, and when the end of the month was near and the news came that the honorable secretary of war was about to visit the corps, the camp of the One Hundred and Sixty-first was ready for any man's inspection.

General Alger's visit to the Camp Cuba Libre was a notable event for the Seventh Army Corps and for the One Hundred and Sixty-first Indiana. The general was accompanied to the city by Surgeon-General Sternberg and General M. I. Luddington, quartermaster-general. The First and Second Division hospitals were inspected and the divisions reviewed; it was after four o'clock when the general and his party reached the Third Division hospital in the rear of the One Hundred and Sixty-first Indiana camp. Not content to allow the surgeon to make these inspections alone, General Alger accompanied him, and together they walked through every ward on the grounds, making inquiry as to needs and conditions, and speaking words of kindness and encouragement to the boys who were sick. The sun was going down as the general left the hospital and walked over into the camp of the One Hundred and Sixty-first Indiana. He gave only a casual glance at the white-washed trees and the well-made sawdust sidewalks but passed to the rear of the camp. It was on this occasion that he pronounced those words which caused the eyes of the whole Seventh Army Corps to turn upon the regiment from Indiana. He said the camp was "a marvel of neatness" and pronounced it a "revelation." It was dark when the Honorable Secretary of War reached the parade grounds to watch the Third Division pass in review before him; it was perhaps the only review of its kind ever held, and was a most interesting spectacle to the people who waited impatiently for the general to come; the moon was vainly endeavoring to get from behind the hazy clouds and was barely successful in keeping total darkness from covering the scene. One regiment could hardly be distinguished from another as they passed before the distinguished visitor, but there was one regiment different from all the rest, and when it had passed the general said to its commanding officer, "*Colonel Durbin, that is the finest regiment I have ever seen.*" After the infantry came the cavalry and the pack mules, which latter afforded great amusement for the visitors as they kicked up their heels and dust and broke away in double time toward the corral which they much preferred to passing in review before the distinguished guest from Washington.

It is needless here to comment upon the satisfaction to officers and men caused by General Agler's commendation of the camp and of the regiment. It shows duty well done and hard honest effort made to bring honor to the great commonwealth from which we came and we have a right to be proud of the record.

CHAPTER V.

CAMP CUBA LIBRE.

October 1-23, '98.

October was ushered in by a Saturday that brought its usual inspection and accompanying quiet while the men lounged around in the shade, or strolled away to the river. The sky was a little overcast in the afternoon and no one would have been surprised if an ordinary storm had blown down upon us, but as night drew its sable gown around us and the men lay down to sleep, none ever dreamed of the things he should behold on the morrow; but the fact was that a hurricane had arisen in the West Indies and was fast sweeping toward us over the south Atlantic coast. The storm struck us in the "wee small hours" of the night; the flags began their slap bang crack as the wind blew "great guns," and the rain poured down in torrents; the poles creaked, the tents swayed and the ropes tugged at the pegs, but they stood it well; yet a few went down in the night and their contents were blown over Duaval county, while a few hats were supposed to have crossed the St. Johns river. No one could sleep and either lay or sat up in their tent, expecting every moment to be buried beneath the groaning canvas. At 5 A. M. the storm abated and all hands were out to see the sights. It was a dismal scene that met the eye, but even while the men were talking of the night's experience, the elements began returning in all their fury; this time every blast that blew discounted one hundred fold anything the night had seen. The storm seemed to grow fiercer with every passing moment; the tall pines moaned and strained their fiber as their tops came bowing to the ground, the flag-pole snapped and falling struck Sergeant Major Starr across the back a glancing blow that saved his life. One after the other the tents went down; the huge assembly tent was torn in shreds as the angry wind first blew it down and then played so fiercely underneath it; the wet soil had gathered tight around the pegs, but the houses were built on sand and true to prophecy fell. There was no waiting on orderlies then, but every man's hand was turned to save his property, and, while so engaged word came of needed help at the Third

STORM SCENE AT THIRD DIVISION HOSPITAL.

Division hospital. At once more men than could be used left their tents to the mercy of the wind, and went to render heroic service in caring for their sick comrades. By reason of their size the hospital tents were harder to keep from going down, but they were held in place by main strength at the ropes while firmer fastenings were secured. Everything in camp was drenched and the men were cold, tired and hungry. Although the storm was abated by 1 P. M., a strong and threatening wind blew all day, and fearful of another night of similar experience, the colonel made arrangements with the Florida Central & Peninsula railroad to furnish passenger coaches for the comfort of the men and when they came out in the evening many of the men availed themselves of this opportunity to secure a good night's rest after the stormy events of that gloomy but stirring October day.

On the 3rd the new hospital mentioned on another page and prompted by the generous impulse of Colonel Durbin, was begun and certainly did prove a blessing to the men who so quickly exhausted its accommodations. About this time a skin concern sent its advance agent into the camp with a proposition to take its convalescents and men with that tired feeling "down the St. John's river for an airing." The price was to be seventy-five cents per man and a fine clamchowder, coffee and ham sandwich dinner free for every man who went. The boat, a fair vessel with "Crescent" written on its prow, left the docks at Cummer's mill at 9:30 o'clock with two hundred and fifty men of the described character on board. The chaplain in charge gave the management credit for honesty, supposed the wonderful dinner was being held in reserve for the men, although sandwiches and coffee were being sold with marvelous rapidity at ten cents each, and when dinner time came the firm was very sorry but everything was gone but chowder, some sort of a red pepper solution through which a clam may possibly have crawled on his pinchers so elevated that the real thing never touched the water. It was also evident that instead of taking the men out for their health they were taken out for a drunk, as beer and whisky were being sold freely; the bar was, however, ordered closed and a guard put over it. The boat finally arrived at Mayport an old stuck-in-the-sand town that betrays its beautiful name, where there was plenty of whiskey but not a thing to eat but dried beef and crackers. Lieutenant Johnson told the management the opinion of honest people in a very emphatic way, and the vessel was boarded for return and we came back a hungry, tired but wiser crowd with only one man wet outside and he fell off the dock in an effort to walk the gang plank. The following day the regiment was rejoicing in pay day and on the 7th the colonel was in possession of communications authorizing him to have his regiment ready to move to Savannah, from which point it was expected embarkation would be made for Cuba. Anywhere to get away from Jacksonville. Its people had been kind and many soldiers will always remember gratefully their introduction into the families and treatment by the good people of that place, but they were anxious to leave. Just what the Savannah trip meant they did not know—grape-vines were sprouting—an immediate departure for Cuba, a winters stay in Georgia—getting ready for muster out—but news of such a definite character was enough to fill the men with new life, for a volunteer hates stagnation and that is what the continued camp life at Camp Cuba Libre was, and so the men waited eagerly for orders to pack.

It was on the 7th that the post exchange was opened for business, the officer in charge being Lieutenant Hanson G. Freeman, Company M, Lawrenceburg. Sergeant C. B. Owens, Company G, was detailed as sergeant in charge and manager. Privates Will A. Taylor, Company M, and Otto Beard, Company C, were detailed as clerks. The regiment having no funds to purchase goods with, the first bill, amounting to one hundred dollars, was bought on ten days' time but was paid off within five days after date of purchase, this being the only bill contracted for and not paid upon delivery during the entire existence of post exchange.

The line of goods handled were always of the choicest quality, consisting of fruits in season, canned and bottled goods, cakes, crackers, fresh pies, nuts, candies, cigars, tobaccos, smokers' articles in general. The drinks served being soda water, lemonade, ginger ale and Hire's root beer; no intoxicants whatever were sold or handled in any way. From starting out with an original invoice of one hundred dollars, the stock on hand at different times would invoice two thousand dollars. Dividends would be declared monthly derived from the profits of the post exchange and distributed to the different companies of the regiment, the band, non-commission and hospital mess. The largest distribution for one month amounted to eight hundred and sixty dollars, this being in the month of March at Camp Columbus, Havana, Cuba. Lieutenant Freeman being the regimental commissary, asked to be relieved as officer of post exchange. Lieutenant Paul Comstock was appointed January 15, 1899, to take the place made vacant by Lieutenant Freeman. No changes were made in the force employed. The largest day's receipts amounted to three hundred and fifteen dollars. Total amount of cash given to regiment in the six months and ten days of its existence amounted to $2,460.00, besides other donations to the regiment amounting to about seventy-five dollars being made. The loss incurred in moving camps by reason of theft or otherwise amounted to five hundred dollars.

One feature of the business in Cuba was the purchase of oranges in bulk by the wagon load, from five thousand to

Post Exchange at Camp Onward.

six thousand being required to fill one of our army wagons. The wholesale prices of this luscious fruit ranged from five dollars to fourteen dollars per thousand, according to quality and quantity on the market. The first month in Cuba the post exchange handled eighty thousand oranges.

Great credit is due both to Sergeant Owens for his careful management and to private Will Taylor for his long and faithful service as clerk.

The first target practice of the regiment occurred on October 8. In the afternoon the regiment went to the rifle range and each company was assigned to two targets, and supplied with a thousand rounds of cartridges. Now was the time to put in practice the instructions given by that officer of the regular army who gathered the commissioned and non-commissioned officers of the regiment in the assembly tent and told them how to shoot; carefully calculating the distance, the resistance of the air and the parabola of the bullet they pulled the trigger; the old Springfields banged back into their shoulders with a vengeance that made them blue; the men looked for the red signals, but the target keepers generally forgot to wave them; occasionally a red sign would appear and describe now a horizontal and now a perpendicular or perchance a circle each of which every man that fired declared meant a "bull's eye." The regiment returned at 6:30 P. M., and a few days later marched again to the range, but found that an order had been issued declaring the practice stopped.

The drills were now being carried out at greater length, but the monotony of the wearisome "column right" and "left front into line," "to the rear" and "right forward fours right" and other preliminary movements was broken by the more interesting and less exhausting skirmish drill, the men dodging about in the bushes, stooping around by twos and fours, and little groups snap-

Second Battalion, Skirmish Drill. Camp Cuba Libre.

ping their rifles and making charges on an unseen enemy with yells that would scare the life out of a whole tribe of Sioux Indians.

The 11th of the month brought with it another division review. General Hubbard, the division commander, was about to leave, and the review of this day was not only his last but it was the last time before leaving Camp Cuba Libre that the regiment was to be reviewed other than by itself, and when it was over the men fell back into the routine of the life to which they were by this time so well accustomed, and wondered when the order was to come in definite shape for the move to Savannah; this order, however, was delayed on account of the coming visit of the Washington board of inspectors. This board consisted of Evan P. Howell, of Atlanta; Charles Denby, of Indiana; Colonel James A. Sexton, of Illinois; D. C. Gilman, president of Johns Hopkins University; Dr. W. W. Keen, of Philadelphia, and General Grenville M. Dodge, of New York, and was appointed by President McKinley to investigate charges pertaining to the sanitary conditions of the army. The party arrived at noon on the 17th, and proceeded at once to the camps of the corps. They examined the sinks, and the baths, and the bakeries and the commissary stores, and thoroughly inspected the condition of every corral, the report returned to the president being on the whole a favorable one.

The following day, at regimental review, General Hubbard was present and witnessed the parade, after which the regiment marched to his quarters, and forming in column of masses tendered him an appropriate farewell.

The closing scenes of Camp Cuba Libre were enlivened by many an evening spent around the "camp fire" during the cool October nights of our last week on the banks of the St. John's river. The men of the various companies were wont to gather round a blazing fire of pine knots and while away the long evenings with song and jest, and many a song of love and home was wafted on the soft winds that blew up from the old ocean. This was an every night occurrence; b..t now and then a general "camp fire" would be held, and around the huge fire a great circle would be formed, and in the light of the blaze the best talent of the regiment would entertain the boys and officers till "taps." Amateur boxers donned the gloves and administered the "solar plexus," Rudy gave his "coon" song and "nigger" dance; Jacobs did his "turn," and Sergeant Wolf delighted the assembled soldiers with his sweet voice. Will those evenings ever be forgotten, whiled away under the tall graceful pine trees and the beautiful night skies of Florida? They were the green spots in the Jacksonville desert, and will grow dear as the years go by "and fond recollections present them to view."

On the 21st the order came directing the First Brigade, Second Division, to which, upon the corps reorganization, the One Hundred and Sixty-first Indiana had been assigned, to repair to Savannah on the evening of October 23, Sunday, of course.

On the night of this same day just after "taps" the camp was aroused by the cry of fire; the guard on post near the railroad platform discovered a small blaze in a heap of rubbish in one of the abandoned stands near the regiment; he promptly gave the alarm and the guard assisted by numbers of the men of the regiment attempted to save the adjoining buildings but to no purpose as the light dry pine burned fiercely and the buildings were soon consumed. The pine trees near by caught fire and added luster to the scene and all the night around us was made as bright as the day while dense volumes of pitch black smoke rolled up to make the heavens darker above us; the whole affair made a very respectable bonfire. The 22nd was a day of packing such as the day before our departure from Camp Mount had witnessed and with the dawn of the 23rd the business of getting out began. At 9 o'clock the signal sounded for the tents to fall and in three seconds every tent was flat. The freight was in and near the camp and by 6 o'clock was loaded and ready to leave and soon thereafter the men were ready also but it became evident that a wait was in store for the regiment and as darkness began to fall camp fires were lighted and every one tried to make themselves as comfortable as possible. A little of this would have sufficed as the men were tired and supperless save the hardtack and such cold lunch as could be procured. The camp ground of the One Hundred and Sixty-first presented a scene that night that will be one of the lingering memories. Every company had from three to four fires as the nights were cold and all must be warm. There was a camp fire at Major Megrew's quarters and one where the colonel's tent had stood; many of the buildings had been reduced to lumber for transportation but plenty were left to burn and everything was ignited; the kitchens and mess shacks that were left standing were fired one after the other and the very sky was illumined by the conflagration while the scene was enlivened by stirring music from the band and then the men began to stretch themselves around the fire to wait while the flames dispelled the darkness and silhouetted their resting forms on the sand of Florida that was soon to be left forever. At 12:15 A. M. the first train came in and the first section, under command of Lieutenant-Colonel Backus and composed of the First Battalion and Companies B and F of the Second, went on board and started; Major Megrew also accompanied this section. The rest of the regiment waited till 2:30 A. M. before their

Waiting for the Train—Camp-Breaking at Camp Cuba Libre.

transportation arrived and hungry and sleepy were soon following the others on their way to the new camp at Savannah.

A few days previous to our departure the regiment had been assigned to its new position in the Seventh Army Corps, which had on the 21st been reorganized as follows:

CAVALRY BRIGADE.

Seventh United States Cavalry.
Eighth United States Calvary.

FIRST DIVISION.

FIRST BRIGADE.

First Texas Infantry.
Second Louisiana Infantry.
Third Nebraska Infantry.

SECOND BRIGADE.

Ninth Illinois Infantry.
Second South Carolina Infantry.
Fourth Illinois Infantry.

SECOND DIVISION.

FIRST BRIGADE.

One Hundred and Sixty-first Indiana Infantry.
Second Illinois Infantry.
First North Carolina Infantry.

SECOND BRIGADE.

Fourth Virginia Infantry.
Forty-ninth Iowa Infantry.
Sixth Missouri Infantry.

CHAPTER VI.

CAMP ONWARD.

SAVANNAH, October 24–December 12, '98.

When the first section arrived at Savannah at 9 A. M. the next morning it found the regimental impedimenta one hour in advance and Captain West's force busily engaged in getting the horses and mules out on "terra firma." In the unloading of the remaining freight the record was broken. The quartermaster and commissary supplies were handled with the accustomary dispatch but the transportation department, altogether out of harmony with the usual "southern hustle," got in a hurry, and backing the cars into the freight yard, pitched the lumber, floors, tables, benches and boxes into a confused, tumbled, jumbled-up heap that looked like it had been struck by a Kansas cyclone or a Jacksonville storm. When the second section arrived one and one-half hours later, like the first it was served with coffee at the station before starting for camp. As the companies marched through the city the men crowded out of their stores and the women out of their homes and while the chambermaids waved sheets or pillowslips from the second-story windows the daughters used their handkerchiefs below and the populace on the sidewalk cheered the boys from Indiana a welcome as they passed, and on out the Thunderbolt road they marched to camp and stacked arms on the site which was to be their "stomping ground" for the next seven weeks; this time the regiment was less fortunate in the land reserved for them; it was low and swampy, cut through by ditches and altogether undesirable for a regimental camping site; objections were made without avail and everybody prepared to make the best out of it. The company streets had all been staked off and an old dilapidated board and wire fence that ran through the length of Company K street was removed; a deep ravine ran along the right of the regiment and a large ditch almost through the center, which necessitated two thirds of the men to pass what they called " over Jordan " to affiliate with members of the First Battalion; the swamp prevented the First Battalion line officers' tents from being

HEADQUARTERS.

pitched in their accustomary place and both these and the battalion commander's tent were pitched toward the road along which ran the staff tents with the exception of headquarters which were more comfortably located in an old house situated nearer the company tents and which has since burned. The colonel's tent was used for a guard house until quarters were prepared, and later, in the second week of November, the tents occupied by the staff were moved near the headquarters house and in a row with the Third Battalion line officers. The tents were pitched without floors and a couple of days were passed before sufficient material could be rescued from the debris at the freight yards to furnish them with that much-needed comfort and the tents that were all too small under Jacksonville conditions had room enough and to spare as the boys hugged up in spoon fashion to pass the night. Camp construction began at once, and while the colored men of chain and stripe cleaned the ditches and drained the camp the carpenters began their work and cook shacks sprang up along the rear as fast as material came in and in a week every company cook was under cover, bridges were built across the ditches, and after the third day the drills were on again.

On the 27th the battalions marched to Thunderbolt, a Coney Island sort of a place; some of the companies fell out and some of the men fell in to a well stocked establishment and after waiting on themselves forgot the eighth commandment and told the men to "remember the Maine" for his pay; the battallions marched down past Bonaventure and returned along the other road by way of Dale Avenue drive. The next day occurred the first regimental formation on Georgian soil; the review, which was not the best ever given by the regiment, was witnessed by General Williston from his tent door.

The drills began on the 29th with their usual regularity; a couple of days at close order and attention was devoted to the more important skirmish drill. A most suitable spot for extended order work was later found back of the cemetery that lay near the junction of the road and street car track, and here in the underbrush and ravines and around the old Confederate breastworks the officers found ample room and excellent environment for scattering their men to the best advantage for such purpose. The last few days of the month brought to the line officers the usual burdensome necessity of getting the rolls in shape for monthly muster and the new month came in with the sound of hammer and saw at work on the commissary, bakery and guard house, while Anthony Montani took his sweater and clarionet and other articles and bid us all a fond adieu.

The substantial structure that rose beyond the ditch to the regiment's right during the first week in November was prepared for the commissary, the bakery and the exchange, and was by conceded opinion the finest arranged building of its kind in the corps.

Sunday was the 6th, and this day, as on other Sabbaths, the One Hundred and Sixty-first camp looked lonely by contrast; while southern regiments were swarming with visitors from Savannah; ours, the nearest to the city, was passed by with a glance over the fence; in this one respect, like the man who fell out of the ballon, we simply were not in it. Why this apparent thusness? is it so hard to forget? Let us be charitable and say they were unthoughtful, but Ivy said the young ladies didn't know what they were missing.

The next day brought Major Wright, the colored paymaster. The major was assisted by his son, also colored, and encountered no embarrassment in disposing to the officers and men of the regiment the coin which the government had seen fit to entrust to his care; the major remarked of his respectful reception.

In the afternoon General Green, accompanied by other distinguished officers of the army, reviewed the division. The six regiments marched to an open field across the way from the Second Division hospital and stood in column of masses at attention for about thirty minutes while whole regiments of armed sand flies enjoyed an undisturbed picnic pestering the patience out of an army of men to whom military etiquette forbade interference, after which the division passed in review before the general, in whose honor it was held, before his departure for Cuba.

On November 11 General Lee arrived at Savannah from his home in Virginia, where he had been in attendance at the bedside of his aged mother during her sickness, death and funeral, and which had necessitated an absence from his official duties for a period of several weeks, during which time the command of the corps devolved on General Keifer of the First Division. The general was accompanied to Savannah by Governor Tyler and a distinguished party of Virginians, both ladies and gentlemen. This was his first appearance at Savannah since the arrival of the corps at that point, and he was given a royal welcome both by the citizens of that beautiful and enterprising city and by his command. He immediately established his headquarters at the DeSota hotel and assumed command of the corps. One of his first official acts was the naming of the camp, which he designated "Camp Onward" in view of the onward march to Cuba.

He immediately issued an order for a review of the corps, including all the troops under his command, which took place the following day in the city of Savannah in what is known as Forsythe Park Extension, and was witnessed by thousands of citizens of Savannah and neighboring cities and surrounding country, for whom it was a gala occasion. Most of these people had never seen any considerable body of troops together before, and were enthusiastic in their demonstrations of approval. The One Hundred and Sixty-first Indiana was tendered little short of an ovation upon its splendid appearance; its full companies, straight lines and excellent marching being commented upon for many succeeding days by its enthusiastic admirers. who were numbered by the hundreds in the city of Savannah; the Press of the city was also effuse in its praise of the work of the regiment, giving it special mention in its account of the review and commenting at length upon its excellent appearance.

The succeeding days brought with them the usual routine of camp life, unbroken by any event of interest. On Sunday, 13th, the camp site was inspected by a surgical board; complaints of a sanitary nature had been made from the day the regiment first saw the grounds and were about to result in an exchange of position between the regiment, brigade and division headquarters which would have furnished excellent locations of sufficient size for all, but owing to the speedy departure for Cuba the inspecting board advised a retention of positions then held. Company E was at this time on duty at the rifle range, having been detailed there the 9th of the month to superintend the target practice of the corps. On the 16th Companies A, K, M and L went to the range for practice, the other companies having been there the day before; five shots at two hundred yards and five at three hundred were allowed each man, and the time was spent shooting at black Spaniards on boards, with results showing remarkable improvements in the art of war since the previous like experience at Jacksonville.

On the 21st the quartermaster unloaded before his store-house twenty-four large boxes, and as the men lined up by companies each one received and was charged with a $11.49 navy blue brass-button caparisoned overcoat. They made every man look like Napoleon, but that wasn't what they were for; they were intended to shield the men from those cold blasts which the colonel told them next day at parade were sweeping over Hoosierdom and which came whizzing over the cotton belt a few days later and sent the men shivering to their tents right glad the authority was wiser than they, many of whom only a few days before had vigorously protested against any such needless and extravagant expenditure. The greater part of the drill during the middle portion of November was battalion extended order.

Nothing of note occurred until the 24th, for which day the boys had been anxiously waiting and wondering what good thing it had in store for them. The day was ushered in with all the beauties of a typical autumn day in the south, and was given up wholly to pleasure. At 10 o'clock in the assembly tent a most excellent sermon was preached by the Rev. Mr. Smith, of the city; this was followed at the noon hour by elaborate spreads in each of the twelve companies of the regiment. The ladies of Savannah were in the dinner serving business out of most excellent motive, but on a plan hardly savoring of the generosity which could so easily have come from so large a populace so greatly benefited by the presence of so great a number of soldiers; we were to raise the money and they were to serve the turkey; but not out of any criticism, but simply with the feeling that the money once raised the serving would be a comparatively easy and pleasant task, while the good ladies were already overburdened with an infinite amount of the same thing, the colonel made the preparation and the serving of the dinner a strictly regimental affair. The ladies were offended, but a due explanation once more bridged the chasm between the north and the south, and sweet harmony was restored.

The boys did not have the ladies but they had warm turkey instead and plenty of it. One thousand one hundred pounds of turkey were furnished by Armour & Co., to be accounted for in surplus meat. There were ninety gallons of oysters that day; there were cranberries and celery and mince pies and other delicacies which appeal to the inner man and which go hand in hand with the day thus observed. For once, hardtack, bacon and canned beef was but a memory which the very next day arose to haunt those who had partaken of the feast in the shape of a life-sized reality and to head off any tendencies to gout by reason of the gormandizing of the boys the day before. Only one kick was registered, and that of an enlisted man who having disposed of nine pounds of turkey, a quart of cranberries, two mince pies and other edibles in proportion kicked because his capacity for consumption went back on him at time so inopportune, but who was reconciled to his fate on hearing of the Thanksgiving dinner which the boys in the hospital had: poor fellows who were given a bit of turkey to chew, on the express condition of spitting it out just when it was in the best condition to swallow, and the cruel part about it was that some one was there to see that they did spit it out. In some of the officers' messes dinner, during which service the table fairly groaned under its load of good things, was postponed until evening in order, as some of the officers asserted, that they might "eat with the boys" but which knowing ones assert they did by reason of the fact that visions of two good dinners were in sight. The afternoon was given over to a diversity of amusements upon which the boys were privileged to attend; many cheered the picked baseball nine of our regiment while it secured a victory over a similarly chosen nine from the First North Carolina on the parade ground of our regiment; others attended the shooting match between picked teams of the best shots from the Seventh Army Corps and the Savannah Gun Club at the rifle range of the latter east of the camp; still others witness the football game in which an eleven from the Second Louisianas contested for supremacy with the First Texas Knights of the Gridiron at the City ball park; not a few attended the matinee at the Savannah Theater or saw the Rough Riders in their exhibition at Thunderbolt.

The day ended most auspiciously in the evening when some of the ladies of Savannah gave an elocutionary and musical entertainment in the assembly tent at which some of the best talent in the city appeared in the various numbers, a favor highly commendable and thoroughly appreciated; and thus the entire day was one joyous occasion that will long be remembered by every man in the regiment.

The aforesaid festivities were followed on November 25th by a sham battle between the two brigades of the Second Division; the First Brigade was assigned to a position behind the huge earthworks thrown up east of Savannah for the protection of the city at the time of Sherman's famous march to the sea; the works in question remain intact although overgrown to a considerable extent by forest trees and shrubbery and are a grim reminder of the fruits of war in the terrible strife of '61 to '65. To hold these works against the attack of the Second Brigade was the duty assigned to the First Brigade; previous to leaving camp both brigades were supplied liberally with blank cartridges; the Second Brigade was given one hour's start of the First in which to afford them ample time to reconnoiter and decide upon their mode of attack; the First Brigade, with band playing and banners unfurled to the breeze marched out and took possession of the earth works and awaited the report of the scouts sent out in all directions to locate, if possible, the enemy and their probable mode of attack; in

the meantime the firing line was established and supports
and reserves held in readiness, the One Hundred and Sixty-
first Indiana being assigned to the firing line; in about one
hour the sounds of occasional shots about one and one-half
miles to our front indicated that our scouts had been discovered and were being driven in; shortly afterward they
could be distinguished across the open country directly to
our front through the undergrowth just beyond, hastily
retreating, closely pressed by an under fire of the advance
guard of the enemy; re-inforcements to cover their retreat
were now sent out; the scouts having reached the edge of
the open space between the enemy and the earthworks,
took advantage of such protection as the country afforded
firing as they came; having advanced to a sufficient distance
to be no longer endangered by a fire from the earthworks,
and a company of the enemy in close order formatoin
having needlessly exposed itself about three-quarters of a
mile directly to our front, Major Peterson, of the Third
Battalion of the One Hundred and Sixty-first Indiana,
which occupied the center of the works, with the Second
Illinois on our extreme right, and the Carolinas on our left,
ordered the squads of his battalion on the firing line to fire
by volley on the company thus exposed and which must
necessarily have been riddled in actual engagement, which
opinion the commander of the company in question evi-
dently shared, for he immediately changed his formation
from a close to an open order; re-inforcements quickly came
up and the enemy continued to advance under heavy fire
which now became general on both sides; they were practically subdued even before the support was ordered to
the firing line, and with the result that much of the reserve
of the First Brigade did not fire a single shot, although the
entire force of the enemy was hurled against the works;
needless to assert that the enemy was called off the field

by the judges of the occasion, competent officials of the regular army, and the battle awarded to the First Brigade as having thoroughly and effectively protected their entrenchments.

During the succeeding few days the overcoats which had been issued a week previous were very much in demand, the temperature having fallen very perceptively, together with cold, drizzling rains, accompanied by biting blasts, which heralded the coming of one of the severest winters known in the south and throughout the states; woe to the luckless soldier whose finance was such that he could not possess the luxury of an oil stove; during the day he borrowed a warm-up from his more fortunate comrade or huddled up in his overcoat, backed up against a tree on the windless side in order that the full energy of the sun's rays might be spent to the best possible advantage in heightening the temperature of his anatomy; darkness overtaking him he huddled around a convenient camp fire in the company street, and at taps crawled between blankets and piled upon him all the sundry articles in his possession, such as trowsers, old shoes, socks, collar buttons and neckties, without even the formality of removing his hat, much less any other article of his wearing apparel. The quartermaster's ability to supply the demand for blankets was taxed to its utmost and he and his chief clerk were the most sought after individuals in camp.

The only instance of note to mar the monotony of the period thus intervening was the issuance of the new United States magazine rifle, which occurred on the 28th; the rifle in question includes all the meritorious points of the Krag-Jorgensen, together with the improvements adopted by the government; the men were highly pleased and they relinquished with pleasure the old Springfields with which they had been armed.

On the morning of the 30th occurred a regimental inspection that was the first and last of its kind. The regiment was lined up in heavy marching order and with open ranks while the colonel and members of his staff with polished boots and white gloved hands marched before them, between them and behind them while the colonel reminded them of neglected points of military toilet and attire and the officers made explanations of the same in writing after which the regiment passed in review and muster for pay began.

On the same day the new recruits began to arrive. The One Hundred and Sixty-first Indiana was the only regiment granted the privilege of recruiting at so late a date, which partially accounts for the unusually large companies that so pleased the visitors when this regiment passed before them in the parades and reviews down in Cnba. On November 5th Captain Stott was sent for this purpose to Indianapolis, the mustering-out place of the earlier regiments; he found only the One Hundred and Fifty-ninth, a very much discouraged lot of men and the work of recruiting went hard; all told one hundred and three men were secured, the larger number of whom left Indianapolis on the 28th, the others starting a few days later and arriving during the first four days of December. Sixty-nine of those who arrived on the 30th were mustered for pay after they stood for a short time in line before the old headquarters building and listened to a few words of welcome and advice from their new colonel; the others were mustered on arrival.

The officers of the regiment were thus kept busy during the remaining days of the month arming the troops and in the preparation of the pay rolls for the month of November. On the morning of the 30th regimental review preceded the muster for pay and in the evening at regimental parade Major M. R. Peterson, of the Third Battalion, severed his official connection with the regiment, his resignation having been accepted by the department at Washington that he might resume his duties in the regular army. His battalion having taken the assigned place on the parade ground, Colonel Durbin requested the major to take the position of honor on the right of the commanding officer of the regiment, who then proceeded in a few well-chosen words to express the regret of the entire command at losing such an efficient and painstaking officer. Major Peterson responded feelingly, expressing his regret at his enforced leavetaking and his best wishes for the future welfare of the regiment; the regiment having passed in review he assumed command of his battalion and in the battalion street formally took leave of the offices and men of his companies.

On the following evening at regimental parade Major Lee M. Olds, past captain of Company A, occupied the post of honor on the right of Colonel Durbin, who, in the presence of the regiment, formally presented the new major with his commission issued to him by the governor of Indiana after which he reviewed the regiment. It was the next day the information became current that the Second Division was to start in a few days for Cuba and Colonel Durbin was notified to have his regiment ready to move by the following Tuesday. During the forenoon of the 5th the regiment took a pleasant march to Savannah's noted " City of the dead." Bonaventure is said to be one of the most beautiful cemeteries in America and the history and romance connected with it make it doubly interesting; the estate, first owned in colonial times by an English nobleman, was sold to John Mulryn, whose only daughter was given in marriage to Josiah Tatnall and the union was typified by planting those now aged and hoary live-oaks in a monogram comprising the letters "M" and "T" still traceable in the shape of the sylvan aisles between the stately trees. Josiah Tatnall was a great soldier, serv-

ing in the wars of 1812 and of 1846 and was commander of the Merrimac in its battle with the Monitor. He became governor of Georgia and lies buried to-day in Bonaventure near the spot of his birth. The place is full of sacred associations and its gigantic trees, hung with their long hoary moss tresses, seem to speak of mourning and of weeping.

In view of the fact that the Second Division was to move so soon, an order for the last corps review on American soil previous to our departure was issued by General Lee. December 6, the day designated, was a delightful one for the occasion; all business was practically suspended in the city during the review, and the residents of Savannah gathered by thousands at Forsythe, the park extension, to witness the imposing spectacle. On this occasion, as on November 12, the review was a complete success, in which the One Hundred and Sixty-first added to its already enviable reputation, again securing special mention in the press of Savannah.

Right in the center of this great field of flashing steel and union blue was the statue of a confederate soldier standing erect on his handsome pedestal. He gave no sign of interest in the passing of so many thousands of soldiers; he saw the stars and stripes go by, but did not uncover; he watched General Lee ride past on his handsome gray charger, but did not bring his gun from parade rest; many a soldier wondered what he thought of it all, but we venture that he was glad to see the Yankees from the north and the sturdy western boys marching with proud step side by side with the men from Virginia and the Carolinas, and in it saw the evidence of a reunited nation, grand and great, and rejoiced with them in the mission they were going to accomplish.

Upon the return to camp the initial preparation for departure began, as the arrival of the transport was daily expected. The company tents were to be left, and all officers' tents were taken with one exception. Captain Guthrie was highly elated over an ingenious contrivance for heating his tent; he knew what destruction a lamp had caused before, but scorning experience he passed many a comfortable night while his less ingenious fellow officers were breathing hard to warm the space underneath the covers. The midnight hour of December 8 had passed when the explosion came which covered the captain and everything inside with burning oil. Unlike the men of another fire who came out unsinged, the commander of

Company I came forth bearing the marks of his disaster, which disappeared in a day or so and left him as good as new, but the tent and most of its contents never went to Cuba. On the 8th Colonel Durbin assumed command of the brigade. The Mobile arrived late in the evening of the 9th, and all the day following all floors and building,

PACKING UP—CAMP ONWARD.

the reduction of which to lumber form had occupied several days previous, were hauled to the wharf, and during the forenoon of the 12th the wagons of the Forty-ninth Iowa and Fourth Virginia, which were at the regiment's service, its own and its mules having been put aboard the Roumania, bound for Cuba on the 8th, hauled the regimental baggage to the docks, and shortly after the noon hour on December 12 the regiment broke camp, and at 1 P. M. the march to the docks began, arriving about 3 o'clock. Owing to the ample facilities for the loading of both troops and baggage on the transport Mobile, now the Sherman, there was little delay in getting all on board. In addition to the One Hundred and Sixty-first Indiana there was aboard the vessel one battalion and the band of the Second Illinois Volunteer Infantry, one or two companies of the signal corps, one company of the Fourth Virginia Volunteer Infantry, the Seventh Army Corps provost guard, General Williston with a portion of his staff and many other officers and men of various detachments, in all to the number of probably two thousand souls with baggage and supplies in endless quantities. Colonel Durbin being in command of the troops, and Colonel Backus being executive officer of the boat, Major Megrew was in command of the regiment. All men and officers being detained on board, the evening was spent in conversation, and at an early hour all were in their berths and bunks. The vessel lay alongside the dock until morning, and at 7 A. M. on the morning of the 13th the tug Marguarite started the great vessel down the river, cutting loose at 9:30; after fifteen minutes more the Estill took the pilot from us and we started on a calm sea toward the "Pearl of the Antilles."

The Mobile is an English-built vessel, and was formerly a freighter and cattle vessel. She was purchased from the Atlantic Transport Company by the United States government and refitted for the purpose of carrying troops. She is a twin-screw steamer capable of making seventeen knots an hour. The dining-room and officers' quarters are roomy and well furnished, while the men were provided with comfortable beds of wire springs and cotton mattresses arranged in tiers three in height. The Georgia shores

having been lost to view, no land was sighted until the following morning. At 11 o'clock the first and each succeeding day inspection of quarters was held; every man

"MOBILE"—OFF FOR CUBA.

was ordered below and proper inspection made as to cleanliness and ventilation.

Major Smith, of the First North Carolina, assisted by Major Longstreet, division commissary officer, and Lieutenant Welsh, of the One Hundred and Sixty-first Indiana, was in charge of the distribution of rations; three times a day the men were served with warm meals. Details from each company went into the kitchen, the food when cooked was placed on tables and the men, two companies at a time, filed by and receiving their portion ate it wherever most agreeable within limits of their restriction, The two thousand men were fed in about forty-five minutes.

During the entire next day the vessel steamed along with the sandy beaches of Florida plainly in sight; at 10:45 A. M. we passed Palm Beach and as darkness again set in we were nearing the southern coast of the peninsular state; the last light-house on the Florida keys was sighted at 9 P. M.; the keys were passed during the night and at daybreak no land was visible until about 8 o'clock when the shores of the stricken island for which we were bound could be dimly discerned in the distance; arriving off Havana we cruised in the waters of the gulf to a point opposite what was afterward the site of our camp, waiting for a pilot to take us ashore when orders were received from General Green directing us to come in to the Havana harbor for the purpose of disembarkation; at about 10 o'clock the Mobile entered the mouth of Havana harbor directly under the guns of the famous Morro.

As we glided along through the narrow entrance to the harbor, the frowning guns of old Morro and the antiquated fortress, Punta, hovering over us, as it were, on either side, not unlike the vultures which soared in countless hundreds, to our front, to our rear, above us and in all directions, the scene was absolutely indescribable and beggars description. Every nook and corner which afforded standing room on the walls of Moro Cubannas or the Punta was crowded with Spanish soldiers looking down on us, silent and sullen. Every house-top, balcony or window, the shores, docks and vessels in the harbor, were thronged with multitudes of a strange looking people representing almost every nationality of the earth, a condition existing in all tropical countries. The cheers of the two thousand of Uncle Sam's boys on board the transport who thronged the upper decks or balanced themselves in the rigging of the vessel, when the two bands on the ship struck up "My Country 'Tis of Thee" was answered in a no uncertain manner by the foreigners on shore and ship.

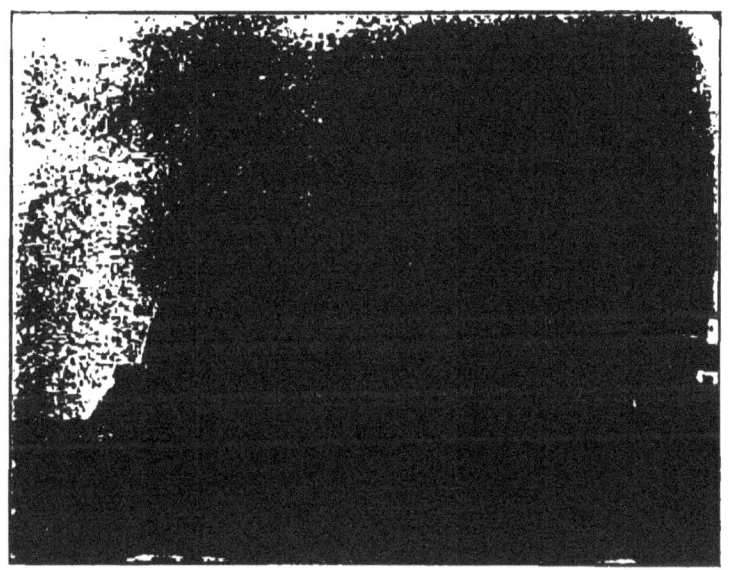

MORRO CASTLE.

Steaming thus slowly down the harbor, the climax was reached when we hove in sight of the wreck of the Maine, the broken and twisted mass of iron, visible above the surface of the water, illustrating as nothing else can do how over two hundred of our brave boys met death and now lie at the bottom of the harbor, victims of the treachery of an unscrupulous foe. Every head was uncovered and not a sound was uttered as the band struck up the "Star Spangled Banner." The stillness was almost oppressive, as all eyes were upon what was once the pride of our navy, now a worse than useless mass lying deserted off a foreign coast, a monument, as it were, to the boys who lie in their watery graves beneath. The sublimity of the occasion and its attendant incidents are beyond description. Heads were bowed and eyes tear-stained and it was with effort that the boys on board controlled the emotions surging through their hearts, and many experienced a choking sensation that they suppressed with difficulty. As if to add to the impressiveness of the occasion, the U. S. Topeka began firing a salute of thirteen guns. Passing a little beyond the charred and blackened wreck, we cast anchor under direction of the harbor pilot; this we had scarcely done when the transport was boarded by Lieutenant Fitzhugh Lee, Jr., bearing messages as to the disposition of the troops aboard. A few minutes later our corps commander, Major-General Fitzhugh Lee, accompanied by members of his staff, in a steam launch of one of the American battle ships in the harbor, hove in sight. His appearance was the signal for a spontaneous outburst by the boys aboard, who made the ancient harbor sound and resound with their cheers for their beloved commander. Shortly after the noonday mess had been served we struck anchor and proceeded to the docks where we lay until the following Saturday morning, during which interval the immense cargo of supplies and baggage had been unloaded and the disembarkation of the troops began, much to the pleasure of the boys, who, having been five days and nights aboard, had grown tired of the transport, the strange sights and unfamiliar scenes about them and were anxious to go ashore.

The regiment had been preceded by a detail of men in charge of the corral contingent and other regimental property. On the 7th Lieutenant Anheier, by order of Colonel Durbin, selected as a detail of men to accompany him on this mission Corporals Imes, Holdridge and Gorman and Privates Stanley, Reynolds and Hurst, of Com-

WAGON TRAIN ON ITS WAY TO CAMP.

pany I, and Private McAdams, of Company H. Sergeant Owens, of Company H, Ralph Robinson, Corporal Wilson and Sam Kahn were also to accompany the party. They went aboard the transport Roumania about 8 P. M. the evening of the 7th. The First North Carolina were on board. Seven regimental horses were in charge, two ambulances, twenty-seven wagons and seventy-nine mules. The vessel left at 5 A. M. on the 8th, arriving before the harbor the night of the 10th, and waited until Spanish law allowed it to enter after 6 A. M. the next morning. By 6 P. M. mules and wagons were unloaded and the mules corraled by a long rope stretched down a wide street.

Those nights were wild ones in Havana—nights of quarreling and wrangling and shooting, and it was the first night that the much-commented-upon riot occurred at the Hotel Inglaterra in which five Cubans were killed. By noon of the next day, all effects unloaded, the wagon train was ready to start for the ground that was to be the camping site for the Indiana regiment. A guide was secured, and under a hot sun the journey was begun.

The camp was reached about 4 P. M. on the 15th. The wagons were used to bring the corps headquarters effects from the wharf to Buena Vista.

When the regiment arrived the property was turned over to proper authority and Lieutenant Anheier reported with his men to the regiment.

CHAPTER VII.

HAVANA TO CAMP COLUMBIA.

The pen seems reluctant to write; not that the heat and dust and final fatigue which belong to the experience of this never-to-be-forgotten day, are things hard of description; such are common place, the mere mention of which suffices, but that the scenes which were ours to witness: the unbounded enthusiasm, the unrestrained manifestation of welcome, the glad shouts of happy-hearted people and the feelings which stirred the soul of the American soldier, are simply indescribable.

The troops were in command of Colonel Durbin, who, with his staff of brigade officers, headed the moving column. The One Hundred and Sixty-first Indiana was in command of Lieutenant-Colonel Backus, while Major Holman G. Puritan commanded the Third Battalion of the Second Illinois, which followed immediately in the rear.

Our regiment alone would have been the largest body of volunteer soldiers that had yet passed through, but with the above-mentioned battalion of the Second Illinois there were in all about fifteen hundred men in column on this memorable occasion.

The One Hundred and Sixty-first band of thirty-two pieces, ten snare drums, four fifes and eight bugles, marched in its accustomed place behind the regimental staff. The Illinois Battalion was headed by their regimental band. The great column began to move at 8:50 A. M. It marched through one or two minor streets, then up Cuba street, until it arrived at Rigla, one of the principal business streets of the city; through this street, or city lane, as they all might be more properly called, by reason of their uncomfortable narrowness, the column passed until it reached the Prado; passing to the left of Parque Central it moved out Principe Alfonso, and from here wound its dusty way for five miles more, until at 2:10 o'clock we were in the vicinity of Quemados, at the allotted place for the staking once more of tents.

It was, indeed, a triumphal entry and passage through the city. If ever there was tendered a more enthusiastic reception to an army of men history has failed to record it. From its beginning to a point far beyond the city limits, at which place the multitudes were turned back by the Spanish guards, its memorable scenes will make a glorious chapter in the history of that people and in our own. Thus far in our experience it was the one thing that paid every soldier of us a thousand times and more for his enlistment. All the heat, all the sickness and homesickof those sultry days at Jacksonville were forgotten in the midst of the glad excitement and grand demonstration that gathered round us on our march.

The man who wanted to go home was now glad he came and he beheld things it is the privilege of few to see.

Other military processions have been longer; many times our number over have followed behind the royal standard of an Alexander, a Cæsar, or a Napoleon. Our own people in the sixties received the boys in blue as they "came marching home again" with a joy and an enthusiasm that knew no bounds and that memorable review of May, '65, when the assembled army of the Union marched through the Capital city of our nation can never be surpassed for glory, or grandeur, or the accompanying display of a rejoicing people; but these were different and this is the first instance in the history of the world where a nation marched its army into a land it had saved from the oppression of a tyrannical master. These people were therefore not only happy; they were grateful and their enthusiasm for that reason the more uncontrollable; was therefore the more soul stirring for every one who witnessed it.

Every one was in high spirits. The band played so well, so much and with so much vigor that the wonder was they had enough wind to reach the camp; the men when in cadence step marched with utmost pride; the crowds shouted and even the horses seemed to catch the enthusiasm which swayed the multitude of soldiers and of people.

It was a proud moment for the American soldier when for the first time he took off his hat to his own beautiful flag on foreign soil. It was waved from a balcony on our right shortly after the march began, the Stars and Stripes that made the people free! It greeted us with a world of meaning. The business part of the city was not so thoroughly Cuban as the residence portion and as our moving column filled the narrow avenues whose only virtue is that the ladies can "shop" from one side to the other, thereby getting a maximum variety of prices at a minimum cost of fatigue, we met the gaze of many who doubtless wished us safe at home, or worse.

Now and then an American flag was unfurled from some of the crowded balconies above us, but as the regiment proceeded the enthusiasm ran higher and the crowd that kept continually pouring in from all sides would have completely choked the street, had such a thing been possible before so large a body of moving men. At the end of Rigla street "halt" was given to rest the men and to clear an entrance for the regiment into the Prado and from this time until the column had passed the Spanish guard-line, the enthusiasm and excitement grew with every square we marched.

It was the chief delight of the barefooted Cuban boys, of the swarthy young men and in fact of the entire Cuban element to clear the way of any obstructing vehicle whose driver chanced to be a little tardy or a little stubborn in turning into the side street to give the regiment its needed room for passing.

It was in one of the wider streets that a heavily laden cart was encountered, but the regiment was marching in columns of platoons and it was evident that either the regiment must turn back or break into column of fours or the driver must right about face and wheel to the rear. The colonel thought it would be easier to move the cart than the regiment and although he had scarcely been on the island an hour he did not experience the least difficulty in making his wishes known; the jubilant Cubans charged upon it with a vengeance. "Fuéra," (get out) they cried and never gave the driver a chance to do it but with an amazing economy of ceremony they siezed the concern by the bridle and by the wheels and hustled the whole lumbering affair into a side street in a way not calculated to leave its occupants in the sweetest possible humor; and they were not, for they were Spanish guards on a cart loaded with commissary supplies; they remonstrated and though they were recipients of some vituperation and a little mud, they did not resist for they had had their day and seemed to know it; but all along the route be the vehicle a Spaniard's or a Cuban's it must needs leave the passage clear and woe betook him who hesitated, especially if he were a Spaniard. The Spanish street car driver had a long gauntlet to run, but it was nothing worse than hisses and biting sarcasm sprinkled with a trifling bit of mud or an occasional spray of Cuban saliva.

As the regiment took up its course through Alfonso street it became evident at once that we were to pass through a residence portion of the city occupied by the more influential class of Cubans. The houses, dressed in Cuba's characteristic colors of white, light blue and pink, presented a better and more substantial appearance, though everywhere was the iron-barred windows which gives to the city at the first impression the suspicious air of a huge penitentiary (and makes one curious to know what is going on within). And now the display of stars and stripes and the Cuban flag grew more profuse. They were run up the flag-staffs, Old Glory always above; they waved from the housetops, they hung from the balconies, they stretched across the porches, or, better still, waved us their salute from the hand of some beautiful senorita. The wealthier and more cultured were satisfied to crowd the porches and balconies, but those whom the world has been pleased to call the common people packed the streets from the buildings to each side of the moving column. They ran before, they followed behind, they pressed along the sides, singing, dancing and filling the air with "Viva Americano," "Viva Cuba." A strange conglomeration of an amalgamated people; some with skins as black as Plutonian night, or ebony, if that is blacker, some as brown as any Malay, and some as fair as any Caucasian can ever hope to be. The eyes of these half-clad people sparkled with unaccustomed luster and delight. They would kiss the American flag and shout "Viva McKinley," while occasionally one more wrought up than others must needs give vent to his feelings in some emphatic oration; with wild gesticulations and a highly-strung husky voice, he would beat his uncovered breast and shout away at an angry woman's rate, stamping Spain into the dust beneath his feet, and lauding Americo and Cubano to the skies; at least we thought he did, for this much we understood: that Spain was "mucho malo" and America and Cuba "mucho bueno."

From the windows and doorways and porches and balconies and steps were waved beautiful silken flags, bright colored handkerchiefs and fancy Castillian fans, accompanied by the nodding heads and gracious glances of Cuba's fairest ladies. We were all acquainted and the formality of etiquette was forgotten, and if any soldier was fortunate enough to faint or fall out *at such a place* he was immediately envied by every stalwart man in ranks.

Frequent stops were made to rest the men and on one occasion the halt was made with the head of the column before what was apparently the residence of a wealthy family. Two large and handsome flags, America's and Cuba's, were crossed before the steps leading to its entrance. As the ladies seized the stars and stripes and waved them to greet us, the adjutant requested the band to play "The Star Spangled Banner." At the first note every hat was removed and the scene that followed can never be forgotten. Every one was loaded with bouquets; the bridles of the horses were filled with roses and every mounted officer covered with flowers as fair as the sun ever shone upon. They carried us the coolest water, the finest wines, and imported brandy and the choicest of Havana cigars. Cheer upon cheer filled the air and touched the heavens with their volume while the band played their soul stirring music, now the One Hundred and Sixty-first, again the Second Illinois and sometimes both. As the column once more took up its march toward its destination a great number who had followed all the way pushed on before, men and women of assorted colors, middle aged and children; they stripped the trees of their long green branches and holding these aloft they led us on out the road through

Cerro, chanting some fantastic air and keeping time with their feet which threw them all into a strange sort of swinging gait which continued 'till they reached the Spanish guard line, where falling to the side they watched the "big soldiers" pass and then slowly took their tired selves back to their humble homes.

The regiment had now reached the Spanish barracks, about six miles from the heart of the city; the band played and the Spanish guard turned out in double column on either side of the road; they came to a "present arms" while we marched past at "port arms." This much must be said for the Spanish officers that they treated American soldiers with all proper respect and consideration, saluting in a most respectful manner when it was proper to do so. If you could put yourself in their place you could better appreciate their feelings and therefore better appreciate their courtesy. The Spanish soldiers had had an experience of which he had long since wearied; the poor unpaid and half starved fellow had grown tired of chasing a foe who, like a phantom, always evaded him while all around him his comrades were dying by the score, of fever instead of falling in open, honorable battle, and when the "boys in blue" came he knew what all the world knew, that he was fighting a hopeless battle. The humblest of them were reserved and respectful. From the Spanish barracks the regiment moved silently along the dusty highway through Puentes Grandes and Ceiba out to its destined camping place by Quemados.

High up on the right, and just beyond Cerro, a Spanish fortification frowned down upon us. Around it was the ingenious and formidable barb wire obstruction, with a depth of eighteen feet, interspersed with posts three feet high and interwoven with wire; it made a difficult and almost imposble approach for the enemy. The exposure while cutting

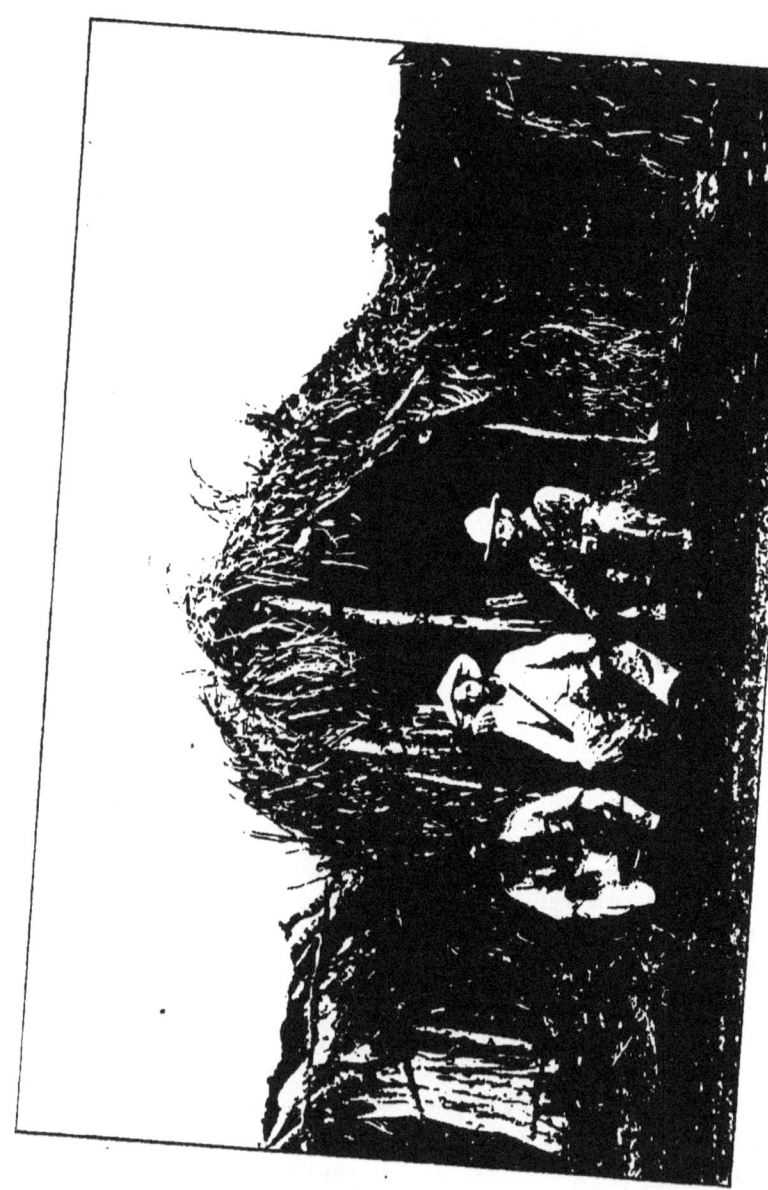

A Cuban Camp. (Seventeen tents are in the row.)

it and the certain entanglement consequent upon any attempt to pass over it when cut, placed the approaching force too completely at the mercy of its foe. With the

BARB WIRE DEFENSE.

proper entrenchment behind, it is hard to conceive of a better device for holding an enemy at bay. It will have a part in the fortifications of the future.

Now and then along the roadside and dotted over the country, there came in view the notorious Spanish "block house," some hexagonal in shape, some round, the majority square; some one, some two stories high; masonry work of no considerable strength whose chief and indeed valuable service consists in affording a shelter place from which to fire. So many were they that it was impossible for any considerable number of men to pass through the country without coming repeatedly within reach of their firing distance.

BLOCK HOUSE.

Nothing further of interest can be noted, save everywhere the beauty and fertility of the country—the stately palms, the bananas, the cocoas and other products of the rich, red soil.

At Beuna Vista the regiment passed the Seventh Army corps headquarters, and in twenty minutes the First North Carolina and the Second Illinois saw us marching by to occupy our allotted place in Camp Columbia. The boys were tired and glad to drop down for a good rest. The day's march was over, but the memory of it will ever be fresh in the mind and its scenes forever live before the eyes of every soldier who participated in it, and Old Glory, too, will always have a deeper meaning and a richer splendor because of the experiences of that day.

CHAPTER VIII.

CAMP COLUMBIA.

December 17, '98–January 31, '99.

Upon arrival Colonel Durbin reported the same and relinquished the command of all troops other than the One Hundred and Sixty-first Indiana Volunteer Infantry. The companies marched each to their places as designated by an officer of the engineer corps and threw themselves down for a rest. The regiment had been given what seemed to us the most unlovely spot on all the island, but around us in every direction was a panorama of wonderous beauty; behind us the green fields adorned with magnificent palms stretched a mile away to Quemados and Marianao, whose red tiled roofs would have been visible ten times as far away, and twenty miles in the distance, over nature as fair as God had ever made, rising in clear outline against the sky to our left were the northern limits of the Blanquizar mountains. On the gentle slope to our right were pitched the tents of the Second Illinois and the First North Carolina and beyond them the brigade and division headquarters, and just before us, three miles that looked like one, lay the shining waters of the Florida straits that washed the shore of the island and lost themselves far in the dim distance that it gave the men day dreams of the land they knew the waters touched far away in the north.

It was the slowest camp pitching the regiment ever experienced, first because the men had nothing to pitch and secondly the next day when the quartermaster's supplies did come the boys experienced great difficulty in driving the wooden pegs into the stone upon which the camp was stationed.

It was one collossal rock here and there sticking its face above the soil, but never sinking more than six inches below. Some one had blundered in the loading of the vessel; the tent poles were at the bottom and it was impossible for the quartermaster to furnish the regiment tents the first day, and that night the boys stuck up their guns and hung them with their ponchos, threw up their little shelter tents or, in good old patriarchial way, took the soft side of a stone for a pillow and slept out under the Cuban skies. Some of the officers did likewise or pitched such old tents as could be found, and night closed over a strange scene, such as might be taken for an army resting from a hot chase of a retreating enemy.

Some of the men received cots for this first night and the next day the issue was completed; this was a new luxury for soldier life and when placed in the large tents, also provided for the first time, one for six men, gave as much comfort as a soldier could reasonably expect. Quartermaster and commissary supplies and headquarter stuff were piled in a seemingly promiscuous heap.

The following day, December 18, was spent in "improving the land." It was quarry work—piles of stone were raked together and hauled away, a stone fence demolished and other necessary but rocky work undertaken.

At the close of the day tents sufficient to shelter the men were up; the headquarters were still jumbled together and remained so for a week. The officers ate what they could procure and paid outrageous prices for it, and the Cuban bread, sweet-meat and orange venders were in clover. They gathered in groups around the camp, a motley set of people, shoeless, the most of them covered with straw hats and linen pants and a part of a shirt and every one with his cuchillo (knife) hung in its leather case inside his pants at the waist. They had oranges dumped on the ground, four for five, jelly in cakes and sweet meats of innumerable variety and color; they jabbered their mother tongue at the boys and taught them Spanish, but the most that most of us learned was to say "quanto" and get skinned a little in the change.

Now was the time for the capturing of prizes and the gathering of relics; the Cuban who could tell the biggest lie was the man who made the sale; later, "machetes" and "mausers" became ordinary weapons of war that sold for a few dollars without a history, but during those early days one could almost see the blood dripping from the famous machete and hear the dying yell of an innumerable host of Spaniards shot down by this or that rifle as they were brought near the camp by some illustrious patriot "del ejercito Cubano." It was in these days that Lieutenant-Colonel Backus made his wonderful find and he didn't ask any one to believe his story; there was the history of the rifle written under his own eye by the Cuban himself, and our own regimental Cuba should read it, which he did, and —"never mind the history!"

On the 22d the headquarters were established in their proper place, but an objection had in the meantime gone to corps headquarters concerning the unfavorable location of the camp, and on December 22 General Lee, accompanied by General Williston, rode over the ground and ordered all clearing work to stop.

For a few days the men seemed to wander at will and began to explore the neighborhood; but reports of yellow fever in the vicinity caused the guard lines to be drawn very close and no one was allowed to leave the camp.

Seven miles south of Camp Columbia are the Vento

springs, beautiful and powerful, which supply Havana with the purest water and from which water was to be furnished the Seventh Army Corps; but until the piping work was completed, all the water used was hauled in barrels from a spring beyond Mariano, two and one-half miles away. There was consequently at first a scarcity of water. One does not need to mention it, but the regiment needed a bath; and on December 23 the entire regiment marched three miles away to the sea coast, near Playa, and turned its coral beach for a brief time into a big bath tub for twelve hundred men. Some got clean and some got something else—they got their feet filled with big black porcupine bristles that stung and caused the feet to smart and swell, and then they got to ride home in the ambulance, as did others who preferred to ride and therefore "didn't feel very well."

Christmas was near at hand—a few selections by the band—a few thoughts homeward, and its eve had gone. The next day ushered in a day like one in August at home. On the knoll among the scattered supplies the chaplain held a little Christmas service. It is said that the staff also had a little time at mess. In his turn each one entertained the rest, save the chaplain, who had gone to take Christmas dinner with one of the companies whose officers had generously provided their men with turkey and other good things. The staff did *not* have turkey—Lieutenant Wilson had purchased one, but it was too fat. He could thin it down a little for New Year's day, so he made a "reconcentrado" of it, and shutting it up in a pen began his cruel process of starvation. By New Year's day he had a dead turkey, and the staff had ham for dinner.

On Christmas day one officer and five men from each company were allowed to be absent from camp till 6 P. M. The same allowance was made in other regiments. The wisdom of restricting passes is at once apparent, considering the existence of three armies whose soldiers might come in conflict, and the serious consequence that might result from disorderly conduct.

Considering the American pretense and what the nation stands for before the world, and the consequent example of sobriety and manliness its soldiers should place before a people whom we have dared to call less civilized than ourselves, it is deplorable that even officers should so conduct themselves in abuse of the above privileges that there must needs come down the evening of the same day an order to the effect that owing to the disgraceful conduct of some of the Seventh Army Corps officers no more passes would be issued. It is not an attempt at self-justification, but due the officers of the One Hundred and Sixty-first to say that investigation exonerated those absent from camp from any suspicion that the above charge rested upon them. A drunken officer is less of a man because of his straps.

It had now been decided to turn the camp about, practically end for end. Such a move necessitated a like change for appearance sake of the two other regiments in the brigade, but when the change was made the entire brigade not only presented a better appearance, but occupied a better and more convenient position. Six companies moved on the 28th, the remaining and the headquarters on the 29th. The 31st brought the last day of the year and the uppermost thought was the long march on the morrow. In the evening there was music and a "Hoosier" watch party, and as the old year died "taps" were sounded with fine expression by musicians Williams and Hays, and as the last note died away in the stillness the band struck up the national tune "America," then they played "The Star Spangled Banner" and "On the Banks of the Wabash Far Away."

"New Year's in Cuba" will bring a flood of memories to the men of the regiment. At 8:30 o'clock the companies were formed ready for the long march to Havana and return. Every soldier wanted to go. Many offered to do double tours of guard duty for the privilege of changing with one of those going. Off up through the camp of the Second Illinois the column moved, headed by Colonel Durbin with his staff and the band. Out from between the rows of great royal palms onto the highway the boys swung into line, happy and proud to be a part of the day's ceremonies that marks such an epoch in the history of the beautiful island. There was little to be said on the way for the first two or three miles.

Probably there were thoughts of those so far away and of other New Year's days. All along the highlands to the cliffs overlooking the gulf, now down into the little green valleys, now up looking down into them, with a brisk salt breeze fanning them, the men of the regiment kept up the march with infrequent halts and short rests.

Down the hill roads to the coast line the long line led into Vedado, the aristocratic suburb of Havana. Here the first long rest was made almost four miles from the home camp. Along the way on every little Cuban cottage the Cuban and American flags had been displayed, but at Vedado the decorations were on a larger scale. Entire fronts of buildings were covered with the flags intertwined with green. Black eyed senoritas in stiff white skirts and fresh ribbons came out from the vine covered verandas and proceeded to capture many hearts with their "Viva los Americanos." A fifteen days' life in Cuba had not given the men a very complete knowledge of the Spanish language, but the pretty girls were assured that they were "mucha buena."

From Vedado to the city all the way is guarded by the

old Spanish forts, which were occupied by American troops and American gunners. At 11:45 o'clock the pontoon bridge was crossed and the regiment was in Havana. Off across the narrow bay Morro stood silent and gray, beating back the waves that forever surge at her feet. Above the stone walls floated the yellow and red emblem of the defeated nation, so soon to be drawn down forever.

As the time drew nearer to the noon hour the excitement among the people increased until they were running about the streets crying, shouting, laughing and singing. Dozens of bombs, exploding high in the air, added to the noise and confusion. There was an intense feeling. The hour they had so long prayed for and fought for was almost at hand. They knew that at that same minute the hated Spanish were leaving the governor-general's palace and that the Spanish guards were being relieved for all time in the Morro. Their fair land, "The Queen of the Antilles," was about to be taken from the hand of the oppressor.

Twelve o'clock!

Boom! The first gun from the Morro ever fired in honor of the American flag.

And the men of the One Hundred and Sixty-first stood on the shore opposite and watched the Stars and Stripes ascend over that stronghold and joined in the cheer that went up with a strong Hoosier yell that was probably heard at the fort.

Just by the regiment the bells of the Catholic hospital, San Lozaro, pealed forth clear and sweet, rung by the black-robed Sisters, heralding the new day in Cuban history. Tears they shed, maybe in sympathy for the mother land, maybe for joy. Farther down the street, at the palace, the old white-haired general, Castellanos, of Spain, was handing over to General Brooke the keys of the mansion, symbolic of the final evacuation of the island.

The scene at the palace was simple and pathetic; the officers who were to take charge of the various departments were instructed by Brigadier-General Clous, the master of ceremonies of the day, as follows: "On the firing of the last gun of the first twenty-one at noon, you are to go to the place assigned you and demand possession of the office in the name of the United States." At 11:10 Major-General Wade and Major-General Butler, of the American evacuation commission, arrived; at 11:30 Major-General John R. Brooke, governor of Cuba, and Major-General Ludlow, governor of the city of Havana, came and at 11:45 Major-General Lee joined them. Just a few minutes before 12 Captain-General Castellanos suddenly entered the salon and after greeting General Brooke and others, moved toward a group of Cuban generals and on being introduced to General Rodriguez shook both his hands according to Spanish custom, and said: "We have been enemies, but I respect you for your correct attitudes and opinions. I have pleasure in shaking your hand." General Rodriguez, replied: "I thank you, General; I feel sorry for the Spanish army which has defended the banner it was sworn to defend. I also have pleasure in shaking your hands." At this moment the big guns began to roar the national salute and at once General Castellanos, addressing General Wade, who was president of the American Commission, the words having been placed on manuscript, said: "Gentlemen: In compliance with the treaty of Paris, the agreement of the military commissioners of the island, and the orders of my King, at this moment of noon, January 1, 1899, there ceases in Cuba Spanish sovereignty and begins that of the United States. In consequence, I declare you in command of the island, with the object that you may exercise it, declaring to you that I will be first in respecting it. Peace having been established between our respective governments, I promise you to give all due respect to the United States government, and I hope that the good relations already existing between our armies, will continue until the termination of the evacuation of those under my orders in this territory."

The address having been translated, General Wade handed it to General Brooke, saying "I transfer this command to you," and General Brooke said: "I accept this great trust in behalf of the government and President of the United States, and (turning to General Castellanos) I wish you and the gallant gentlemen with you a pleasant return to your native land. May prosperity attend you and all who are with you." General Castellanos immediately retired from the throne room and turning to his officers said, with tears in his eyes: "Gentlemen, I have been in more battles than I have hairs on my head, and my self-possession has never failed me until to-day. Adieu, gentlemen, adieu." The old man bowed his head as he walked down the stairway and out into the plaza. Some American ladies waved their handkerchiefs to him and bowing he kissed his hands to them and accompanied by General Clous and by his own staff he started toward the wharf; all the way he was hooted and jeered by the Cubans and there was no Spanish soldiers to do his bidding had he cared to notice them, but those of better hearts looked quietly on and pitied the faithful old servant of his country. At the wharf he thanked General Clous and as he stepped into his launch that was to take him to his vessel he wept again while the docks were crowded with Spaniards, men and women, all dressed in black, weeping with him. Not a shout was raised, not a handkerchief was waved, but men and women wept together.

It was almost 1 o'clock when the regiment was ordered forward. The review of the American troops by General

Lee, General Brooke, General Ludlow with the staff of each, drawn up in front of the Ingleterra, was in progress and the Indianians marched onto the Prado, ready to carry off the honors. The regiment was formed in platoons and there were a third more in the regiment than in any other organization that passed the stand. Cheers that were hearty before increased two-fold when the One Hundred and Sixty-first passed.

Down the Prado they marched, every man a soldier. On to Reina street the column was directed and there it was halted for the noon-day lunch. The men fell out of ranks and for an hour and a half the neighborhood was filled with soldiers, visiting scenes they had read of, maybe, but had never seen. Then on home, back to a hot supper and cots and blankets that never seemed more comforting and more comfortable, and the great day was over.

Cuba was out of the power of the Spanish.

On the morning of January 2, the boys turned out of bed and discovered their legs were a little stiff from the previous day's hike; it was a day of well-deserved rest, for all drills were suspended and the men spent the day lounging about camp making "pipes" and "grape vines" on the next move.

The month of January, apart from New Year's day and the 31st, was in one respect an uneventful one. There were no marches, no reviews and only one battle, on the 6th in which the score was fourteen to three for the Cubans, seventy dollars gate receipts and that sore feeling for the boys. The panacea for all ills came next day when Major Havens visited the regiment with the good government's crisp paper and yellow gold.

The boys were determined, however, to hold their good record at the drill and on the 9th began to drill twice a day, from 8:30 to 10 A. M. and from 3:30 to 4:30 P. M.

This was immediately followed by regimental parade; it was quick time and if the first sergeant does not remember, the men do; it was "company dismissed"—get ready for parade"!! and as quick as it takes to tell it the men were on their way to "pass in review, take full distance, guide right, harsh." !!!!

But there were some things which made even January an important month historically, and these are found in the camp improvements, the outcome of that spirit which has always by conceded opinion made the One Hundred and Sixty-first Indiana camp the model one.

The 10th of the month saw the erection of the first company kitchen and for a week of time incessant hammering sounded an invitation for the company cooks to

Soupee! Soupee! Soup! Soup!

leave the sun and the wind and the dust and the temporarily erected "flys" and come into a commodious shack which sprung up along the regimental rear, one for each company, in a line as straight as human science could make

THE WAY MOTHER USED TO DO.

it. At the same time the headquarters went down one tent a day, and "Dude Allen" with his force constructed those elevated floors and tent skeletons which made that row look like the street of a deserted village when we had gone.

As fast as lumber arrived, and God and the government knows it came slow enough in spite of the fact that the quartermaster had receipted for sixty thousand feet in the states which went into government buildings and the regiment consequently had to wait, but it came by degrees, and as it did come was hurriedly worked up into floors for the company tents, but all tents however were not floored until the middle of March, when those of the home bound Maine artillery were brought to us for that purpose. In the meantime the grounds throughout and in the immediate vicinity of the regiment were being thoroughly policed; every shrub and root grubbed up, and every loose

and protruding stone removed till the whole place was as neat and clean as human hands and labor could make it.

Then came the "ornamental period" when companies vied with each other in making their quarters attractive. Had there been any Spaniards to fight all this camp embellishment would have been unknown, but it is certainly a great credit to any regiment and indicative of an enterprising spirit, the essence of which will make good soldiers under any circumstances, that a portion of the men's time was spent in an endeavor toward attractiveness. Great loads of sand were hauled from Playa beach and along headquarters, around battalion quarters, along the captains' and the company streets sand walks were made and

CAMP COLUMBIA.

bounded by uniform stones covered over with whitewash. At the head of each company appropriate designs were made by scratching up the red soil, by lettering and designing upon it by small bits of white limestone blasted from the hard earth by our Cuban sink diggers, who from the first day startled the camp by their cannon-like explosions and filled the air with flying stones which came hailing down ofttimes all too near for comfort or appreciation. On a certain Saturday (21st) a prize of $5.00 offered by the officer of the day for the neatest interior and surroundings was awarded to Corporal Joseph L. Luse, privates Frank E. Oaks, B. S. Kellenberger, Robert E. Ketner, Ralph McCallie and Elbert M. Blake, who occupied tent No. 10 in Company K.

The band quarters, the hospital especially, and the First Battalion coral star, the product of Lieutenant-Colonel Backus' creative genius, all deserve mention, but the one work of note that made all the kodack fiends hurry to our camp, that made other regiments look our way with envious eyes and wonder why they "hadn't thought of it" was, is and always will be the One Hundred and Sixty-first Indiana Volunteer Infantry Monument. It stands there to-day in its lonely grandeur, growing more endurable with the passing ages; a monument to the enterprise of the regiment whose name it bears. It is the first monument ever erected on foreign soil to the memory of an American Soldier and the honor of its origination and general design belongs to the inimitable Backus, to whose inherent aptitude for such things and untiring energy the One Hundred and Sixty-first Indiana owes much of the credit bestowed upon it for the example it always set as the model camp of the Seventh Army Corps; and would it not be well to confess that some of us looked a little wise and doubted a little bit the success of what seemed to be a hard task to make out

Regimental Hospital at Camp Columbia.

of rough material a monument creditable to the reputation of the regiment; but the lieutenant-colonel simply remarked "Just let the old man alone" and when the work was finished every man in the regiment was proud of it. It was begun on the 21st day of January and completed the 5th day of February, and every stone was hauled, hewn, lifted and put in place by a soldier of the regiment.

Its base is sixteen feet square and four feet high; surmounted by a second base twelve feet square and three feet high and rising from this is the shaft, sixteen feet high, being four feet square at its base and two and one half feet square at the top where rests a twelve-inch steel shell making in all a total height of twenty-four feet. The shells and cannon balls upon and around its base were secured from the landing place on Playa coast. The shaft is a heavy frame work covered with brain coral and set in cement. Imbedded in the four faces of the second base are huge limestone slabs bearing the four inscriptions "One Hundred and Sixty-first" "Indiana" "Volunteer" "Infantry." Set in the north side of the lower base is a plate of limestone bearing the names of Colonel Durbin, Lieutenant-Colonel Backus and Captain George West as builders. In the front lower base is another limestone shield bearing the date 1899. In the upper left hand corner of the lower base immediately under the lower left hand corner of the upper base is the corner stone concerning the laying of which and its contents the following is quoted from the "Times of Cuba."

"Yesterday morning the corner stone was laid, not with any formal ceremony but in a business-like way. The corner stone is one of great size, and after being chiseled out a tin box was placed inside. The box was about fifteen inches on each side, and when filled contained a remarkable collection of papers, very different from any that

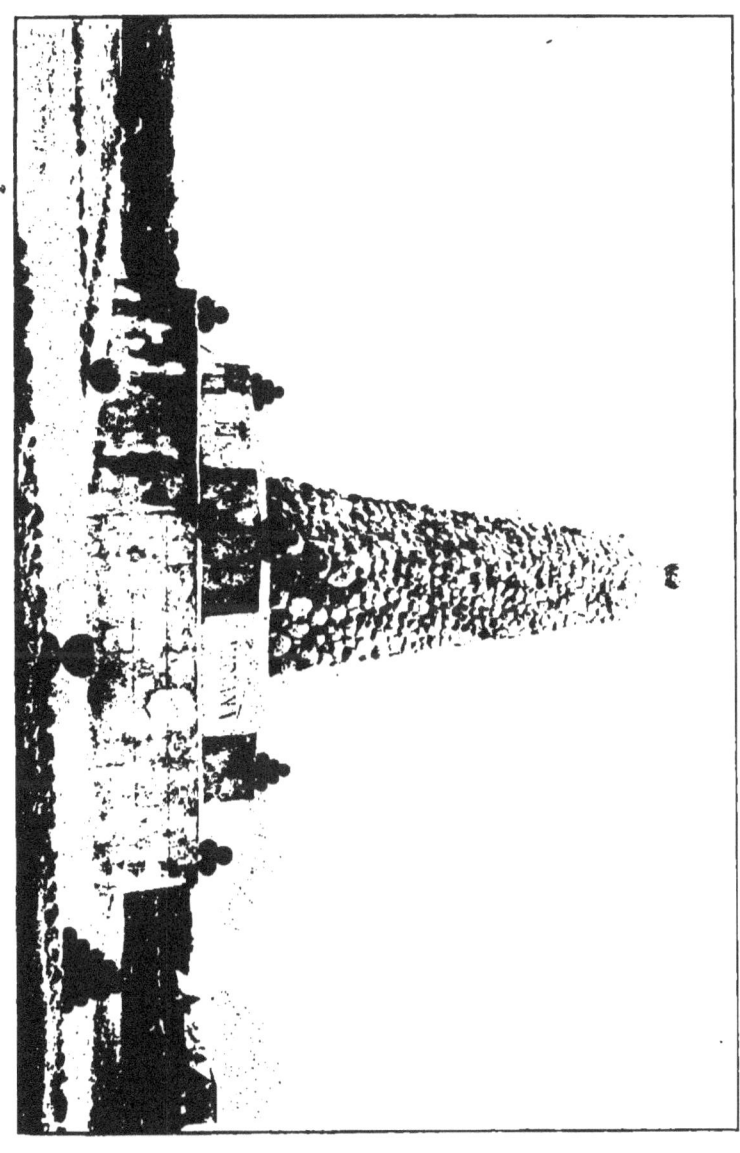

history records, and the man who will open this stone in centuries to come will marvel at the wonderful sight that will greet his eyes when he removes the cement that now so well protects the assortment of mementos that the Indiana men covered with a massive slab. A complete roster of the regiment was first placed in the stone. Then came a copy of the drill regulations and the manual of arms, followed by the photographs of a number of the officers of the regiment, all the newspapers published in Indiana which could be procured, a few small coins, a piece of rope from the lamented Maine, one cigar in a box, a brief history of the regiment, copies of the New York, Cincinnati and Chicago papers, and lastly a copy of the Times of Cuba, of Tuesday, January 23, which contained the first account of the unique memorial of the Indiana regiment."

Captain West deserves great praise not only for his share in the monument's design but for the attention and assistance given to its erecton, and the men who worked so hard for so many days ought also to be remembered. It is not the only monument of its kind but it is and always will be the *first* one. It is told of a southern colonel: There were fourteen baptized in another regiment; he forthwith ordered the adjutant to make a detail of twenty men, to take them down to the creek and baptize them, for he "wasn't agoin' to allow any regiment to get ahead of him;" and so there are other monuments, at least one,—a creditable work, too, by the way.

January also contained the "bloody period," a time when the patriots' fluid was drawn upon every man, a time out of which the future brought much intense suffering, a time when one thousand two hundred Hoosier soldiers bared their strong left arms to the surgeons' little·bone slivers, with poison points like Oriental daggers, dipped in some mysterious concoction, that for effect might have been, for all the soldiers knew, drawn from a cauldron mixed up by Macbeth's witches, and in plain vernacular beat a tarantula bite all hollow. There was smallpox in camp, of which later mention will be made, and every man was vaccinated, beginning with Company A, on the 16th of the month. The men were driven up to the dispensary like sheep to the slaughter-house—there was no getting out of it. There were more " Ohs! " and "damns!" and like emphatic exclamations in this month than in all others together, as those beautiful rose-colored sore arms hanging so carefully and tenderly down would run against the hand of some thoughtless fellow who wanted to tell him something on the confidential; but they were glad of it for it doubtless prevented what might otherwise have been a period of much and serious sickness, *at least so medical science use to say.*

Many of these January days were wisely employed in visiting much of what there was of note on the island. On the 21st fourteen officers; including the Colonel, "saw the sights." They reported a time of great interest. They did Morro and Cabannas and the city thoroughly and were in the act of bringing the Maine from its wreck spot in the bay to camp but stopped suddenly after procuring enough to supply a few museums. On the following Saturday ten more under charge of Major Olds made a similar excursion. It was another pleasant and profitable day; Major Smith found a dollar on the tomb of Columbus in the old cathredal. The privates had their outings, too. Colonel Durbin who has always been considerate of his men, conceived the idea of sending each day, ten men from each company to the country in army wagons for a day of recreation and acquaintance with the country's beautiful appearance. Accordingly at 7 A. M. on January 29th the first excursion went out. They drove over a fine macadamized road past

A MIXED RACE.

trotting ponies, dusty stage coaches, lumbering burrow carts, cane and pineapple fields and banana groves, past a thousand palms and cocoas and other tropical growths, through peculiar Cuban villages to the mountains sixteen miles away and back again at six o'clock in the evening. Nature certainly has a lavish way of doing things in Cuba and as one looks upon the luxuriant landscape he thinks of something that Emerson said,

> "Happy, I cried, whose home is here;
> Fair fortune to the Mountaineer;
> Dame nature round his humble bed
> Hath royal pleasure grounds outspread."

Still appearances ofttimes deceive, and even the Cubans never raised enough as the import statistics on rice, flour, potatoes, salt, etc., plainly indicate; but the chief thing now is that nature does it all or nearly all, for the wooden plow and antiquated ox goad; show the rude and barbarous stage out of which their agriculture has never emerged; but now while all over the island where once magnificent estates are

in ruins and the country has gone to waste, the time has come for the replanting and rebuilding and under an American protectorate or at least the influence of her civilization which is bound to come, agriculture will become an American science more in harmony with nature's demand that will usher in an era of prosperity such as the island never yet has known.

Squads of ten, accompanied by a commissioned officer, from time to time also visited the city and surveyed its points of interest; there was grim old Morro with its walls hewn from the rocks in 1589; its famous O'Donnell lighthouse on the seaward corner and its frowning batteries crowned with sixty cannon and the famous "twelve apostles." And there is traditional and worthless old Cabana, dating from 1763, at a cost of fourteen million dollars. There is the unrivaled view encircling the bay, the tragic spot where rests the Maine, the old Catholic cathedral, and, best of all, the life with all its peculiar characteristics that flows through the city's narrow streets. The value of seeing the country, the city and the people, will always be to every man, from an educatioaal standpoint, a reason for rejoicing that the destinies of war took him to those shores.

If January began with a significant event it was also to end with one. An order came to prepare for a corps review on the 31st. The reviewing officer was to be the inspector general of the United States Army, Brigadier-General Breckenridge. The general had inspected our camp the day before, the 30th, and on the 31st, the parade ground being next and nearest our regiment, every man who could shoulder a gun turned out. Beside the infantry of the Seventh Army Corps there were present the Seventh Cavalry and the Second United States Artillery. In all over thirteen hundred men passed in review at 3 P. M. before the distinguished visitor who was there for that purpose in company with General Fitz Hugh Lee.

The review was one that showed the results of hard training on the part of every regiment present; in fact it was remarkable the way those men did march. The Indiana boys were there. Said one fellow from another regiment, "Those d—d Hoosiers can have typhoid fever, smallpox and everything else and then turn out bigger companies and march better than any regiment in the whole d—d corps." That he was about right, forgetting the indelicacy of his expression is clearly proven by the following letter.

HEADQUARTERS 1ST. BRIG., 2D. DIV., 7TH A. C., }
CAMP COLUMBIA, HAVANA, CUBA, FEB. 1, 1899. }

THE COMMANDING OFFICER, 161st IND. VOL. INF.

SIR:—The brigadier-general commanding directs me to inform you in his opinion your regiment presented the finest appearance of any in the corps at the review before the inspector-general yesterday, and to express to you his gratification thereat. Also, that he considered the condition of your camp as worthy of especial commendation, which he takes pleasure in transmitting to you. Very respectfully,

R. G. PAXTON,
Assistant Adjutant-General.

The men were proud of this deserved tribute; it was the result of intelligent and hard work and every future parade showed they meant to hold the distinction they had so honorably acquired. And thus the first month of 1899 came to an end. February was at hand and entered upon, every man wondering what its four short weeks would bring forth in the experience of the army to which he belonged.

CHAPTER IX.

CAMP COLUMBIA.

February 1, '99–March 31, '99.

February came and brought with it twenty-eight days of atmospheric changes; for a day or a few the sun was at his best and then for an equal length of time or longer the clouds that hid the hot old orb poured their torrents down upon the thirsty ground; for a time we were warmly reminded of our equatorial proximity and then with a gale that sprang up in the night the wind would turn and bring us chilly reminders of that for-years-unequalled winter they were having in our Hoosier home up north. It was not necessary to wait for the "rainy season" to discover that Cuban skies had fine raining facilities; they were too generous to deal in "drops;" they poured it out in torrents and then some. The north wind that rose in the night and played those beautiful tunes with the flies, that blustered around the tent and blew an occasional one down, just to show what it could do, was a little reminder of what we might expect when the real time came for the wind to blow. But the night of the 13th was not so slow. At 2 A. M. on the morning of the 12th the wind began to rise; it had been blowing from the north for a day and all through the 13th it kept rising higher till it sent the ocean breakers in white dashing billows against the coast of Playa. By 8 P. M. there was a heavy wind growing hourly stronger and by 2 A. M. of the coming morning a regular hurricane was having its own way all over camp. The night was awful; the flies banged the tent with a vengeance, the frames creaked, the shrinking ropes pulled hard at the pegs and everywhere destruction was imminent. Many of the division hospital tents went down, all the assembly tents fell, and our own was irreparably ruined. The guard tents fell and from one to several tents in every company. The men were used to it, however, and when the wind got through they put them up again and were ready for drill.

The month was full of history, though not all of it pertaining directly to the regiment; there was, however, the usual drill evolutions and the month's share of camp construction.

All through the month there was in course of erection, in the rear of camp, a commodious and much needed, but, alas, never used bath house, a most convenient arrangement surpassing anything yet provided; a regular double decker. The upper story was provided with nine shower baths, the lower with one large tub for twenty-five men, besides which there were other complete toilet arrangements for twenty-four men. Other regiments were also provided, the work in this case being done not by the men of the regiment but by the corps of engineers, Second United States. They made a fine bath house, but were a mighty long time at it. That it was ready for use sometime after the regiment left is to be presumed.

On the 5th Colonel Backus drew the plan for the One Hundred and Sixty-first Indiana band stand. It was to be octagon in shape, to be built of bamboo, and to surpass in uniqueness and beauty anything in the Seventh Army Corps. Would it be hard to substantially join the bamboo? Yes, but the colonel would do it. Forthwith wagons were sent into the country to procure the Cana Brava (bamboo), for the frame and the palm leaves for its characteristic thatched roof. It is not necessary to relate the adjutant's war with the Cuban farmer whose bamboo he had innocently appropriated, nor how the chaplain's mules ran away while he was pulling a mahogany post four feet out of the road side, but the poles and leaves were brought and the work began. When nails would not hold the poles were wired together; each of the eight sides were ten feet wide, seats edged with bamboo were put in place, the floor was made of famous Playa sand, the palm branches were strapped upon the roof and it was finished, a shining green Kiosque with accommodations for forty musicians. Of course the green faded out, the leaves were brown in a day as if to remind us that man is like the grass of the field; in the morning it flourisheth and groweth up; in the evening it is cut down and withereth; but when the band played we forgot all about that. The companies were yet without dining rooms and February saw their erection. Lieutenant Johnson, of Company A, had returned in time to complete the music stand, and February 13, began work on the eating shacks. Ten feet in front of each kitchen was built a long narrow frame work and covered with paulines. Each was twenty-five feet long and fifteen feet wide, providing fifty men on either side with seating and table room.

The drill was mostly battalion; for ten days it was battalion drill in the morning and dress parade in the evening; then came a few days of company drill, and the latter part of the month was devoted to battalion extended order drill and to "advance and rear guard work," in which latter the battalions marched into the enemy's country, threw out their skirmishers and advanced for points of attack; now toward some thatched hut, or some ravine or even God's holy house in Marianoa, but failing to find an enemy returned to camp and left the bewildered Cubans wondering what they had in mind to do.

Major Havens paid us his accustomed visit on the 6th. The major was always welcome. On the 10th, at dress parade, the regimental photograph was taken on the hillside, near the division hospital. Picture business paid better than a commission in the army.

Among other events of peculiar interest to the army in general was the burial, on the 11th, of the remains of General Calixto Garcia, an imposing ceremony, marred only by the childish action of the quick-tempered and pharisaical-dispositioned Cuban officials. The following is taken from La Lucha, of February 13:

"The funeral of the Cuban general, Calixto Garcia, which took place on last Saturday afternoon, was altogether an imposing ceremony, not only on account of the divers elements which figured in it, but also on account of the immense number of people of all classes who literally covered the balconies and terraces of the houses and invaded the sidewalks and even the streets through which the mournful cortege was to pass.

"Clubs to the number of eighty-three formed in the procession, in which were also to be seen four splendid hearses, respectively drawn by four, six and ten horses, the coaches laden with part of the floral crowns dedicated to the memory of General Garcia, whose body had been placed on the caisson of an American cannon.

"In compliance with President McKinley's instructions, General Brooke ordered that the honors of a general who had died in campaign should be rendered to General Garcia; accordingly four companies of cavalry and four batteries of artillery of the United States formed in the funeral; General Brooke with his staff and escort also attended.

"The caisson with General Garcia's body was followed by three priests on foot; then came General Garcia's sons, in a carriage; Generals Brooke, Chaffee and Humphreys and Colonel Richards and the secretaries, in three carriages; General Brooke's staff and Lee and his staff, mounted, a cavalry troop; General Ludlow in a carriage, his staff mounted.

"The two corps of Havana firemen, that turned out in full at the end of the procession, greatly attracted attention, on account of the fine look of their personnel, and brilliant uniforms.

"It is really a pity that the misunderstanding occurred at the last hour, owing to which the delegates of the Cuban assembly, part of the members of the city council, all the Cuban generals and troops withdrew from the funeral, thus defrauding public expectation of seeing armed Cubans formed for the first time in this city; and a sentiment of uneasiness, as to the future consequences, became general."

Four days more, and the 15th, bringing up the sad memory of a year ago, was at hand. It was the anniversary of the destruction of the Maine. The following order was received:

HEADQUARTERS SEVENTH ARMY CORPS,
CAMP COLUMBIA, HAVANA, CUBA,
February 14, 1899.

GENERAL ORDER NO. 12.

To-morrow being the anniversary of the loss of the United States battleship Maine, all duty in this command excepting the necessary guard and police, will be suspended.

By command of Major-General Lee.

R. E. L. MICHIE,
Assistant Adjutant-General.

It was the night of February 15, 1898; it was 9:40 o'clock. The sky was overcast, but now and then the soft rays of the clear moon would break through to kiss the placid waters of the bay as they gently washed the sides of the great vessel as if to say, "All is well." Taps had sounded and the boys had "turned in," and while they were sleeping and dreaming, perhaps, of home or perchance of how they were bravely manning the guns in some

WRECK OF THE MAINE.

great and honorable naval conflict, listening with pride in their dream-bound imagination to the thundering of the big twelve-inch guns, there was consummated the fiendish perfidy of an enemy, who did not dare to meet the defenders of Old Glory in fair and honorable battle, and therefore chose the cover of darkness to touch the lives of innocent men.

Two hundred and fifty-four men were lost that night. A few of the one hundred rescued died shortly after. February 17 nineteen bodies were interred in Colon cemetery; others followed, until more than a half hundred rest beneath that sacred mound.

A year had passed since the tragic event, and a fitting memorial service was to be held in Colon cemetery.

At 9:30 marines from the Brooklyn, the Resolute and the Lebanon, accompanied by a detail of sailors and their band, formed in front of the United States Club in the Prado, and with a troop from the Seventh Cavalry and a large procession of carriages and army ambulance containing ladies with numberless wreaths of beautiful flowers, they started at 2 o'clock for Vedado. At the entrance to the cemetery they were joined by General Brooke and his staff. At the same hour a battalion from the First Maine Heavy Artillery, one battalion from each division, one troop cavalry and one battery of light artillery formed in the road leading to Havana with the head of the column resting at Puentes Grandes bridge. When this escort with General Lee reached the cemetery part of the ceremony had been finished. The marines and sailors had drawn up, and as the Brooklyn band rendered a few selections they filed past the graves, each placing upon them some beautiful flowers. Then came the ladies with the other floral offerings. General Lee's party then came and rendered similar tribute; a national salute of twenty-one guns was

THE MAINE GRAVES.

fired and the crowd passed out under the colossal arch of Havana's holy field, leaving the dead heroes sleeping beneath a wilderness of flowers. It was impressive, solemn and pathetic; it was all that could be done to honor our country's dead, but the United States will have done its duty only when somewhere on the Prado or on some other suitable spot a beautiful and imposing monument rises to their memory.

Since the narrative has entered the Havana cemetery it will be interesting to take the reader to one corner of this huge burying place, and there look upon one of the most shocking sights in Cuba—the "Human Bone Yard"—a cut of which is given on the following page. This enclosure is over seventy feet square, and the depth of the bone pile is over forty feet, containing, to-day, the bones of many millions of people. The rich man is hauled to his grave with highly caparisoned livery; the poor man carried in a rude coffin on the shoulders of four young men; according to his wealth, he is buried in his coffin, or, as is more usually the case, taken out and lowered by a rope into his resting place in mother earth's bare bosom. The coffin-bearers each pick up a piece of dirt, kiss it, throw it upon the corpse, pick up their coffin and take it back to be used for the next poor man. A little lime is then thrown over the corpse and the grave-digger takes his hoe and scrapes in the soil to a depth of about eight inches above the poor fellow's remains, and the SAME grave is then ready for another occupant, who is not long in coming. If this is shocking, what follows is more so: For centuries the established church of that island has imposed a yearly grave tax, an exorbitant sum which the poor, of course, cannot pay, and as the poor predominate in numbers the hideous bone pile is the result, and every cemetery has its ghastly corner into which the grave-digger is busy throwing the

HUMAN BONE YARD.

bones while he empties the grave for another tenant. The day of this heathenish practice is over! Up to Washington has gone the cry of the Cuban people, asking the privilege for their dead to rest undisturbed, and the influence of the starry flag, the ideas of the American nation, will make it so.

In the regiment a corps review had been ordered. The first order for this review, dated February 8, corps headquarters, called for a review of the corps on the 11th inst., at 3 o'clock P. M., on the open ground in the vicinity of the camp of the One Hundred and Sixty-first Indiana Volunteer Infantry by the major-general commanding, division of Cuba. The drill ground in our vicinity was the largest and best available; it was thoroughly prepared by Cuban labor, giving to the One Hundred and Sixty-first Indiana the best practice ground in the whole Seventh Army Corps.

Many of the regiments were on their way to execute the above order when it was revoked because of rain, and the men, already drenched, went back. It was ours to wait in the dry. On the same day, from regimental headquarters, general order No. 6 was promulgated, stating the review would be held Monday, the 13th, with battalions ready to move at 2:30 P. M. All men able to bear guns to be in line and no one excused except in writing by the major-surgeon.

Again the men were on their way. Again it poured and again came the order of postponement until Friday, the 17th. This time the elements were threatening, but the review was on. The First Division was followed by the First Maine Heavy Artillery and then the Second Division, of which the One Hundred and Sixty-first Indiana was the last regiment, passed in review, followed by the Light Artillery Battalion and the Cavalry Squadron, which last, for the satisfaction of the people, passed a second time, in running order. This was the first time in which General Lee himself, with his staff, passed the reviewing officer. In all, there were fifteen thousand soldiers in line. The troops were given a critical inspection, and a judgment that was favorable rendered for them all; the men were on their nerve that day and it would have been hard to find a better body of marching men. The spectacle was imposing and the impression was general that it would be the corps' last review.

The 22d brought another anniversary and also an order for the suspension of all military duties. The men were allowed to go out in considerable numbers. Many officers were also absent, and it was a quiet camp all day. At 12 o'clock the national salute of twenty-one guns was fired, under the direction of the commanding officer of the Light Artillery Battalion, from the eminence on which the headquarters of the Second Division is located.

At the same hour in the city of Havana occurred a review of the Regulars; the Cabanas guns fired a salute and the Seventh Cavalry Band played "America," which was the signal for beginning the march of three thousand men, who passed in review before Generals Brooke and Ludlow, who, with their staffs, had their reviewing positions in front of the "Inglaterra."

The order was: Seventh Cavalry, Second Artillery and Tenth Infantry; the Eighth Infantry and two companies of engineers bringing up the rear.

The review only lasted about twenty minutes, the men returning immediately to camp.

Salutes from the Texas and Brooklyn were fired in response to that of Cabanas.

The next day brought Gomez to Marianao. The old chief had skulked in the woods long enough; he had made terms with America for the payment of his army and was on the way to stand before the people whose cause he had espoused. The One Hundred and Sixty-first band had been asked to meet him and escort him through the city at 1:30 P. M., he was expected and the band was there, the populace was there, hundred of soldiers in blue were there and the Cuban army was there, seven hundred infantry and five hundred cavalry, a strange mixture of color and age; we have remarked upon the color before; but there were young boys, children not over thirteen and some that were nearer twelve riding bony ponies small of stature, soldiers in the Cuban revolt. Every half hour brought a train, but not the general, and when the crowd had waited three hours and a half a special bearing the "stars and stripes" and the Cuban flag came rolling up from Quemados; every one knew it bore the expected chieftain and immediately a scene of greatest confusion reigned, the bands played and the multitude yelled. The mayor of Marianao had driven his handsome pony and carriage to the proper exit to receive the old hero, but some excited Cuban who knew it all persuaded him to quickly drive to the other entrance and about the time he got there Gomez came where the carriage first stood. What, no conveyance to meet the old battle-scarred veteran ? and the crowd bearing down upon him! near the entrance stood an antedeluvian shay with a skeleton between the shafts and an ebony faced driver on the seat. They jerked his old rattle-trap half way and the general the other half and would his posterity ever believe it the "peseta" hack-driver was to drive the great Gomez through the streets of Marianao. Just then the mayor spun around the corner, and his angry passions rose; it was "carramba" with one hand and then "carramba" with the other, and then "carramba" with both and Mr. Know-it-all expostulated, and the mayor expostulated and said "carramba" again, and just then four drops of rain fell from the sky and the old warrior of many a storm was in his mackintosh before it could be told and the dusty buggy top dropped over him and he was off before a third of the crowd who had stretched their cervical vertebra so hard had a chance to see him. The One Hundred and Sixty-first band went before him playing "The Stars and Stripes Forever," while his Cuban followers came behind him and thus he was escorted to Cuban headquarters; in the evening a reception was given and later in the theatre a ball. The general wore a slouch hat and around his neck was tied a silken handkerchief; he was a trifle stooped and his face bore signs of the hardships he had suffered in his late campaign. The next day he entered Havana and received the ovations of a grateful populace while the political charlatans were whetting their knives to stab him in the hour of his triumph.

This suffices for February, unless it be to mention the 26th, when the privates had an opportunity to watch and laugh while the line officers drilled, practicing sword salutation *a la* regulation; or perchance to tell of how the boys of the Seventh Army Corps changed the schedule on the "Ferro-Carril de Marianao." It is a simple story of a simple plan. The trains didn't stop where the boys wanted to get on, and they "soaped" the track. The train stopped and the boys got on, but it caused General Lee the trouble of writing General Order No. 18, and then, of course, the boys stopped.

During the latter part of February officers and men were in daily expectation of an order from brigade headquarters sending the brigade out for a ten days or a two weeks' practice march. The Second Brigade had just returned from such a march, and it was generally understood that the First Brigade was to proceed upon a similar one, going, however, around the city through the Havana province, instead of the southwesterly direction taken by the Second Brigade. On February 27 (Sunday) Colonel Durbin, Major Smith and Major Olds made a prospecting tour, selecting suitable roadways and camping spots.

In the meantime, however, the surgeon had, on February 25, sent up to division headquarters a protest against the plan. The protest received the approval of the acting chief surgeon of the division, but after going to the chief surgeon of the Havana province, was returned practically disapproving the protest, and recommending preparations for the march, which, though not yet ordered, had been set for March 1st, but the major's protest was too sensible and weighty, and word came on March 1st that the proposed practice march had been postponed, but the fact was that the idea was altogether abandoned. In the meantime the colonel had planned another march, that of a day's pleasure trip to Vento Springs. The adjutant, in company with Captain Fortune, picked the way on Wednesday, March 1st, and in the early morning of the 2d, with Company A as advance guard, the regiment started on its way. When they came to the Second Division hospital the nurses and convalescents and all of Company M turned out to see them as they passed. The bugle corps did its best from the top of the hill till the railroad was crossed, when the band struck up "The Indiana State Band," and kept it up in a way that meant business till Real street was reached. The regiment marched out past the sugar factory to the main railroad, where the ambulances waited while they pushed on one and one-half miles to Vento. The band played a tune and the boys were turned loose. They took a swim, had lunch at 12, went down into the basin, went through the tunnel, and while some lounged others went over to visit the insane asylum, one-half mile away.

At 3:30 the regiment took its way toward camp, arriving at 5:45.

Before the construction of the Vento springs the city had been inadequately supplied with water from the Zanja and Ferdinand VII aqueducts; the magnificent aqueduct of Isable II, or of the Vento, was begun in 1859, deriving its supply from the pure and inexhaustable Vento springs on the edge of the Almandares river, nine miles from Havana.

The aqueduct itself has already cost three million five hundred thousand dollars and is still incomplete, being temporarily connected with that of Ferdinand VII. It will cost three million dollars to complete it. The Vento spring is a wonderful construction, being a large stone basin open at the bottom, through which the spring bubbles. The aqueduct is a tunnel of brick, eliptical in shape, placed under the ground and marked by turrets of stone placed along its course, carrying the water to two great reservoirs near Cerro and from thence to the city. An attempt was first made to pipe water for the camp from Havana, but the elevation interfering, a big elevated tank was built near the Fourth Illinois by means of which the water was to be forced through the camps. On Sunday night, January 22, a tremendous crash was heard and as the men went flying toward the sound conjecture was running wild; it was generally conceded that a frightful wreck had occurred and Bruce of Company K declared he saw the train just go up and the head light just go out, but as they drew near they found the huge water tank smashed to splinters in a flood of water and mud. The water was afterwards piped from the reservoirs and every camp furnished with the clear, pure water of Vento.

The asylum visited by the boys has a sad history; when war came its inmates were neglected; at General Lee's departure two thousand barrels of a wheat preparation, a

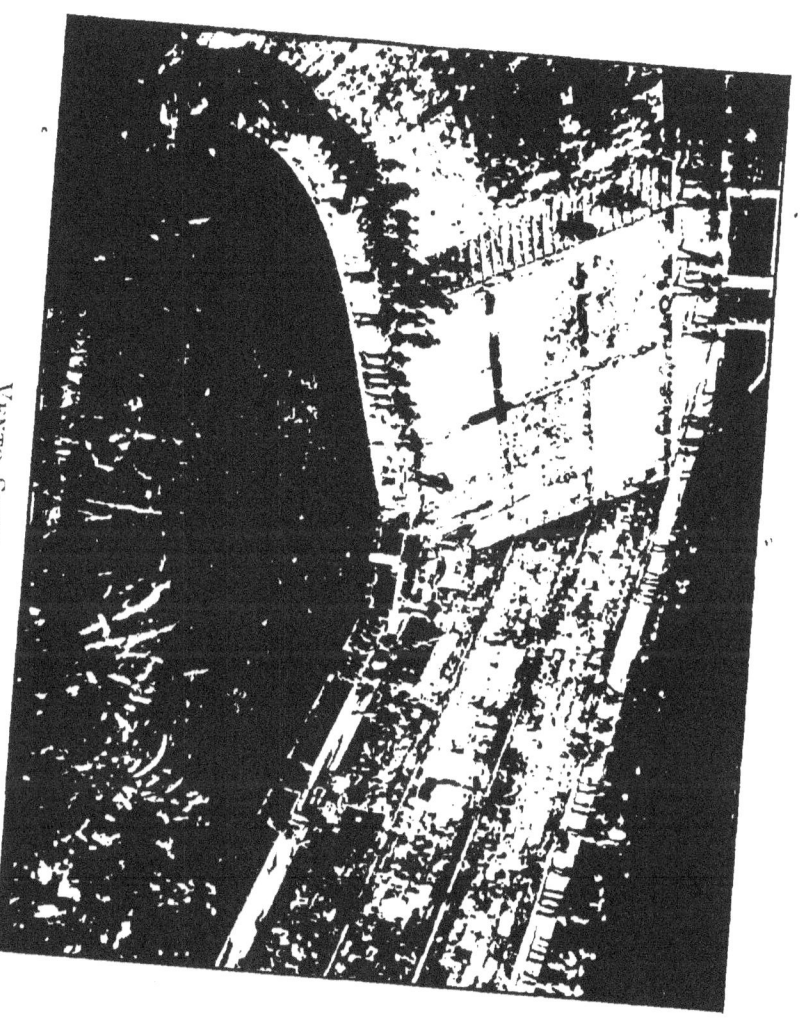

Vento Springs.

portion of America's gift to the starving people of Cuba, was left in the sheds at the wharf. This the Spanish authorities seized and divided it equally between three institutions of which the asylum referred to was one. There were then one thousand and seventy-five inmates and from then until the fortunes of war changed no other provision was made to sustain their life and less than two hundred lived through that awful period of starvation—starved to death! The surviving ones are all nearly dark skinned, showing their superiority of physique and consequent power of endurance.

A week of usual camp routine followed next. There was drill and parade, an issue of clothing by the quartermaster and a sermon by the chaplain. At dress parade on the 6th General Lee was present and was stationed at Colonel Durbin's left, while Lieutenant-Colonel Backus passed the regiment in review. The general, in company with Admiral Sampson, passed through camp again the following day and again on the 9th, in company with Captain Sigsbee of the Texas, visited camp, witnessed the review and stopped for conference with the colonel. Among other things the disposition of the Maine artillery tent floors was a matter in question. The Maine boys had left on the 8th and many of our own tents were still without floors; that evening a few floors found their way over the hill by mistake; the mistake was a simple one. Our regiment had been asked to put a guard over the much coveted property; the instruction to the guard was to allow no one to carry away the floors, but when he gave the instruction to his relief he said " no one is allowed to carry these floors but the One Hundred and Sixty-first," and the floors began to move. However, the next day they were given us by proper authority and were accordingly moved and made up for the regiment what it lacked in floors for its men.

GOVERNMENT WAREHOUSE AT QUEMADOS.

On Friday, the 10th, at 2:15 P. M., the battleships New York, Brooklyn, Indiana and Texas passed, in order named, along the coast on their cruising expedition to Cienfuegos and Santiago. Thirteen guns were fired by the light artillery from the eminence near division headquarters and the salute returned by the guns of the New York. On the 10th the Exchange was moved out of its weedy corner and obscure surroundings and taken to the "Midway," so dubbed by the boys, for here was the band, the assembly tent, the post-office, and the exchange and here the officers sent for their men when they were wanted and couldn't be found, spending idle moments listening to band practice, playing games, writing letters, buying stamps and soft drinks at the Exchange. It was also on the 10th that cir-

MIDWAY.

cular No. 5 was issued from corps headquarters authorizing regimental commanders to replace the drill on Tuesdays and Thursdays with athletic exercises.

Instead of fours right and column left there was to be dashes and hurdles, pole vaults, hammer throwing, shot putting, wrestling, base ball and foot ball. The athletic fiends were in high delight—great things would be done to other regiments—but while all the men were glad for a change they were not looking for a change of this kind; it was a change of country and this announcement savored of a longer stay than the most satisfied had hoped for, but the time of departure was too near at hand and the authorization of such a programme, which, had it come earlier, would have produced a most excellent and acceptable

OFF FOR THE MAIL.

change, was too untimely, for in less than two weeks preparations for "goin' home" were in progress.

The next day, Saturday, March 11, brought Major Kenner, the paymaster, and also a new order of company inspection. Every tent was emptied and then taken down; it was the inspection order only, but it looked like something else, and the yells sent up by the boys made the neighbor regiments believe we were; then the floors were raised, the soil underneath them scratched and everything left to ventilate, after which "as you were" was executed and inspection was over.

Sunday was the 12th. The colonel and Major Smith had gone to Mantanzas; Chaplain Watts, of the First Texas, preached in the assembly tent; the officers at a meeting decided to give a reception, and on Wednesday the following

invitation was sent to all the officers of the Seventh Army Corps:

"The officers of the One Hundred and Sixty-first Regiment Indiana Volunteer Infantry request your presence on Monday evening, March the twentieth, at the headquarters of the Corps of Engineers.

"At eight o'clock.

"Dancing."

The rooms of the building were handsomely decorated with branches of the royal palm, and the affair, by all who were there, was pronounced the best kind of a success. Light refreshments were served, and in the court arbor a peculiar but excellent quality of lemonade was at the disposal of all throughout the evening; the officers did not stay late *and showed fine consideration for their sleeping comrades by the quiet way in which they came into camp.*

On Monday, the 13th, Lieutenant John R. Ward, with a detail of six men, accompanied Paymaster Major Benjamin F. Havens on his pay trip among the regiments outside Havana province. They visited regiments at Mantanzas, Cardenas, La Union, Batabano and minor points, returning to the regiment the 26th. In January Lieutenant Durbin and in February Lieutenant Pitman, each with a detail of men, made similar trips with the major. It was an excellent opportunity to see the country and a privilege that every one coveted. The detail was selected from the One Hundred and Sixty-first Indiana each time, and caused a little concern on the outside, but our friend, Major Havens, is a Hoosier and no other explanation is needed.

Tuesday, 14th, Major Blow, of the Fourth Virginia, an officer of the regular army, came into camp for investigation and instruction concerning the condition of company books; the officers gathered in the band stand and with mustering out in view were carefully reminded of the exactness and completeness of all record necessary for acceptance by the authority on that day. Nothing of serious consequence occurred during the next few days save Kimmel's white collar at dress parade and the report that several men strained their optic nerves looking out to sea for transports.

For Friday, 17th, a brigade review was on. It was a farewell review for Colonel Joseph F. Armfield, commander of the brigade and colonel of the First North Carolina. Colonel Moulton, of the Second Illinois passed the brigade in review, and Lieutenant-Colonel Backus was in command of the One Hundred and Sixty-first. Colonel Armfield and his regiment left the following day, a week, for Savannah, Georgia. On Monday, 20th, instead of the usual regimental parade the battalions were reviewed by their respective commanders.

On the evening of this day there was organized "The Society of the Seventh Army Corps—Spanish-American War," of which Major-General Fitzhugh Lee was chosen president; Colonel Durbin was chosen as a member of the executive council. By article V of the constitution "all officers and soldiers who have served in the Seventh Army Corps in the war between the United States and Spain, possessing a good moral character and an honorable military record, shall be eligible to membership in the society."

On Tuesday, 21st, at regimental parade, the regiment heard the following notification was read to them by the colonel:

Commanding General,   Havana, March 20, 1899.
     Buena Vista:

Secretary of war directs the Second Illinois and the One Hundred and Sixty-first Indiana be prepared to go to States after regiments already ordered get away; you will be notified later when transport will be ready. Regiments should get their records complete.

       By command of Major-General Brooke.
              Signed RICHARDS,
              Asst. Adjutant-General.

The men heard these words in silence and marched back to quarters; they wanted to go home, of course, but neither at this time nor later when the information was definite as to time did there occur the joyful and noisy demonstration which characterized other regiments of men under the same circumstances. The *esprit de corps*, the pride of reputation, the excellent health and fine feeling of the men and the entire environment made them satisfied and the certainty of a recall before the extreme heat set in made them willing to await what the department thought the proper time; nevertheless twelve hundred glad hearts beat under army blankets that night and twelve hundred imaginations were busy living through the scenes that were soon to occur in the homeland far away.

COMPANY G STREET BY MOONLIGHT.

Thursday was a day of picture taking; the chaplain was busy preparing a regimental history and Waterman's photographer was busy with his camera; it was turned upon the sergeants and corporals and other such groups as could be called together, and then from an elevated construction hauled about in a wagon photographs of the regiment and views of camp were taken. In the afternoon Lieutenant-Colonel Backus passed the regiment in review before Colonel Durbin, adjutant in command of the First Battalion.

The next day morning drill was replaced by camp

Next!

cleaning, and at parade the men were told they might be in expectation of an order to move any day, and they were also given the pleasing information that small boxes containing their additional effects in the way of Cuban relics, etc., would be transported for them.

In the evening the First North Carolina men, who were to leave the following day, paid us their parting respects by way of a noisy tin can serenade; the whole howling regiment, frantic because of home-going, came down upon us and made night hideous as they marched through the headquarters and battalion streets. It was indicative of the kindly feeling existing between the regiments of the brigade and made our boys glad to see the North Carolinians shout because they were going back to the cotton and the pine trees of their native state. The next day, Saturday, 25th, Major Blow again met with the officers; in the afternoon Major-General Brooke sent to the commanding general at Buena Vista the following information which was forwarded to this regiment, in substance that on the 29th and 30th inst. the Second Illinois was to leave and that efforts were then being made to secure the Ward line to land the One Hundred and Sixty-first Indiana in Tampa, Florida, by 12 o'clock, March 31. On the same day all ammunition and extra ordnance stores were turned in and Quartermaster Brunt took them to the government ordnance store at Fort Principe.

On this Saturday an execution occurred under the "hangman's tree," without an account of which and a picture of the tree the history of the regiment would be incomplete. The tree in question grew especially to hang people on; it has only one limb for the reason that so continuous has been the weight of bodies hanging from it that all the strength of the tree must be concentrated in this one limb to be able to bear the strain. The first use of this marvelous tree was when a band of bandits robbed a Spanish trading party and hung them all from the limb, tying the ropes about the trunk, and then not long thereafter the civil authorities having captured the bandits hung them all in turn, seventeen of them, from the self same limb; the Cubans hung many a Spaniard there and in the recent war the number of Cubans strung up to this noted limb varies according to report, some declaring fifty; others seventy-three and still others one hundred and fifty, and no doubt Weyler, the assassin and butcher, hung a whole town of reconcentrados to the limb in question. The grass grows greener under the tree because the blood has fertilized the soil. At night a wise man always avoids passing it. Spooks and ghosts laugh at you with a fiendish laugh and apparitions of hanging bodies dangling there knock against each other as they are blown about by wind that comes up from Playa beach.

On the day in question a man was stood against the tree; ten rifles were leveled at him twenty feet away. The man could not be recognized from camp, one-quarter mile

HANGMAN'S TREE.

away for his bandaged eyes disguised him, but it could be no other than the poor Louisiana soldier who in a drunken row had killed a comrade and was waiting death sentence in Marianao jail. Would they shoot before the men and officers who saw them could get there? "After all do I want to see a poor fellow shot down?" "My! its awful." "Why couldn't they give him a life sentence?" "I tell you its sad, boys." "I don't know whether I want to go any farther or not, but if it's got to be done I guess I'll go on just to say I saw it." But before the men got more than half way the fatal moment came. There came a sharp metallic click and the awful deed was done, the rifles were lowered and the poor boy in blue threw up his hands and— took the bandage from his eyes—the photograph was taken. Under the circumstances it is not policy to mention every name, but if Captain Osborne and Captain Gwinn and Major Olds had caught Lieutenant Dority just then another man might have been hung from that famous tree.

Monday forenoon, the 27th, an order came calling for a corps review, by the secretary of war, that day at 4:30 P. M. The arrival of the secretary of war in Havana and his conference with the heads of departments was an occasion of great moment for the military administration of affairs in the island. The corps review was held in his honor; it was the last review of the corps, and it was fragmentary, there being only seven regiments, besides the artillery and cavalry, to participate. Seventeen guns, the proper salute for a member of the cabinet, was fired by the batteries as the secretary, with his escort, arrived upon the field. The Fourth Illinois, Ninth Illinois, Third Nebraska, One Hundred and Sixty-first Indiana, Second Illinois, Forty-ninth Iowa and Sixth Missouri passed in review in the order named. The cavalry and artillery passed the reviewing stand twice, as usual; but this time, as if it were their last opportunity, showed the secretary and everybody else how fast they could go. It was a fine exhibition of military horsemanship, and a whole circus and hippodrome to see them dash by with just danger enough to make it real exciting. In view of who the reviewing officer was, the One Hundred and Sixty-first Indiana had a record to sustain. How eyes did open at the sight of those big companies and straight lines! The secretary only said to the colonel, as he retired, "It beat Jacksonville"—three words big with meaning.

In the evening General Brooke tendered the secretary a reception. Prominent officers of the army and navy and their wives and many leading citizens were present. The Seventh Cavalry band furnished music, and the occasion was one of the most pleasant social events held in the city since the evacuation. While Colonel Durbin was in attendance at this reception, Major Megrew being in command of camp, a telegram was received stating that the command would leave camp at daybreak on Wednesday morning and embark on the steamship Logan for the United States. All next day the camp was a busy scene of men hurrying to and fro, packing boxes and getting things in readiness for the long looked for and hoped for event.

The evening was one of preparation for the morning's departure. The chaplain was holding nightly services in the assembly tent, and that night was an unexpected farewell service. Fires were consuming all combustible leavings, and the whole camp was lighted by the flames. There was not much sleep that night. The men's brains were busy, and they were restless for the coming of the morning. One man mistook 2 o'clock for 5 and began to wander about beating upon a washpan in an attempt to raise the camp, until either the sight of the Third Battalion commander in his night shirt or his mighty voice commanding silence scared the fellow back to his cot. At 4 A. M. reveille sounded, a hasty but good breakfast taken, the wagons loaded, assembly call given at 5:45, and at 6 A. M., promptly, the colonel commanded: "Forward, march!" The wagon train had gone before, and the regiment marched past Buena Vista Station and formed in line of masses before General Lee's headquarters, where the general was standing to see the One Hundred and Sixty-first Indiana march away. Colonel Durbin dismounted and, saluting, said: "I have the honor to report the departure of the One Hundred and Sixty-first Indiana Volunteer Infantry." The colonel had in mind to say other things, but the occasion was one of deep emotion and he could only grasp the old general's hand and say: "Good bye, and God bless you!" and he turned away. The tear in General Lee's eye spoke for him as he watched the colonel mount and the regiment move away.

The regiment then proceeded out on the road to the city, marching by way of Vedado, where they came to "port arms" in passing General Brooke and other officers before headquarters, arriving at San Jose wharf at 9:30, after a three and one-half hours' march, where the men piled themselves up in the shade to rest and wait for the order to move on board the transport.

CHAPTER X.

THE DEPARTURE, VOYAGE AND ARRIVAL.

The wagon train had come in before them and the dock men were busy loading the effects upon small flat cars, pushing them out on the pier and preparing them for the hoist that carried them up and down into the two hatchways of the vessel; if the regiment and its effects could be on board by 4 o'clock or thereabouts, the transport was to make for Savannah, which port it could reach by noon of the 31st in time to avoid quarantine; otherwise we were to reach the states by way of Tampa, and be necessarily inconvenienced by a ten days quarantine.

To be ready by any ways near 4 o'clock seemed impossible, according to the progress usually made in moving a regiment on board a vessel, but it is doubtful if ever a transport was loaded with greater rapidity than this, and the wonder is that more boxes and a few heads were not smashed. Boxes, trunks and barrels were piled together in the net or looped within a single rope, the cog wheel began to play and away they went with a swing and a bang and a chorus of Cuban ejaculations; they made new bundles while the one just sent up swung in the air above them. Now and then a bundle came back with a smash, but always missed a Cuban, or if it reached the hatchway hole beat the rope to the bottom with a bang and scattered their contents on the floor. The boys lounged under the wharf shed till 3 o'clock and then began to board the vessel. Lieutenant-Colonel Backus, executive officer of the vessel, superintended their embarkment.

SAN JOSE ESPIGON (WHARF.)

They came with guns and knapsacks and canteens, but they came with more. The beasts and the birds were there; this fellow had a dog and another one a rabbit and company F's snake charmer had his mammoth serpents; there were yellow breasted canaries and game roosters, green parrots in wire cages; one fellow had a cat with kittens; he had taken puss with him from Savannah and while on that productive soil she gave birth to nine kittens; each one was worth its weight in gold, for it was born in "Cuby," and mother and all should go back to Freedom's holy land; and there were canes and small portable boxes of this, that and the other thing, and what the men didn't have heaven knows they did have in their boxes among the heavy baggage. Company officers stood at the foot of the gang stairway and noted the men as they passed and quite a few failed to pass, not One Hundred and Sixty-first men, but discharged soldiers, fired teamsters and cooks and an

A Few of Them.

occasional speculator who had gone broke, all seeking passage back to a better land. They were a persevering lot of fellows and when turned down once would try again until some officer was charitable enough to disobey orders and allow an occasional one to slip along. A rope ladder lowered for a couple of late passengers brought up the rest and all on board, at 5.05 P. M., the well loaded vessel, assisted by the tug Gladisfen, slowly turned its prow to the north and started for the harbor exit close by Morro's massive walls.

The band played "The Stars and Stripes" and "A Hot Time;" the vessels that lay at anchor in the harbor filled the air with the shrill noise of steam whistles; the Paris' decks were filled with tourists who cheered us loudly as we passed; a steam launch ran out to cheer us on our

GOING ON BOARD THE LOGAN.

way, and the band of the Resolute played "Home, Sweet Home;" there was a moment's quiet and a piercing Indian yell came from behind that caused every man on board to turn toward the wharf; it was "Broncho John," the man with the record of the plains, a familiar figure in the Seventh Army Corps, who added a little romance to its history; he was astride his horse at the end of the pier bidding us good-bye with his characteristic yell and a wave of his coat, and the boys returned it with fine imitation and a rousing spirit. Past the Maine, past Cabana, past Morro at 5:23 and out into the ocean the steamship went and we were "goin' home." Things were different than when we entered; Cabana's walls were not lined with Spanish soldiers and Old Glory waved from Morro. Scenes that

186   HISTORY OF THE

three and a half months before were strange were then familiar, and a mission, the idea and purpose of which when we first came into such environments played upon the emotions of the American soldiers, no longer moved him as before, but left him alone with his musings of where he was going.

The vessel was a government transport, formerly the Manitoba, but re-named the Logan. It was four hundred and fifty-seven feet long, several feet shorter than the Mo-

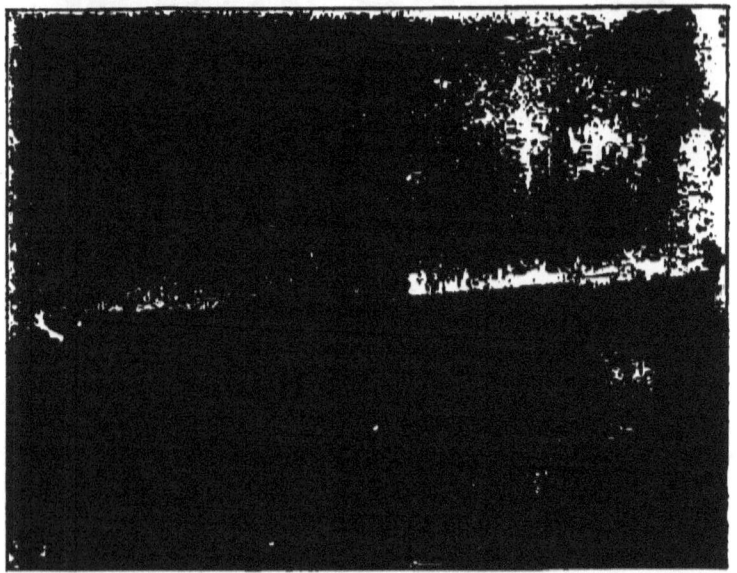

LOGAN.

bile, and, although a comfortable and substantial vessel, it could hardly be called the Mobile's equal. It had, however, more deck room for the men than had the Mobile, while the officer's quarters were smaller. In place of cots for the men, hammocks were provided, which arrangement allowed better ventilation. The vessel made sixteen knots an hour over the bottom, and thirteen and a half feet through the water, dropping anchor at the quarantine station in the Savannah harbor at 9:15 A. M., Friday, the 31st—forty hours since 5:05 P. M., Wednesday, the 29th, when the line was cast off at San José pier. From Savannah to Havana and return, allowing eight hours for loading, it was the fastest record yet made by a government transport. The sea was just a trifle rough the first morning out, and officers and men, who had voluntarily thrown up home

Not Feeling So Well!

and friends and position for suffering Cuba's sake, began to throw up again simply because they couldn't help it for their feelings' sake. The sea grew calmer and the vessel grew steadier and the politicians, so long out of practice, realizing the early return to their profession, called a mock convention to determine by their knavery the political destiny of some of their comrades.

Vick M. Backus imposed himself upon the convention as self-constituted chairman. Oratory was on tap and flowed like greased liquid. Much opposition was encountered to "old man" Gwinn's nomination for sheriff of Rush county, but the gallant old veteran's record of daring bravery in the Mexican war was too deserving of recognition, and at the end of a hot debate, was given the unanimous nomination for said position. Percy Welsh, of Hooppole township, Posey county, was made a nominee for coroner of his township, but so far forgot himself as to insult the chairman, whereupon Ward, of White, arose and startled the convention by masterly eloquence, in which he repudiated the man Welsh, who quailed into speechlessness under the scathing denunciation. The new discovered Demosthenes closed his phillipic by placing Congressman Brunt's protege, Sam Cahn, in nomination, who was thereupon chosen by the convention amidst wild acclamation. Messages of condolence were to invalid Hudgins and the convention adjourned to meet in the saloon at 7:30 P. M. Wickliff Smith was unanimously chosen chairman, but Backus intimidated the convention at the point of weapon and when Smith started for the chair he found himself starinto the depths of a pistol in the hand of the determined and now desperate Backus; Smith was afraid to take his seat, whereupon he was vehemently denounced as a traitor to his convictions a proceedings began with Backus in the chair. Harold Megrew and Albert D. Ogborn, by appointment of the previous sitting, reported a draft of resolutions denouncing all intoxicating liquor but whiskey, advocating all kinds of money as long as there was plenty of it, and granting the toiling millions leave to toil. The scene that followed was a stormy one. Waterlilly Kimmel led the race for congressman of the Sixth district, and Ivy, of police fame, was made the convention's choice for justice of the peace of

Clark county. Welsh was there with blood in his eye—the time for vengeance came when Ward, of White county, was made a nominee; he defamed his character and his well-known reputation for honesty and truthfulness carried the opinion of the representatives present, but when the man from White arose to acknowledge his defeat, he did'nt do a thing to the man from Posey, and the convention adjourned after firing Welsh from the salon.

The next morning at 8 o'clock, the Logan was nearing the muddy mouth of the Savannah river. As she drew near her mooring place the indispensable tugs were there to help the big boat to her place. There was the "H. C. M. Smith," whoever that referred to, that brought the inspecting surgeon on board, and there was the "Dauntless" of filibustering fame, that ran her twenty miles an hour and cost the governments of Spain and United States so much in vain endeavor to catch her; huge lighters were pushed alongside and the work of unloading began. At 12:10 the Santee, a strange bulk of a boat came and took the First Battalion over to the dread fumigation plant; what they would do to us was the supreme query all the way from Cuba. Strange stories of that mysterious place had been circulated; the men were to be stripped and steamed until all the Cuban brown would leave their skin and they were to go home as fair faced as a new-born child. Some of the men had come into possession of little pieces of hardened shapeless rubber purported to be fumigated buttons—relics were to melt and run together and every parrot, cat, canary, rooster and dog would be cleansed beyond recognition if he came out alive. The First Battalion returned at 3:15 and all the satisfaction they gave the rest was "what they'll do to you 'll be a plenty," and they were towed to the city along with the commissary goods that were not subject to fumigation. At 4 P. M. another load went over and passed us on their way to Savannah, with the message "they wont do a thing to you when they get you."

Night fell over the Logan, a Company C man fell into the water, and in the morning the rest of the regiment started in two bodies to the place of torture. We were first subjected to a long wait, in which they let loose on us about sixty millions sand gnats, that bit and stung worse than Morro fleas; then the men marched in to an open space and prepared such baggage as they carried with them for the cauldron. It is only fair to say the fumigating authorities had their own way about it all; not the least concession of any character would they make unless some petty condition was complied with. If you only had one laundered shirt it must have all the starch steamed out of it in the fumigatory process, unless you wore it, in which case it didn't need fumigation. Blankets which were aired almost every day must be steamed into worthlessness, but clothes and overcoats that hung for months in the tents passed without it. At first men were stripped and dressed in pajamas to stand around like hospital convalescents, while their every piece of clothing went in the cylinder; but this got wearisome for the management and such carefulness was afterward dispensed with, but such articles as were steamed got two hundred and twenty degrees for twenty minutes, and the most skeptical had but to lay the tip of his little finger on them as they emerged to be most thoroughly convinced that every flea, United States grayback and every vermin of every kind, carrying concealed about his person any contagious microbes of smallpox or yellow fever, had suffered a most horrible death; but they deserved it all for what they did to us in Cuba. Any leather that went felt in awful little when it came out, as the accompanying cut will fully demonstrate to a careful observer.

Most leather goods were dipped in a solution of water, bichloride of mercury and sodium chloride and dirt, while boxed articles were sprinkled with sawdust, moistened with a solution of formaldchyde or some such concoction of similar name; it was a big nuisance and a regular April fool but no doubt a great life saving station and all its attendants worthy a medal of honer from its superintendant to the small boy who slipped the officers red chalk to O. K. unfumigated goods, for if those terrible microbes who came with us, transportation free, from Cuba had ever got loose, the entire south would have been overwhelmed with an appalling loss of life. We might in return for courtesy received, suggest to its worthy proprietors an excellent motto "a thing worth doing is worth doing well." Personal fumigation being over, at 2:40, with empty stomachs, we embarked on the Santee and, assisted by the Dauntless, made our way up to the city wharf. Wagons were ready to haul us to camp and at 6 P. M. we came up with the rest of the regiment gone on before, with a camp laid out on the ground formerly occupied by the Forty-ninth Iowa. The tents were old ones of every description, left behind by the regiment that had previously gone to Cuba; at camp Columbia we had better tentage than any regiment in the Seventh Army Corps, besides the men, the officers also having each one a large (hospital) tent, but here we tumbled into what ever was at hand and, unwashed and unkempt, froze around till our washpans and blankets were released from quarantine. The regiment came over without a sick man and this deprivation caused more sickness than the steaming of those imaginary bacterial microbes ever prevented, but a soldier must have a heart for any fate and so with hearts that were cheerful because the time was short and because the stiff winds that chilled them through and through were American and therefore better than the balmy breezes and warm sunshine of Cuba, the men began the last chapter of their experience in the war they had undertaken to assist.

CHAPTER XI.

MUSTERING OUT MONTH.

CAMP HOMEWARD, April 2-30, 1899.
The evening of April Fool's day found the regiment once more together and when Sunday, the 2d, dawned, a month of hard work stared everybody in the face; the guard *played* guard mount, and next day the regiment *played* parade, after which the colonel said a few words and business was on in earnest thereafter. There was plenty eating every where and the messes were never formed, but at a meeting of officers on the 5th it was announced that suitable arrangements could be made with the genial Holmes couple who had been in the restaurant business all the way to Cuba and back, and a decision reached which drew all the regimental officers around their well spread table three times a day for $5 a week. The same day the baggage came from the place of its retention by the fumigating authorities. The officers had gone frozen by night and unkempt by day, until the bedding and wash-pans arrived; the stuff came and every man had to hunt his own—it brought with it a smell that hasn't left it yet and which so infected the bedding that when a man tucked it under his nose for the night he expected to wake up in the morning axphixiated or chloroformed or in a condition that might be worse. But the rough part of it all was that many articles of value never came at all; one thing is evident, they were either lost or stolen—the reader may form his own opinion, but in either case the responsibility is not hard to fix.

The first week was intensely chilly, especially at night for men fresh from Cuba, and all the rusty oil stoves of former Savannah days were started on the burn; a certain lieutenant of Company F, with honors fresh upon him, built his camp fire upon the floor of his tent, but the majority of the officers spent the nights in town previous to the arrival of their blankets.

Captain Beckert, of the Sixteenth United States, the mustering out officer for the regiment, had made his appearance and was busy with the inspection of company books and records. While Surgeons Gerrish and Wilson were busy at medical inspection of the Fourth Virginia men the men of the One Hundred and Sixty-first were marching by companies to a building in the camp of the Two Hundred and Second New York, where a board of medical examiners, consisting of Surgeons Pead and Old, of the Fourth Virginia, and Tetamore, of the One Hundred and Second New York, under direction of Surgeon Howard, of the United States Army, endeavored to find out how many of those who enlisted able bodied were crippled at the close of the war. The men who reported themselves as sound were passed with little or no examination, while those who reported unsound were tested as to the genuineness of their disability. The arrangement was a mutual protective concern; it began Friday, the 7th, with Company G, and ended Monday, the band and the staff being examined the last day.

The day for turning in ordnance stores had been set for Wednesday, the 12th; accordingly, Tuesday was the last day with guns and good use was made of the time. At 9 A. M. the regiment marched to the Dale Avenue camp with the purpose of making a regimental call on the First North Carolina and the Second Louisiana; Colonel Durbin, in a neat speech, spoke of the good feeling entertained by the Hoosiers for the men from Carolina, of the pain in breaking associations that had been so friendly and wishing Colonel Armfield and his men God-speed, he said good-bye for the regiment. There were cheers for the regiment, cheers for the brigade which Colonel Armfield commanded and cheers for the Seventh Army Corps. Arms were stacked, and while the men spent half an hour talking of Cuba and of home, the officers of the regiments mingled in social and farewell intercourse. On the return march a like scene occurred at the camp of the Second Louisiana, where the Indiana men were warmly welcomed by the "Tigers" from the south. Lieutenant-Colonel DuFour made a touching little speech which was warmly and loudly applauded by the men in ranks. He declared that he was glad to see that all sectional feeling had been wiped out and that the northern men had it in heart to thus visit the regiments from the south and wished that everything good might attend the Hoosier boys as they went back to their homes in the north.

Wednesday was a picture taking day and in the midst of the greatest rush of business, for the order had come for the turning in of all ordnance stores; before the captains' tents the guns were stacked and the knapsacks, haversacks and canteens were placed in piles of five, and after Lieutenant Guignard, of the Fourth United States Artillery, had passed along to inspect them they were snugly packed away in boxes and Uncle Sam's wagons came along and took them away. Each company was in possession of ordnance stores to the amount of about three thousand dollars. Six companies completed this work on the 13th, and six on the 14th. On the 13th the first attempt since leaving was made to mount the guard without arms; it was not an easy thing to do and the men that gathered round to watch had a little fun at the guard's expense. During these days neither pen can describe nor words can tell the awful agony of toil through which the captains and their clerks were passing, burning the midnight oil out of their lamps and the energy out of their lives in preparing the muster rolls for the men to sign; there were only five of them for each company and the men pitched horse-shoes while the officers worked and when they were signed, every one of the five by every man in the company, they were subjected to a board of examiners composed of the lieutenants, who labored through them and sent them back for needed correction.

For the men the following week was one of monotonous waiting, going out perhaps at drill time for a little exercise and spending the rest of their time at the popular game of quoit pitching or in trying to borrow a dime to take them to town and back. In the forenoon of the 17th the officers of the One Hundred and Sixtieth Indiana paid their respects to the regiment by a visit to its officers. They called at the colonel's tent where it was suggested that Chaplain Vigus, of the visiting regiment, excuse himself in order to call on the chaplain of the One Hundred and Sixty-first, who was at that time in his own tent; the chaplain *considerately* did so.

In the evening of this day the flag pole that was set up in front of Colonel Bryan's headquarters at Camp Cuba Libre in place of the one that was not set up met with a sad fate; other men have secured lumber for canes, but it was in the bright light of day, but this was done under the cover of night; it only goes to show what crimes are committed in the name of politics; the said flag pole had come all the way from Jacksonville intact, but the Bryanitically inclined officers who, in army life generally, live pretty close to where the flag pole ought to go, could not resist the temptation to reduce it to walking-stick lengths which will now come into possession of Bryan disciples and 16 to 1 will make them believe all the harder in his principles because they have a cane made from his flag pole, and Major Smith is willing to leave it to all sound thinking people if that was not a greater crime than losing eighteen dollars on a bluff or smuggling mahogany posts out of a hospital tent.

The next day the colonel went to Washington; the men did not know exactly for what, but they knew all railroad agents had been forbidden to do business in the regiment and they were a little curious and anxious to know what the commanding officer would have to say when he returned; he came back on Sunday, the 23d, and after dinner the officers' call was blown and the Colonel told them in substance the purpose and result of his mission. It had resulted in an invitation from the President of the United States for this regiment to return home by way of Washington, at which place he would take pleasure in reviewing it. The Secretary of War had also expressed a desire to see again the regiment whose splendid appearance and marching had called from him on previous occasions words of such high commendation. The trip was to cost the men no more than a ticket the shortest way home and would afford to them perhaps the opportunity of their lifetime to see the capital city of the nation with its interesting and historical sights. The officers then gave an expression, after which the men were called before the colonel, and he told them the same things requesting them to think the matter over and give their company commanders an expression at retreat and roll call. It was accordingly done and the answer came in an almost unanimous desire to accept the President's invitation.

The next morning witnessed a new departure in the guard mount: Lieutenant-Colonel Backus was officer of day, Major McGrew mounted the guard, Adjutant Tichenor was

acting sergeant major, and the captains accompanied each
the detail of men from his company; the boys expected o
have a laugh but the major fooled them; however, they
had it the next morning when Colonel Durbin was made
officer of the day and Lieutenant-Colonel Backus took his
turn at mounting the guard; the boys meant no discourtesy
to their superior officer, but they simply couldn't help but
laugh. In the morning Lieutenant Johnson distinguished
himself by championing the cause of the despised and
abused colored woman. The Fourth Virginia men were
engaged in the unmanly and shameful conduct of tossing
a poor defenseless colored washerwoman in a blanket.
For shame! Let it be a man, boys, even though he be white,

Kangaroo Court

but a woman is a woman, be her color what it may, and a
good black woman is a thousand times better than a bad
white one. The Savannah Morning News of the 27th,

said: "It was reported last night that a woman who was in a delicate condition was tossed in the Fourth Virginia camp day before yesterday, and that yesterday she died." How true this report was we do not know, but apart from any serious consequence the act was a disreputable outrage, indecent and disgusting, and the conduct of those men a disgrace to their own color; to a man of true sentiment it was funny, but gratifying, to see the colored washwoman run to the Indiana camp because she knew the Hoosiers would protect her.

On April the 10th General Lee had issued his last General Order to that portion of the Seventh Army Corps still in Cuba. It was as follows:

HEADQUARTERS SEVENTH ARMY CORPS,
CAMP COLUMBIA,
HAVANA, CUBA, April 10, 1899.

GENERAL ORDERS NO. 24.

The order has been received which moves the last regiment of the Seventh Corps across the sea to be mustered out of the service of the United States. The ranks of its organization are forever broken. The record made by the officers and men will be forever preserved. The pages of military history of their country will inscribe the deeds of no troops who won a greater reputation for discipline, drill, and manly discharge of duty, soldierly conduct and cheerful obedience to all orders.

The President's assurance, had the war with Spain continued, that the Seventh Corps would have been selected to lead the assault upon the Havana lines, proves that the Corps possessed the confidence of the Commander-in-Chief of the Army and Navy, a confidence shared by his fellow countrymen.

It is gratifying to review the career, and remember the

harmony which existed among the forty thousand soldiers who answered the roll-call at Tampa, Jacksonville, Savannah, and Cuba. Whether it were the "Volunteers" who afterwards at various times broke ranks, and resumed the duties of American citizenship, or the "Regulars," whose standards are still flying, and who are now the advance sentinels of American progress and civilization,—soldiers of the North and South took the sunshine and storm of camp together, and marched side by side under one flag, in one cause, for one country.

Their cordial support and unvarying kindness to the Corps Commander will be gratefully cherished, and though his military connection with comrades and soldiers be severed, the connection that binds him to what concerns their lives, their prosperity and success in days that are to come will never be broken.

May health and happiness crown their days, and when their thoughts sometimes wander back to Camps Cuba Libre, Onward, and Columbia, may their hearts beat quicker as they remember they once marched under the banners of the Seventh Army Corps.

FITZHUGH LEE,
Major General U. S. Volunteers, Commanding.

This order was communicated to the One Hundred and Sixty-First Indiana Volunteer Regiment by the Colonel on the morning of the 22nd and with it came also his own last General Order:

HEADQUARTERS 161st IND. VOLUNTEER INFANTRY,
IN CAMP NEAR SAVANNAH, GEORGIA,
April 22, 1899.

GENERAL ORDER NO. 8.

In communicating to you General Order No. 247, Havana, Cuba, April 10, which is the farewell order of our recent corps commander, General Fitzhugh Lee, your commanding officer desires to add his personal testimony, and convey to you in order his parting words of commendation of your services to your country—leaving your homes and your civil pursuits with only one thought and ambition, and that to answer the call of our President to maintain the honor of our flag and punish the insult offered in the destruction of the battleship Maine and the murder of part of her gallant officers and crew. You gave to the world that you were ready, willing and anxious to make any sacrifice required of you, coming as you did unacquainted and uneducated in military affairs or training and attaining to a high degree of proficiency speaks more than words of mine can convey. Your services have been truly honest and faithful; by your intelligence, desire, devotion and hard work, you were quickly made acquainted with the details of drills and maneuverings necessary. By your conduct and soldierly deportment and bearing you attracted to yourselves favorable notice. In your camp conditions, in which none excelled you in neatness, tidiness and sanitary conditions, you received the favorable commendation of your suerior. In your drills, tactics, parades and reviews you have had the plaudits of men, the compliments and highest praise of officers of the highest grade, including the Honorable Secretary of War. These favorable expressions belong to you. They have been honestly and honorably earned and will be pleasant memories in years to come. You are not returning to your homes battle-scarred, and I believe I voice the feeling of each one of you when I say that our regret is that no opportunity was afforded to add to honors, bravery and gallantry under fire and in battle, and we must quit the service with the consolation that what was given us to do we did cheerfully and to the best of our ability. In parting as soldiers, let us always cherish the kindliest feeling and consideration for each other, that feeling of comradeship which in after years will link us together as brothers. In going to your homes in the pursuits of civil life carry with you the assurance of your colonel that you are enshrined in his heart's affections and for each officer and man of the regiment he has the highest personal regard and his prayers and strong desire shall always be for your welfare, and wherever you may go may heaven's choicest blessings be yours.

Thanking you for your willing obedience to orders and requirements, whatever their character, at all times.

Your Colonel.

On Wednesday evening the officers were the guests of Colonel Durbin at an elaborately spread banquet in the banquet hall of the DeSoto. Sergeant-Major Starr was the ranking officer in camp and between the hours of 7:30 p. m. and 1 a. m. wore his "blushing honors full upon him" in a manner becoming the only sergeant-major who ever commanded a regiment. The officers went to the city at 7:30 in two cars especially reserved for them at Liberty street, marched to the hotel and were soon gathered around tables formed in a hollow square and most beautifully decorated with potted flowers. It was a notable and joyous occasion, every man was happy, and yet every one was touched with a solemn feeling as they realized that the gathering was a farewell one and that the associations that had for the past ten months bound them together were about to be broken and the habiliment of the soldier laid aside for the dress of civil life. Between the servings there was jovial conversation and fun poked at everybody, and at the close of the repast the following toasts were responded to:

The American Soldiers—Lieutenant-Colonel Backus.
The Volunteer Soldier—Captain Ogborn.
Indiana and her Soldiers—Captain Fortune.
The Indiana National Guard—Major Megrew.
Our War with Spain—Lieutenant Welsh.
Phenastine, and why he fed us Quinine—Major Smith, followed by Lieutenants Gerrish and Wilson.
The Old Army Mule—Quartermaster Brunt.
Cuba and her Senoritas—Lieutenant Ward.
The Value of a Pair of Deuces—Captain Scott.
What we Should Think of Ourselves as Soldiers and Citizens—Chaplain Biederwolf.
How we Won a Home—Major Olds.
The Lieutenant and How He Got There—Lieutenant Comstock.
How the Tenth Infantry made Good Soldiers—Lieutenant Owens.
The Folks at Home—Captain Guthrie.
The One Hundred and Sixty-first Volunteer Infantry—Col. Winfield T. Durbin.

It was one of those long-to-be-remembered events; everything was said that could be said and just those things that should have been said; and it is needless to here state the deep appreciation of every one present for the regard and courtesy shown to them by their commanding officer. The hour hand was at the smallest figure on the dial when the evening was over and the officers returned to camp.

The hard work had slowly come to an end and the few remaining days gave to every one a chance to make any desirable purchases in the city and to pack everything in readiness for the coming of the great day. Arrangements had been made for the trip to Washington, the regimental horses were sent north over the shortest way, the officers had sworn before Captain Beckurts concerning their responsibility for government property and there was nothing more to do.

The last regimental formation was held in the open space by the road. The battalions formed three sides of a hollow square and the colonel spoke to them. He first told them all about the arrangements for leaving; the mustering-out was to begin at 9 o'clock the following morning, after which the men would be paid and be at liberty, all reporting at 2 o'clock at the Plant System depot ready to start; he gave to the officers such instruction by which they were to effect with order and dispatch the business of the morrow. He then spoke a few words of parting to the regiment asking that all grievances be laid aside and that the spirit of manliness which had characterized them in their military career go with them into civil life. He wished them all God speed and asked that if in the future by reason of their changed uniform he should fail to recognize them they should pull his coat tail and tell him who they were and he would—the chaplain standing near deterred him he said from saying what he would do. Lieutenant-Colonel Backus called the officers to the front and told Colonel Durbin of a meeting of the regimental officers at which two committees were appointed, one of which was then ready to report. The other committee appointed for the purpose of selecting a suitable remembrance for the regimental commander was reported at a later date after muster-out, but Major Olds, chairman of the committee on resolutions, stepped out and addressed the colonel in the following appropriate remarks:

COLONEL DURBIN: The meeting which brings us here this afternoon is indeed a sad one. We come here knowing it is to be the last formation of an organization which has grown dear to the hearts of each and every one of us.

Friendships formed in the army are stronger than those formed under any other circumstances. This is doubly true of the friendships formed in this regiment. Ten months ago when we assembled in the city of Indianapolis for the purpose of organization scarcely any of us had acquaintances in the regiment outside of those members who came from the immediate vicinities of our home towns. We go forth bearing friendships stronger than any we have ever formed. There are many circumstances which have brought this about, but we, the officers of this regiment, believe it mainly due to the untiring devotion and the efficient and honorable methods pursued by our regimental commander. True we have put forth our best efforts and have tried to do our duty, but all that would have gone for naught had we not had an efficient and capable leader,—but we had such a leader—a leader who by the strength of his personality, by the earnestness of his purpose and by the support which he was able to command, could unify and strengthen our efforts.

Moved by these sentiments, we, the officers of the regiment, offer you the following resolutions.

The following resolutions were then read and handed to the colonel:

WHEREAS, The One Hundred and Sixty-first Regiment of Indiana Volunteer Infantry has been brought to a high degree of efficiency through the energetic and telling efforts of Colonel Winfield T. Durbin. Therefore be it

Resolved, 1st, That we, the officers of the regiment, express to Colonel Durbin our friendship, loyalty and gratitude for his untiring devotion to the welfare of his command.

2d, That we are profoundly grateful to him for the sacrifices he has made in response to the dictates of patriotism and for his many acts of kindness and consideration shown us.

3d, That in the muster out of the regiment, the Volunteer Army loses a faithful, energetic and able commanding officer; the officers and men a true and noble friend.

4th, That though he is called upon to lay aside the habiliments of a soldier for duties of a citizen, we wish him unbounded success in civil pursuits, and that our hearts will ever be with him.

>LEE M. OLDS,
>RICHARD W. BUCHANAN,
>JOHN R. WARD,
>OLIVER M. TICHENOR,
>JAMES W. FORTUNE,
>Committee on Resolutions.

It was evident that these words had gone to the right spot and moved the colonel with deep feeling, and after a moment's pause he responded with words of thanks and appreciation for what, he said, he felt was more than he deserved. The men went back to their tents and after supper every one sat up long into the hours of night reluctant to retire because they knew it was the last night they would sleep as soldiers. The tension of strict discipline was of course relaxed and the first half of the night was made noisy with the songs of happy soldiers, and only when the repertoire of familiar songs was exhausted, the past ten months retrospected, and the future prospected, did the men roll into their blankets for the purpose of trying to sleep till morning.

Early in the day that followed, the big affair began. Talk about hustling—the day saw it in all its fury. The place was turned into a scene much like a county fair.

Peddlers of every description were on hand. Trunk selling was the chief paying business, and before the camp was up great piles of trunks had been hauled into the grounds and arranged by sizes ready for the men to take their pick. Waterman had a special tent in a conspucious place, and his big sign for Cuban photographs helped his business out and the side show appearance of the affair as well. On three of the headquarters tents were huge colored signs telling the boys where to get their tickets while the ticket wagon was ready to wait on all who were going direct home.

Aunt Chloe was there with her melodious voice crying "nice cool lemonade, two glasses for five," while another with huskier tones cried, "hyar's de place whar you git your lemon pies; dey is as fresh as you make 'em an dey haint no joke 'bout dat neither." Other edibles were carried about mixed up with sand that filled the baskets because of a spanking wind that whizzed around the tents and peppered everything with flying dust. At every tent door was a sable face inquiring if dey was any old thing de soldier wa'nt gwine to tote up north; and the old Confederate loon was there cackling for a nickel, and if he got it he God-blessed you and said you had a true soldier's heart for helping a poor old Confed., and if he didn't get it he said it the other way and said you had a stingy heart like every other d——d Yankee in the army. The photograph man was there, the venders of relics and of parrots were there, and of canaries and dogs too, all warranted to have come from Cuba. Three paymasters were on the ground, one in each of the battalion commander's tents.

Promptly at 9 o'clock the procession began. It was started by Company A. They lined up by the mustering-out office, the captain called the roll and each man cried "here" and stepped out at the sound of his name to fall in a new double rank forming at right angles to the first—this was all—he was mustered out. Then in line for his pay; then at the proper place for his railroad ticket and off to the city to await the starting of the train to Washington. It was 1 o'clock before the staff and band were paid; the camp was rapidly being deserted, hacks were in demand and the once private was as swell as the swellest in his transit to the city.

One by one with a parting glance the soldiers left the place—camp life was over, a strange feeling filled the men—no one could say "do this" or "do that" and every one did what he chose to do.

For an hour a great crowd of soldiers surged about the Plant System depot. Those unable to get tickets at camp after much trying of the patience, got them here. The fact is, the regiment had too much executive ability that worked too well for the railroads. They did not understand how it could be done and were not prepared to take their part as per agreed calculations.

At 2:10 P. M. the first section moved. It carried Companies A, I, L and M; also Colonel Durbin, Majors Smith and Olds and Lieutenants Brunt and Tichenor. The second section started at 2:40 P. M., loaded with Companies F, G, H and C; Major Megrew, Lieutenant Wilson and Chaplain Biederwolf accompanied this section. The third section left soon after, carrying Lieutenant-Colonel Backus, Lieutenant Gerrish and the remaining companies.

Three trains full of happy soldiers—a few happy soldiers full too, but in general an orderly set of fellows who did not steal silver spoons from railway restaurants and always paid for what they ate—three big crowds of happy Hoosiers on their way to Washington—alas so soon to be disappointed! It was very evident we had met our Waterloo simply because an honorable contract was made with a concern that had no conscience. The railroad concern had no intention of carrying out their contract; it was a shameful robbery by an unprincipled management. The baggage car arrangement for preparing coffee was a deception; water and other needful things could not be procured half of the time, but all the inconveniences could have been endured with little complaint had any effort been made to get the train to its destination with any reasonable limit of the appointed time. The trains dragged along the rails at a freight train rate and side tracked for everything that had a whistle to it, and instead of arriving at Washington at 9 A. M., the first section pulled in at 4:30 P. M., the second two hours later, and the third correspondingly behind the second. Great preparations had been made for the reception; crowds had gathered around the White House long before noon and waited until long in the afternoon, and after waiting in vain they left the place where the reception was to occur—the regiment did not come. The Indianans at Washington were as disappointed as the regiment; they had taken much pains in the matter and were going to do the affair in a way worthy of Hoosiers, but the railroad had the soldiers' money and it was no concern of theirs *when* the soldiers got to the place they had paid to go. However, had the regiment arrived on time a disappointment would still have been in store for it. Every arrangement had been made as Colonel Durbin had announced, but unforeseen circumstances prevented President McKinley from returning to the capital on the day appointed for the reveiw.

The following telegrams will be of interest in this connection:

"WASHINGTON, D. C., April 29, 1899.
"To Colonel Durbin, One Hundred and Sixty-first Indiana Volunteer Infantry, Savannah, Georgia.

"Upon arrival of your regiment at Washington, President will review it at portico of White House, and afterwards receive members in the east room of the executive mansion; please give early notification of time of departure, route traveled and expected hour of arrival in Washington. Acknowledge.

"HEISTAND, Assistant Adjutant-General."

On the train going to Washington the colonel received the following not far from Fredericksburg:

"WASHINGTON, D. C., May 1, 1899.
"Colonel Durbin: Your telegram stating you will arrive at 4 o'clock received. The President is unavoidably detained in New York and will not be home until to-morrow. Secretary of War also absent from city. These facts are communicated to you to enable you to determiue upon your line of action. Acknowledge receipt.

"HEISTAND, Assistant Adjutant-General."

The pleasure and satisfaction of the review would thus have failed the regiment in any event of arrival, but the rest of an interesting program could have been carried out much to the satisfaction of all concerned. The first section was met by the marine band and escorted to the White House. Before entering the colonel told the men of his own bitter disappointment, which was perhaps greater than that of the men.

The second section came in not long before the first was ready to depart, and later the third. The first section left about 7 o'clock. The men of the other sections spent some time about the city, and near midnight and morning started west, the trains breaking up at Cincinnati and

Louisville. Company M left the first section at Cincinnati and Companies I, L and A came on to Indianapolis with the colonel. Expected here in the evening as per scheduled time, again extensive preparations were made for the reception of these three companies. In the State House a stand trimmed with the colors had been erected for music and speakers, a supper had been prepared and waiting for the train that did not come was next in order. Early in the morning we awoke and found that the train had actually arrived in Indianapolis. At 6 A. M. the boys marched to the State House where the good ladies who had lost all the night's sleep waiting, had come at this early hour to give the boys their breakfast. The boys were ravenously hungry and after being assured that any one of them who choked to death would be given a pension, they went at the table in a way that always pleases a woman when she has worked hard to prepare a good meal. Breakfast, over Governor Mount, who, with his good wife, had come so early to the State House to meet the boys, stood to address them. He told the men how proud the state was of the regiment to which they had belonged, and gave them in the name of the commonwealth a cordial welcome home. Colonel Durbin responded, first thanking the ladies for their goodness and then emphasizing the fact that the regiment had tried to do its duty well; he then presented to the state through the Governor the regimental colors and the flag. Governor Mount briefly responded, telling the men the flags would be kept in the State House where, when in the city, they could come and look upon them. Senator Fairbanks then spoke briefly and after the men made the marble corriders ring and echo with rousing cheers, they went slowly back to their train.

From this time on the experience of one company was the experience of them all, and something like the experience of Company Q, of the Two Hundredth Indiana, in which Si Klegg was a corporal. "The Company Q boys received an overpowering welcome at home. The people from the village and the adjacent country turned out *en masse* to greet them as they alighted from the train. Farmer Klegg and his wife and Maria, proud and eager, were there; and joyful tears flowed unchecked as they twined their arms around son and brother and pressed him to their beating hearts. Annabel was there, with moist eyes and a flush upon her soft cheek.

Si had grown brave now, and as soon as the family embrace relaxed he advanced and put his arms around her as unflinchingly as if she had been a rebel battery.

Tumultuous cheers rent the air, the band played and banners waved in honor of the soldiers' return from the war.

A sumptuous dinner was served to them in the town hall, and the village orators exhausted their eloquence in giving them welcome and glorifying their deeds of valor.

By the time the speakers got through, the veterans were pretty well convinced that if it had not been for Company Q the war would have been a failure—on the Union side.

Then the boys were taken in charge by their respective friends. In anticipation of Si's return, his mother and sister had for days done little except cook, and he found himself in a land flowing with milk and honey.

That night Si had the "best bed" in the house. As he threw himself upon it he sank down in a sea of feathers that almost covered him. Of course he could not sleep in such a bed, and in the morning when his mother went to call him to breakfast, she was amazed to find him lying on the floor. "Tell ye what 'tis mother," he said, "I didn't like ter go back on yer nice bed, but 'twa'n't no use. I swum 'round 'n them fethers purty much all night, but I couldn't git to sleep t'll I bunked down on the floor. That's a leetle more like the beds I slep on 'n the army. I b'liev t'night I'll rig up a pup tent, put down some rails ter lie on, 'n take my old U. S. blanket 'n crawl in."

This is all pretty much right, but the pup-tent and the rail racket—just put up a common A tent and put down some Florida pine and we guarantee the boys will sleep, though feather beds *aint* so bad to swim around in either. We wish every man who fell a victim to the connubial epidemic all the success that Si had and in the walks of civil life health, happiness and prosperity. The habiliment of a soldier has been laid aside for the apparel of a citizen; the thought of citizenship should come to every member of the One Hundred and Sixty-first with a profounder meaning because of this experience in the service. So glorious has been the past of the American Republic, so significant is its present, so grand is its prospect that to be a citizen of such a nation is a proud distinction.

No time in all its history has the nation needed more men of sterling worth than in this present time; with the glory of victory adding fresh luster to its flag of stars and stripes there has come an added burden and consequent responsibility of government that shall strain every fiber and tax every energy of this nation we proudly call our own. Questions are about to arise involving the most enormous interests, and if the true force of manhood and right citizenship is not brought to bear upon them they will be solved by those with baser motives than ought to prompt a man of genuine patriotism, and in it all the honor of the nation is at stake; and as we have done our duty well wherever duty called, as the excellent *esprit de corps* that has moulded our experience as soldiers has brought to us the highest commendation that could rest upon such a body of men, so let us follow the walks of civil life, giving to our nation and to our state our best thought, our best interest and unselfish endeavor, counting it always a high privilege to serve a flag the most beautiful, the most noble and the most powerful that ever kissed the sunshine of God, OLD GLORY, THE FLAG OF THE STARS AND STRIPES.

COLONEL WINFIELD T. DURBIN.

Winfield T. Durbin, of Anderson, was the man upon whom was placed the honor and the responsibility of commanding the last regiment of men that went out from Indiana. The glory of what a thing becomes belongs severally to those whose influence helps to shape it and the enviable reputation acquired by the One Hundred and Sixty-first Indiana belongs in a degree to every man, be he an officer or private, who took a pride in his regiment and tried to do his duty well for his regiment and for his country's sake, but the man who occupies the place of greatest responsibility, the man upon whose mind depend the ideals toward which an institution shapes itself and upon whose ability to execute depends the final approach to those ideals is the man to whom the greatest honor must fall when he proves himself worthy of his position. A regiment is generally and to a great degree always what its commanding officer makes it and the fact that the regiment whose superior officer was Winfield T. Durbin stood so high in the estimation of the highest army officials, that it was worthy of such recognition as that given by the honorable secretary of war, when he declared concerning the cleanliness and condition of the One Hundred and Sixty-first Indiana camp that "it was a revelation," a "marvel," and in a public manner declared on the reviewing field and twice afterward that the regiment was the finest he had ever seen,— this fact certainly does reflect the greatest honor on the man who controlled its movements and accordingly made its name a reminder of all that a body of thirteen hundred soldiers ought to become.

Colonel Durbin did not seek the position; the position was seeking for the man, and it found him puzzled over some needed repairs amid the noise and rattle of

Colonel Winfield T. Durbin.

machinery in the works of the Diamond Paper Company at Anderson. The call came quick and unexpected. His wife and son were on the Continent; without the possibility of consulting them or apprising them of his intention, he decided; he did not leave his plow standing in the field, but he did leave the old smashed up engine lying in the factory and started for the capital city of his state whence he had been called. The CALL was his marching orders. Colonel Durbin was born at Lawrenceburg, Indiana, May 4, 1847, when he was but three years old his parents moved to New Philadelphia, and there he spent his early days, securing such educational advantages as were offered by the village schools of his boyhood home. He was fourteen years of age when the Civil war began; one by one he saw his five older brothers enlist to fight for the Union, and his young heart stirred him to offer himself. Accordingly in 1862 he endeavored to enlist in the Sixteenth Indiana, but owing to temporary disability was not accepted, but went with the regiment and participated with it through part of the Vicksburg campaign, rendering good service in the battles of Vicksburg, Arkansas Post and elsewhere. He then enlisted in the One Hundred and Thirty-ninth Indiana. This was in the following year, 1863, and at the close of war he remained for four years with his father who was at that time engaged in the tanning business. In 1869, a young man of twenty-two, he went to Indianapolis and entered upon a clerkship in one of the city's large jobbing dry goods establishments; he held position with the firm for ten years, and when at the expiration of this time he was prepared to leave, he had by his faithful industry and business ability become the head manager of the office force.

On the 6th of October, 1875, he married Miss Bertha McCullough, of Anderson and went in 1879 to the city of his bride to engage in mercantile and banking pursuits. That he was a successful business man his present connection with the business interests of that place fully attest. He is president of the Anderson Foundry and Machine Works, vice president of the J. W. Sefton Manufacturing Company, and general manager and treasurer of the Diamond Paper Company.

For six years he was a school trustee of Anderson during which time he materially aided in the erection of several of the finest school buildings in the state.

No figure has been more prominent in political circles during the past fifteen years than Colonel Durbin; his fine executive ability and sound judgment has placed him in constant demand of his party. He was a presidental elector in 1888, a delegate to the National Republican convention at Minnaepolis in 1892, and was chairman of the committee that notified Whitelaw Reid of his nomination to the Vice Presidency. He was also a delegate to the same convention in St. Louis in 1896. He is now a member of the national Republican committee for Indiana and a member of the executive committee.

Colonel Durbin always had a high ideal for his regiment and was solicitous for its interests in every particular; he so placed this ideal before the men until every private had taken unusual pride in the appearance and reputation of his organization. The health of the men was always a subject of deep concern on the colonel's part; he used every precautionary means to keep the camp in the best possible sanitary condition, attending in person with the surgeon on his tours of camp inspection, and in Jacksonville when malarial indisposition rendered so many of the men unfit for duty, scarce sick enough to be sent to the hospital, yet needing special nourishment and more comfortable sleeping quarters, Colonel Durbin at his own expense erected what might be called a recuperation hospital, a large and substantial frame building, into which the men were sent and where cots and milk diet, so far as the latter was procurable, were furnished them.

Colonel Durbin did not know the men personally; and consequetly there was no partiality and no favors for special ones, but the humblest private was always welcome to his tent and men who may have hesitated to approach him always came away feeling they had been treated with all due kindness on the part of their regimental commander.

He is versatile and a man of jovial disposition, but could be stern to severity when, in his judgment, it became necessary, and under such circumstances when he spoke every one knew that he meant what he said and he was obeyed. That the regiment has received its well-known recognition and its favors the men have always felt has been due to the influence of the man at its head.

At the organization of the Society of the Seventh Army Corps March 25, 1899, Colonel Durbin was chosen a member of the executive council.

OLIVER M. TICHENOR.

Oliver M. Tichenor, first lieutenant and adjutant, was one of the regiment's busy men. No commission less than a captain's should ever be given an adjutant. This ener-

OLIVER M. TICHENOR.

getic young officer was born near Princeton, Indiana, April 21, 1864. He received the excellent training that is found in farm life, and entering Princeton's high school, graduated in 1883. He was at once appointed deputy treasurer of Gibson county. From 1889 until 1894 he held the position of postmaster at Princeton, and then for four years traveled as freight and passenger agent of the Peoria, Decatur & Evansville railroad, which position he resigned to accept the appointment of chief deputy collector of internal revenue, and July 12, 1898, he placed in the hands of his employer his resignation that he might accept the commission urged upon him in which he was made adjutant of the One Hundred and Sixty-first Indiana Volunteer Infantry.

Lieutenant Tichenor was journal clerk of the Indiana legislature in 1886-7, and but for his youth would doubtless have been elected to the clerkship of the supreme court of Indiana, for which position he was a candidate in 1894.

JOHN RICH BRUNT.

First Lieutenant and Quartermaster John Rich Brunt is a man fitted for the responsible position he held by a life of varied business experiences. He was born in Madison

JOHN RICH BRUNT.

county, Indiana, July 29, 1845, and is consequently the oldest man in the regiment. His grandfather was Nathan Lee, of Virginia, and was killed in the war of 1812 at

Sackett's Harbor. When twenty years old Lieutenant Brunt went into what was then the far west, where for five years he remained, leading the life of a hunter and scout. It was his intention to return for a collegiate course, but the fascination of frontier life changed that intention, and until 1870 he was a scout and guide. In this year he was united in marriage to Miss Lois C. Vanlandingham, daughter of a cousin to Hon. Clement L. Vanlandingham. After his marriage he gave up the adventurous life he was leading and became bookkeeper and manager for a railroad contractor at what afterwards became Chanute, Kansas, in which place Lieutenant Brunt built the first house ever erected. He then served four years as under sheriff at Osage Mission, Neosho county, Kansas, and followed this by a four years' term in office as sheriff. He then embarked in business at the same place, and a few years later bought the Neosho County Journal, which he successfully managed for eight years. During Cleveland's first administration Lieutenant Brunt was postmaster at Osage Mission.

In December, 1889, after an absence of twenty-four years, he turned his face toward his native state, and made his home at Anderson, Indiana, which place, on the organization of the One Hundred and Sixty-first Indiana, he left to accept a commission as quartermaster of the regiment. While at Anderson he was secretary and treasurer of the Anderson Iron & Bolt Company, and its receiver for two and a half years after its failure, and upon its reorganization was made secretary and manager, resigning this position in February, 1898. In 1886 Lieutenant Brunt was the Democratic nominee for congress from the Eighth

Indiana district, and made an excellent race against overwhelming odds.

Upon the organization of the regiment he was appointed to the position of ordnance officer, which office he held in addition to his position as regimental quartermaster. On February 24, 1899, he was made acting regimental commissary officer during the illness of Lieutenant Freeman, and he accordingly was responsible for the work of three positions. He continued in this latter position one month.

During the months of September and October, 1898, at Camp Cuba Libre, he was acting brigade quartermaster of the First Brigade, Third Division. Quartermaster Brunt understood his place; he got for his regiment what others in a like position did, and usually a little more, and if the staff and line were in large tents as well as the men; if, in fact, the One Hundred and Sixty-first Indiana was the best tented regiment in the corps, it must be placed to his credit that it was so. He is a plain man, without boast, but what he does he does well.

WILLIAM E. BIEDERWOLF.

Captain William Edward Biederwolf, chaplain of the regiment, offered his resignation to the Broadway Presbyterian church, in Logansport, Indiana, that he might go to

WILLIAM E. BIEDERWOLF.

care for the spiritual needs of the boys of the One Hundred and Sixty-first Indiana. He was born in the year of 1867, on September 29, at Monticello, Indiana. Graduating from the high school of his native place, he taught school for one year, and then, in the fall of '86, entered Wabash College, Crawfordsville. After four years' work in this institution, he entered Princeton University, at Princeton, New Jersey. Upon graduation here, he began his theological course in the seminary of the same place, receiving his degree in 1895. After a year's evangelistic work with Rev. B. Fay Mills, the evangelist, in April, 1896, he was married to Miss Ida Casad, of Monticello, Indiana. They went at once to Germany, where for eighteen months he enjoyed the privilege of study in New Testament Greek, as Fellowship scholar from Princeton Theological Seminary. After traveling to the Holy Land he returned and accepted the pastorate of the Broadway Presbyterian church, in November, 1897. Captain Biederwolf, during his study at Princeton, devoted his vacations to rescue work in the slums of New York city. He is a lover of athletic sports, and was for four years a member of Princeton's athletic and gymnastic teams, and in other ways connected with her athletic interests. Chaplain Biederwolf took delight in his work and the men called him their friend.

Writing of a chaplain's work from an experimental and retrospective view point, one sees discouragements and hindrances unthought of at the initial stage of that experience, and which in spite of any further recognition of the man and his work which is justly due from the highest military authority must still depend for their alleviation upon circumstances of character with which the war department has nothing to do. The efficiency of the chaplain's work depends upon other things besides "what the chaplain makes it," which nothing but the grace of God can remedy. Some men have written that army life is a character moulder. 'Tis false—the drift, or better still the current, of army life is anti-moral and anti-religious; neither space nor appropriateness of place permit any defense of this statement, but experience proves it in spite of exceptions. The chaplain of the One Hundred and Sixty-first is not elated over his work. He is, however, *on the whole* proud of the morale of the regiment it was his privilege to serve; it was as *good* as any and *better* than many, due more to the make-up of the men than to anything he was permitted to do. But he knows the ministrations in the hospital among the sick and the dying, the friendships with the men, the words of counsel and the utterances from the place of worship were not in vain, and that even results unseen below eternity will reveal in rich fruition.

And yet much of the chaplain's work does depend upon what he makes it and with this in mind early efforts were made to purchase a suitable tent for assembly purpose. Nearly all the towns from which the boys came donated liberally, a large 50 x 80 tent was purchased, and through help from the Christian Commission, furnished with an organ, with reading, games and writing material. At times peculiarly appropriate for letter writing, from six hundred to seven hundred letters a day were written from the tables of this tent. The first ten days in Jacksonville, nightly evangelistic services were held by Fred Schivera. Services were held every Sunday by the chaplain, usually morning and evening. An occasional concert given and such other meetings held as were legitimate for such a place. Elbert M. Blake, of Company K, was detailed to care for the tent and was a most valuable aid to the chaplain. After the severe storm the center piece was left out and the tent became circular with a fifty-foot diameter. At Savannah, Fred C. King, Company G, had charge of the work; in Cuba, Chas. Sheller, Company G, for one month, and John Coates, Company A, for a few weeks, when Mr. Blake was again put in charge.

Some of the most precious moments and glorious hours were those spent by the cot side of sick in the wards of the hospital.

There was much of this to do in Jacksonville and when the regiment left for Savannah, eighty-seven men were left behind in the tents of the Third Division Hospital. The chaplain was granted the privilege of staying with them, and the writing of letters for them, furnishing them with such delicacies as medical authority would allow, the moments of serious conversation and the bidding them good-bye as they were helped into the hospital trains bound for the north, were experiences for which one may well be grateful and feel that his ministry was worth its while.

It was hard to sympathize with many of the men who took up their lodgings in the quarters shown in the following cut. It was all voluntary, the men didn't have to go there, that is, at a period considerably prior to their registration, but when once there resolutions were readily made that they would never go again nor recommend its accommodations. These resolutions and promises, whose place if not the chaplain's to help the men to keep them, and as so many would have it that the building on opposite page and similar institutions belonged to the ecclesiastical department, its cut is appropriately and with pleasure inserted here.

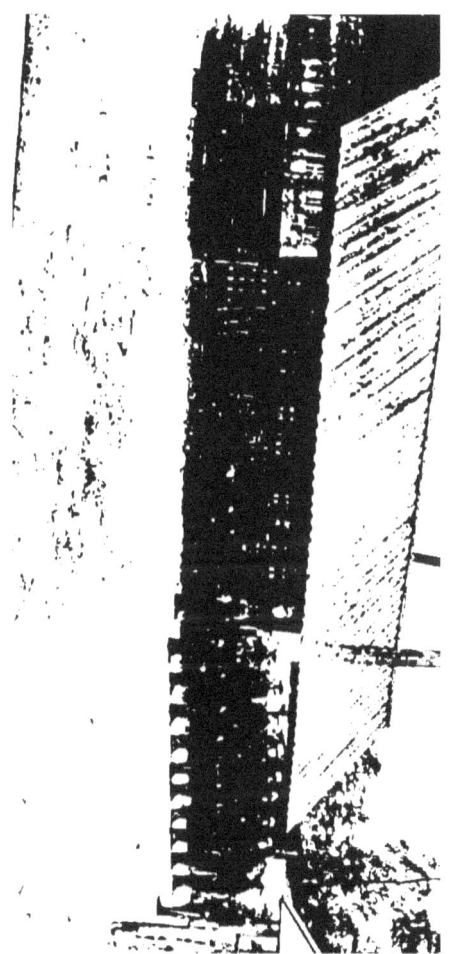

FIRST BATTALION

K, M, A, E.

VICTOR M. BACKUS.

Lieutenant-Colonel Victor M. Backus is a born soldier. His grandfather was an officer on Napoleon's staff, his father was a soldier and Colonel Backus himself a hard

VICTOR M. BACKUS.

Union fighter in the war of Rebellion. He therefore brought with him into the recent service a large experience of army life and this with his peculiar genius and characteristic earnestness made him an invaluable officer of the regiment in which he served.

He was born at Williamsburg, New York, the 27th day of March, 1850. When six years of age his parents came to Franklin, Indiana, and six years later moved to Indianapolis. His school education was meagre, being interrupted by the war, where he felt, young as he was, that he was needed and therefore belonged. He was only eleven years old, he waited two years and then succeeded in gaining enlistment in the Seventeenth Indiana Regiment, then a part of the Army of the Cumberland. General Wilder commanded the brigade and General Gerrard, the division. He was a brave and daring soldier and although but a boy, bore well the part of the strongest man. He fought at Dalton, Resaca, Rome, Big Shanty, Noonday Creek, Kennesaw Mountain, Peach Tree Creek and many other battles. In all he was actively engaged in nineteen battles and fifty-one skirmishes. It will be remembered that it was Wilder's brigade that made the famous charge against the breast works of Selma. Assault after assault had been made when Wilder hurled his men against the stubborn resistance and went over the works at a great cost of life, but thereby making possible the almost complete destruction of General Forrest's command.

At Macon, Georgia, Colonel Backus was made one of a picked detail of sixty men to effect the capture of Jefferson Davis, who it was learned was attempting to escape to the west. This detail came up with another within an exceedingly close distance from where it had captured the fallen Confederacy's president, and together they brought him back to Macon and with him another prisoner of distinction then, and of still greater fame to-day—fighting Joe Wheeler, the hero of Santiago.

At the close of the war the fifteen-year-old soldier was

mustered out at Macon, August 12, 1865, and taken to Indianapolis for final discharge. He had reason to be proud of his record. He never missed a battle in which his regiment was engaged and from beginning to end was never once in attendance at sick call.

There was no more fighting to be done and the youth entered the Shaw Company Carriage works as an apprentice at seven dollars per week; but in ten years after taking this position, he had by his constant diligence and earnest application acquired a one-half interest in the concern, and a few years later he had purchased Colonel Shaw's interest and the firm was known as V. M. Backus & Company.

In 1890 the colonel was nominated by the democratic party for county and city treasurer of the county of Marion, and the city of Indianapolis. He was elected by a handsome majority. At the expiration of his term of office he turned his attention wholly to the business of contracting, undertaking and satisfactorily completing some of the largest and most important systems of sewerage and other works in the country.

When the war with Spain came on Victor M. Backus raised a regiment and offered it to Governor Mount two days before the president issued his first call for troops. The members of the state militia being already sufficient in numbers to furnish the state's required quota, the colonel's regiment could not be given place. Upon the second call for troops the One Hundred and Sixty-first Indiana was created and the position of lieutenant-colonel tendered him, which he accepted and which position he has filled with the greatest acceptability.

His experience in contracting has made him an invaluable part of the regiment. He cheerfully assumed that which properly was the duty of others; he was always busy and always had some scheme to keep others busy.

To him must be given much of the praise for the building and adornment of the camp. The seven-pointed cement star, the bamboo band stand, the monument and the Backus garbage burner, warranted to cremate anything from water to a stone, will always be connected with his name.

He was commander of the First Battalion, but was often in command of the regiment while Colonel Durbin commanded the brigade. He made a capable officer, and a good disciplinarian; he was not hard to approach and his easy-going manner made for him friends throughout the whole regiment.

COMPANY K.

WILFRED T. STOTT.

Captain Wilfred T. Stott, son of Dr. W. T. Stott, president of Franklin College, was born March 6, 1869, at Columbus, Indiana. He was graduated from Franklin College at the age of twenty-one and soon after became engaged in the newspaper business as a reporter. In this profession he continued until the outbreak of hostilities against Spain. His first work was done on the Indianapolis News. Later he entered the University of Chicago and took a three years literary course at that institution, supporting himself in the meantime by reportorial work on the Chicago Tribune. Afterward he was employed on that paper for a number of years. In 1897 he returned to his native city and purchased the Republican, a daily and weekly paper, which he published for a year.

During the stay of the regiment at Savannah, Georgia, Captain Stott was detailed as recruiting officer for the regi-

Captain Wilfred T. Stott.

ment and was absent in Indiana on that duty for one month. He has served in the Indiana National Guards for five years and is a son of a veteran, his father being a captain in the Civil war.

CHARLES C. SMITH.

First Lieutenant Charles C. Smith was born December 22, 1871, at South Bethany, Indiana. He was educated in the public schools of Columbus, Indiana, and soon after completing his education became engaged in the pen-

First Lieutenant Charles C. Smith.

sion business. He continued in this business until 1893, when he formed a partnership with Samuel W. Daugherty under the firm name of Daugherty & Smith, and purchased the business of his former employer, to which real estate and insurance business was added.

Lieutenant Smith has served three years in the Indiana National Guards and is the son of a soldier.

TEMPLE H. OWENS.

Second Lieutenant Temple Hubert Owens was born in Noblesville, Indiana, July 14, 1876. He was educated in Columbus, graduating from the high schools of that city in 1895. Since that time until entering the service he was engaged in newspaper work, being employed on the local papers of his home city, besides acting as correspondent for many of the metropolitan dailies.

For three months during his service with the One

SECOND LIEUTENANT TEMPLE HUBERT OWENS.

Hundred and Sixty-first Indiana he was detailed on duty with the Tenth United States Infantry at Havana and Mantanzas, serving as lieutenant in Company F, and also as adjutant of the Second Battalion.

Lieutenant Owens also acted as adjutant of the First

Battalion, One Hundred and Sixty-first Indiana, at Camp Cuba Libre. His father was a veteran, having served during the entire Civil war.

COMPANY HISTORY.

Company K was organized at Columbus, Indiana, April 28, 1898. At the meeting at which the organization was perfected two hundred men were enrolled.

W. T. Stott was elected captain and C. C. Smith, first lieutenant, and T. H. Owens, second lieutenant. A strenuous effort was made by the officers and men and citizens of Columbus to have the company ordered out on the first call for troops. Feeling confident, however, that it would later be called into service, the organization was maintained, though a number of the members enlisted in the regular army and in the volunteer regiments already accepted.

The second call for troops found the company in readiness, the armory having been converted into temporary barracks and daily drills having been conducted for several weeks.

In accordance with orders from Governor Mount, the organization reported at Camp Mount July 4, 1898, after having undergone a preliminary physical examination at the home station. Company K, which designation was later given, arrived at Camp Mount with a greater number of men than any other company, there being one hundred and thirty-two in the ranks. It was also strongest in point of numbers when mustered in, July 13, 1898, entering the service with one hundred and five enlisted men.

The company was assigned to the First Battalion, and at the time of muster-out was the ranking company of that

COMPANY K.

battalion. It has been fortunate in having a complement of good non-commissioned officers. The list of sergeants remained unchanged during the service of the company. This organization bore distinction for its many tall men and for its excellence at drill.

COMPANY K ROSTER.

WILFRED T. STOTT, Captain, Columbus, Ind., Reporter.
CHARLES C. SMITH, 1st Lieutenant, Columbus, Ind., Insurance Agent.
TEMPLE H. OWENS, 2nd Lieutenant, Columbus, Ind., Reporter.

SERGEANTS.

Thompson, William A., 1st Serg't, Columbus, Ind., Civil Engineer, promoted to 1st Serg't Nov. 3, 1898.
Bray, Charles, Q. M. Serg't, Columbus, Ind., Mechanic, promoted to Serg't Nov. 3, 1898.
McGovney, Charles S., Columbus, Ind., Student.
Voris, G. Ashley, Columbus, Ind., Clerk.
Carr, Frank, Columbus, Ind., Miller.
Wynegar, Eugene, Columbus, Ind., Stenographer.

CORPORALS.

Haislup, Harry H., Columbus, Ind., Cabinetmaker.
Oliphant, Wilfred H., Noblesville, Ind., Painter.
Ghrist, Orlando P., Columbus, Ind., Tailor.
Allison, Franklin E., Hope, Ind., Teacher.
Day, Elmer C., Columbus, Ind., Mechanic.
Cobb, Edwin A., Columbus, Ind., Student, discharged Feb. 4, 1899.
Pruitt, Elmer T., Edinburg, Ind., Laborer, discharged March 13, 1899.
McCoy, Harry, Columbus, Ind., Clerk, transferred to 3rd Div. Hosp. Corps Aug. 20, 1898.

Sergeants, Company K.

Luse, Joseph L., Edinburg, Ind., Stenographer, appointed Corp. Aug. 29, 1898.
Von Willer, Adolph R., Columbus, Ind., Laborer, appointed Corp. Aug. 29, 1898.
Tobrocke, Frank A., Waymansville, Ind., Clerk, appointed Corp. Aug. 29, 1898.
Roth, Louis A., Edinburg, Ind., Laborer, appointed Corp. Sept. 26, 1898.
Pursfield, Forest, Columbus, Ind., Hostler, appointed Corp. Nov. 4, 1898.
Phillips, Joseph F., Edinburg, Ind., appointed Corp. March 24, 1899.
Beatty, William J., appointed Corp. March 24, 1899.

MUSICIANS.

Israel, Horace B., Edinburg, Ind., Laborer, appointed Musician Aug. 30, 1898.
Clark, Alexander, Columbus, Ind., Student, appointed Musician Aug. 30, 1898.

ARTIFICER.

King, Edwin, Columbus, Ind., Carpenter.

WAGONER.

Bruce, Herbert R., Nortonsburg, Ind., Farmer.

PRIVATES.

Abell, Samuel, Seymour, Ind., Student.
Abernathy, Robert, Seymour, Ind., Laborer.
Adkins, James, Columbus, Ind., Molder.
Ayers, William A., Seymour, Ind., Engineer.
Barmes, Frank H., Hope, Ind., Farmer.
Beabout, David, Columbus, Ind., Laborer.
Betterly, Benjamin, Seymour, Ind., Clerk, discharged Sept. 27, 1898.
Blake, Elbert M., Columbus, Ind., Student.
Branaman, Henry, Becks, Ind., Farmer.

CORPORALS, COMPANY K.

Bruce, Mell, Lexington, Ind., Farmer.
Brumfield, Gurtis, Columbus, Ind., Mechanic.
Burns, Samuel, Columbus, Ind., Printer.
Coats, William T., Shelbyville, Ind., Student, transferred to
    Co. C Jan. 26, 1899.
Carr, Harry C., Hartsville, Ind., Student.
Carter, Allen, Columbus, Ind., Laborer.
Collins, Samuel, South Bethany, Ind., Farmer.
Cook, Joseph L., Columbus, Ind., Mechanic.
Coy, Lora E., Pikes Peak, Ind., Farmer.
Craig, Clifford, Seymour, Ind., Laborer.
Cron, Henry, Indianapolis, Ind., Handlemaker.
Dill, James R., Columbus, Ind., Laborer.
Dillman, Harry, Bedford, Ind., Mechanic.
Dinkens, Thomas, Liberty, Ind., Laborer, discharged Jan. 30,
    1899.
Dobson, James M., Columbus, Ind., Farmer.
Downs, Charles M., Edinburg, Ind., Laborer, discharged
    Feb. 3, 1899.
Ehlers, George C., Columbus, Ind., Brakeman.
Fawcett, Oliver, Columbus, Ind., Laborer.
Fuller, William, Columbus, Ind., Clerk.
George, John S., Scipio, Ind., Farmer.
Grove, Clarence B., Columbus, Ind., Student.
Haislup, Charles A., Columbus, Ind., Laborer.
Hardesty, Sylvanus G., Nebraska, Ind., Stone Cutter.
Henderson, Edward F., Columbus, Ind., Laborer.
Henderson, Walter E., Seymour, Ind., Mechanic.
Hodler, Charles H., Ogilville, Ind., Cook, discharged Feb. 7,
    1899.
Hodler, Samuel S., Columbus, Ind., Mechanic.
Huffer, Welden, Newbern, Ind., Student, discharged Jan. 13,
    1899.
Jones, Percy, Hope, Ind., Farmer, transferred to Reg. Band
    Aug. 20, 1898.
Keethler, James, Ogilville, Ind., Laborer, transferred to 3rd
    Div. Hosp. Corps Aug. 20, 1898.

Kerth, Franklin, Cincinnati, Ohio, Mechanic.
Kellenberger, Bertram S., Columbus, Ind., Clerk.
Ketner, Robert E., Hartsville, Ind., Laborer.
Kroencke, Henry F., Columbus, Ind., Carpenter.
LaForce, David E., Bedford, Ind., Clerk.
Lambert, Arthur S., Conway, Ky., Farmer.
Lathrop, Lyman G., Hope, Ind., Student.
Lockman, Cecil, Bedford, Ind., Laborer.
Lunsford, Robert A., Indianapolis, Ind., Laborer.
Manuel, Andrew, Christiansburg, Ind., Farmer.
McCallie, Ralph, Newbern, Ind., Laborer.
McKee, Melvin, Columbus, Ind., Carpenter.
Marlin, Temple, Hope, Ind., Farmer.
Marlin, Nathaniel W., Hope, Ind., Farmer.
Myers, Jacob, Edinburg, Ind., Laborer.
Oaks, Robert F., Edinburg, Ind., Mechanic.
Payne, Charles B., Columbus, Ind., Teamster, discharged Jan. 30, 1899.
Pickens, John M., Columbus, Ind., Mechanic.
Potter, Charles, Columbus, Ind., Laborer.
Pruitt, Leslie, Edinburg, Ind., Farmer.
Quick, George W., Columbus, Ind., Carpenter.
Richey, Alonzo, Indianapolis, Ind., Laborer.
Repp, John F., Columbus, Ind., Moulder.
Rich, John W. D., Columbus, Ind., Teamster, discharged Feb. 16, 1899.
Romine, John D., Ogilville, Ind., Farmer.
Rowell, Fred C., Columbus, Ind., Cabinetmaker, transferred to Hosp. Corps Aug. 20, 1898.
Seeger, John F., Columbus, Ind., Farmer.
Skinner, Elihu M., Brownstown, Ind., Farmer, discharged Feb. 4, 1899.
Stiner, Harry E., Taylorsville, Ind., Laborer.
Stuckey, Erastus, South Bethany, Ind., Farmer.
Schierff, Olif, Chicago, Ill., Clerk, discharged Feb. 15, 1899.
Thomas, Charles E., Taylorsville, Ind., Farmer.
Thomas, Martin R., Taylorsville, Ind., Engineer.

Thompson, William H., Columbus, Ind., Barber.
Turner, Joseph, Modora, Ind., Laborer.
Twaddell, Forrest, Columbus, Ind., Clerk, discharged Feb. 1, 1899.
VanArsdal, Evert, Taylorsville, Ind., Farmer.
Western, William C., Columbus, Ind., Engineer.
Yerger, John, Bedford, Ind., Barber.
Young, Hallard G., Columbus, Ind., Laborer.
Everson, Charles, Columbus, Ind., Moulder, died Dec. 2, 1898.
Carr, Victor M., Hartsville, Ind., Cook, transferred from Co. A Jan. 17, 1899.
Gifford, George H., Indianapolis, Ind., Clerk, transferred from 159th Ind., deserted March 17, 1899, at Camp Columbia, Cuba.
Koehne, George H., Evansville, Ind., Machinist, transferred from 159th Ind.
Miller, Isaac J., Clifford, Ind., Laborer, transferred from 159th Ind.
Swartwood, Sherman B., Columbus, Ind., Farmer, transferred from 159th Ind.
Schaufler, Charles, Evansville, Ind., Potter, transferred from 159th Ind.
Ruby, Edward T., Indianapolis, Ind., Cook, mustered as Cook Dec. 8, 1898.
Cole, Bert A., Bloomington, Ind., Civil Engineer, transferred from 159th Ind. Vol. Inf.

COMPANY M.

GEORGE A. WEST.

Captain George A. West is the oldest man among the officers of the One Hundred and Sixty-first Indiana Regiment. He was born at Lawrenceburg, Indiana, February 14, 1844, and received such education as could then be obtained in the public schools of his native town. In 1861 he went to New Orleans and remained there until the outbreak of the Civil war, when he hastened north, coming

CAPTAIN GEORGE A. WEST.

on the last steamer that came up the Mississippi river, and enlisted at once.

He served during the entire war, re-enlisting in the Second Indiana Battery at the expiration of his first enlistment.

During a greater part of his service Captain West was engaged as a scout west of the Mississippi river and while serving in this capacity was wounded five times. He was also wounded at the battle of Prairie Grove. Special authority from the war department was granted in order that Captain West could be commissioned in the Spanish-American war. In re-entering the service he forfeited a pension of fourteen dollars per month.

Captain West has a son, John B. West, who is no less a fighter than himself. John B. West was a bugler in the army at Santiago but asked for a gun and went on the firing line and was severely wounded, being shot through both legs.

FIRST LIEUTENANT GEORGE W. FITCH.

GEORGE W. FITCH.

First Lieutenant George W. Fitch was born at Lawrenceburg, Indiana, March 24, 1868. He was educated in the high school of Lawrenceburg and later was employed in his father's bank. Afterwards he held a responsible position with the Adams Express Company, and still later he was identified with the Potter, Parlin Company, of New York, as assistant secretary and treasurer for a number of years. At the opening of the Spanish-American war he was city engineer of Lawrenceburg.

HANSON G. FREEMAN.

Second Lieutenant Hanson G. Freeman was born October 30, 1859, at Prattsburg, Indiana. He graduated from the Lawrenceburg high school, and later took a two years' course at Moore's Hill College. Soon after completing his education he engaged in the coal business at Lawrenceburg, in which he continued until the outbreak of the war.

On September 5, 1898, Lieutenant Freeman was detailed as regimental commissary of subsistence and remained in that capacity until the muster-out of the organization. The father of Lieutenant Freeman served during the entire Civil war.

HISTORY OF COMPANY M.

Company M was organized early in April, 1898, by George A. West, George W. Fitch and Hanson G. Freeman as a battery, as it was expected it would be first to

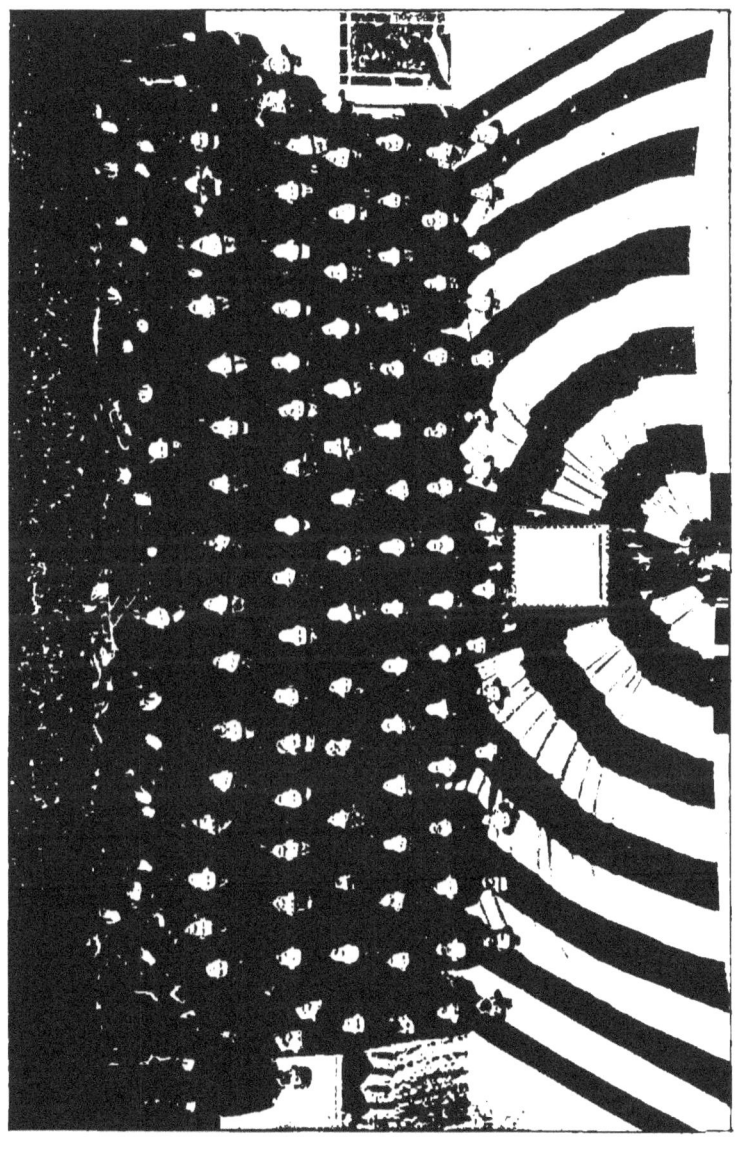

Company M.

see service in our partly unprotected coast cities. The company was tendered to the Governor April 8, 1898, but when in a few days the situation developed that a battery would have no chance to get into the service, the company was quickly changed to a company of infantry.

Lieutenant Freeman's coal office, at the corner of High and Vine streets, was the company headquarters. There the plans were often revised to outwit the opposition of many others who were anxious to split the organization that they might have the honor of leading the only company that Dearborn county would get to furnish during the war. In union there was strength, and Company M stood loyally together and all opposition either fell by the wayside or extended a helping hand.

The company tried to get in under the first call, wanting to represent this part of the state in lieu of the Aurora company, whose place was vacant in the state guard, but failed, as larger counties were given the preference. The company kept up their organization, replacing with new men those who dropped out to join other companies that had been more successful in being recognized, some going into the regular army. A member of the company was found at Indianapolis at every change of events or rumor, that no doubt might exist of the company getting in, and on June 15, 1898, the Governor rendered a final decision that the company would be accepted. An hour later a telegram was posted in Lawrenceburg and the news spread like wildfire. June 24th, the Governor notified Captain West, sending the examination blanks. June 27th, 28th and 29th were consumed making physical examinations by Dr. James D. Gatch, after which the Governor was notified that the company awaited his orders. The company received instructions to leave Saturday, July 2d.

July 1, 1898, after the company had made their fare-

Non-Commissioned Officers, Company M.

well parade over the city, they were presented with a handsome flag by the ladies of Lawrenceburg, Mrs. Ezra G. Hayes making the presentation in a strong and touching speech, which was responded to by Lieutenant Fitch, after which the members of the company went to their homes, some for the last time. The departure of the company, on the morning of July 2d, was an event that will live in the memory of every citizen as the most touching scene the city had witnessed since the dark days of 1861.

The company arrived at the Indianapolis fair grounds at noon and was quartered in cattle barn F. After re-examination, the company was mustered into the United States service July 13, 1898, and lettered Company M, after which the history of the company was about that of the regiment. September 5th, Lieutenant Freeman was detailed as regimental commissary officer, which place he filled until the regiment was mustered out.

October 17, 1898, at Jacksonville, Florida, death parted Private Henry H. Stille from his company after a brief sickness with typhoid fever. The remains were sent to his home at Sunman, Indiana, for interment. February 17, 1899, in Cuba, the dreaded small-pox, after a two weeks' struggle, claimed as its victim Private Andrew Gould, and he was interred the same day with military honors in the United States cemetery, between Marianao and Playo, in grave No. 26.

All other events of the company can be looked back upon, no matter how unpleasant at the time, as having some pleasure connected with them save the deaths which parted two good soldiers from the company.

The company was detailed as provost guard at the Second Division, Seventh Army Corps, Hospital, near Marianao, from February 18, 1899, to March 27, 1899.

Company M was mustered out at Savannah, Georgia, April 30, 1899, and returned home *via* Washington, D. C., stopping there two hours and marching through the White House. The company arrived home at midnight, May 2, and were received with open arms, welcoming them home in a happier way than they had bid them Godspeed and success, just ten months before. The reception prepared on the arrival of the company was postponed till the evening of May 3d. The company paraded the principal streets, escorted by all the uniformed ranks of the city, when they marched to Odd Fellows' Hall. Mayor O'Brien made the address of welcome to the company and Captain West responded in a few well-chosen words, after which the company retired to the banquet hall and partook of a feast such as only the ladies of Lawrenceburg know how to prepare. At a late hour the company separated and went to their homes to take up the lives of civilians.

COMPANY M ROSTER.

GEORGE A. WEST, Captain, Lawrenceburg, Ind.
GEORGE W. FITCH, 1st Lieutenant, Lawrenceburg, Ind.
HANSON G. FREEMAN, 2nd Lieutenant, Lawrenceburg, Ind.

SERGEANTS.

Rief, Jacob J., 1st Serg't, Lawrenceburg, Ind., Bookkeeper.
Evans, Edwin J., Q. M. Serg't, Lawrenceburg, Ind., Fireman, appointed from Corp. to Q. M. Serg't Jan. 5, 1899.
Seekatz, John, Lawrenceburg, Ind., Shoemaker.
Sparks, Charles D., Moore's Hill, Ind., Machinist.
Marshall, Edward, Lawrenceburg, Ind., Cooper, appointed from Corp. to Serg't Jan. 5, 1899.
Spencer, Cyrus M., Moore's Hill, Ind., Dentist, discharged.

CORPORALS.

Scofield, John J., Milan, Ind., Telegraph Operator, discharged Feb. 80, 1899.
Wilson, William, Moore's Hill, Teamster.
Cissna, Adrian H., Chillicothe, O., Butcher.
Fleck, George J., Lawrenceburg, Ind., Laborer.
Young, Clarence, Hornersville, N. Y., Butcher, promoted to Corp. Aug. 16, 1898.
Laswell, Jesse L., Versailles, Ind., Cook, promoted to Corp. Dec. 20, 1898.
Webster, William S., Sunmam, Ind., Liveryman, promoted to Corp. Dec. 20, 1898.
Bell, Charles H., Milan, Ind., Carpenter, promoted to Corp. Dec. 20, 1898.
Landers, Edward, Lawrenceburg, Ind., Cooper, promoted to Corp. Dec. 20, 1898.
Schnetzer, George, Lawrenceburg, Ind., Laborer, promoted to Corp. Jan. 5, 1899.
Truitt, Edward A., Lawrenceburg, Ind., Moulder, promoted to Corp. Jan. 5., 1899.
Wingerberg, Henry J., Lawrenceburg, Ind., Laborer, promoted to Corp. Feb. 20, 1899.
Winkley, Martin, Guilford, Ind., Railroader, promoted to Corp. Feb. 20, 1899.

MUSICIANS.

Strauss, John M., Lawrenceburg, Ind., Piano Tuner, discharged Feb. 8, 1899.
Kelsey, Charles L., Moore's Hill, Ind., Telegraph Operator.

ARTIFICER.

Fleck, John J., St. Bernard, Ohio, Blacksmith.

WAGONER.

McAdams, William, Lawrenceburg, Ind., Hod Carrier.

PRIVATES.

Abdon, James W., Cochran, Ind., Laborer.
Andrews, Henry, Elizabethtown, Ohio, Farmer.
Aprill, Frank, Lawrenceburg, Ind., Laborer.
Aylor, George J., Lawrenceburg, Ind., Paper Hanger.
Barrow, Charles, Rockdale, Ind., Farmer.
Berry, Clyde C., Milan, Ind., Laborer.
Billingsley, Nicholas, Aurora, Ind., Laborer.
Brumblay, Thomas B., Moore's Hill, Ind., Engineer.
Christian, Henry, Lawrenceburg, Ind., Stone Mason.
Clark, Ira W., Milan, Ind., Brakeman.
Clark, John C., Lawrenceburg, Ind., Farmer.
Clark, James, Hartford, Ind., Farmer.
Connelley, Bertram, Sunman, Ind., Stenographer.
Cox, Edward S., Aurora, Ind., Laborer.
Cooper, William, Aurora, Ind., Laborer, discharged Jan. 26, 1899.
Daily, Andrew, Lawrenceburg, Ind., Laborer.
Davis, Milton C., Lawrenceburg, Ind., Laborer.
Donner, George, Lawrenceburg, Ind., Laborer.
Downs, Samuel, Lawrenceburg, Stationary Engineer.
Emchiser, Leroy, Santa Fe, Ind., Lumberman.
Enke, Charles F., Cincinnati, Ohio, Blacksmith.
Fahy, Luke, Aurora, Ind., Laborer.
Frazier, James M., Bright, Ind., Butcher.
Frost, John, Cohoes, N. Y., Fireman.
Flush, Henry C., Lawrenceburg, Ind., Cooper.
Gerkin, Albert C., North Vernon, Ind., Moulder.
Gould, Andrew, Lawrenceburg, Ind., Sawmaker, died, Havana, Feb. 17, 1899.
Gould, George K., Lawrenceburg, Ind., Printer.
Givan, Paul, Lawrenceburg, Ind., Blacksmith.
Gray, Harley, Aurora, Ind., Laborer.
Hauser, Peter, Lawrenceburg, Ind., Tailor.
Hayes, George M., Lawrenceburg, Ind., Farmer.
Hayes, Charles, Lawrenceburg, Ind., Farmer

Hitchcock, Edward M., Hope, Ind., Laborer.
Huntington, Homer, Moore's Hill, Farmer.
Jeffries, Thomas B., Lawrenceburg, Ind., Moulder.
Johnson, Albert L., Dillsboro, Ind., Farmer.
Johnson, Clifford, Moore's Hill, Ind., Farmer.
Johnson, Hal, Dillsboro, Ind., Bricklayer.
Jones, Walter D., Moore's Hill, Ind., Photographer.
Kepper, George C., Shelbyville, Ind., Clerk.
Ketcham, George P., Chesterville, Ind., Laborer, discharged Feb. 4, 1899.
Knagge, John W., Dillsboro, Ind., Farmer.
Knippenberg, August H., Lawrenceburg, Ind., Farmer.
Kunkel, John M., Lawrenceburg, Ind., Cigarmaker.
Lawrence, William R., Lawrenceburg, Ind., Cooper.
Losey, John F., Lawrenceburg, Ind., Laborer.
Laird, George W., Greensburg, Ind., Stockdealer.
Marshall, Benjamin, Lawrenceburg, Ind., Laborer.
Mason, Henry, Guilford, Ind., Farmer.
McCartney, Charles W., Lawrenceburg, Ind., Miller.
Meyer, Ralph A., Dillsboro, Ind., Farmer.
Montooth, Charles E., Vevay, Ind., Laborer.
McElfresh, George R., Lawrenceburg, Ind., Clerk.
McCartney, Frank, Lawrenceburg, Ind., Clerk.
Pate, Henry C., St. Louis, Mo., Farmer.
Purnell, Minter, Lawrenceburg, Ind., Laborer.
Ratekin, Emery J., Richland, Ind., Farmer.
Reed, Amos B., Lawrenceburg, Ind., Stove Moulder.
Roemer, Fred C., Lawrenceburg, Ind., Machinist.
Rolf, Frederick, Lawrenceburg, Ind., Blacksmith.
Rief, Charles H., Lawrenceburg, Ind., Carriagemaker.
Schwab, Edward, Lawrenceburg, Ind., Stone Mason.
Speckman, Frank E., Lawrenceburg, Ind., Laborer.
Stewart, Walter S., Elizabethtown, Ohio, Farmer.
Stille, Henry H., Sunman, Ind., Telegraph Operator, died, Jacksonville, Oct. 17, 1898.
Suit, Calvin, Elizabethtown, Ohio, Farmer.
Stricker, George W., Lawrenceburg, Ind., Painter.

Spencer, Henry A., Moore's Hill, Ind., Dentist.
Taylor, Charles J., Lawrenceburg, Ind., Blacksmith.
Taylor, William A., Lawrenceburg, Ind., Express Agent.
Taylor, William, Lawrenceburg, Ind., Laborer.
Thompson, Edward, Aurora, Ind., Laborer.
Temke, William, Spader, Ind., Laborer.
Tudor, Gidion H., Caleast, Ky., Farmer,
Ward, Marcus, Lawrenceburg, Ind., Laborer.
Wesler, William J., Lawrenceburg, Ind., Cooper.
Zimmermann, John G., Cincinnati, Ohio, Baker.
Siemantel, John J., Lawrenceburg, Ind., Blacksmith.
Moody, Curtis, Indianapolis, Ind., Railroader.
Slageter, Karl, transferred from 159th Ind. Vol. Inf. Dec. 1, 1898.

COMPANY A.

GEORGE M. SILVERTHORNE.

Captain George M. Silverthorne was born at Chicago, in 1877, and after finishing a grammar-school course he entered the Michigan Military Academy, from which institution he graduated in 1896. Later he went to Northwestern University and had just completed a two years' law course when war was declared against Spain.

He was commissioned as first lieutenant of Company A, and later was made captain to succeed to Captain Olds. During the first part of his service, Captain Silverthorne acted as adjutant of the First Battalion.

CAPTAIN GEORGE M. SILVERTHORNE.

AUGUST H. W. JOHNSON.

First Lieutenant August H. W. Johnson was born at Hinsdale, Illinois, January 9, 1869. He was educated in the public schools of La Grange, Illinois.

Lieutenant Johnson is a contractor and builder, and from 1892 until 1895 he had charge of the construction work of the Grassila Chemical Company, of Cleveland and Chicago.

He was promoted from second to first lieutenant to succeed First Lieutenant Silverthorne. On October 25, 1898, soon after the arrival of the regiment at Savannah,

First Lieutenant August H. W. Johnson.

Georgia, Lieutenant Johnson was taken sick with typhoid fever, and was confined in the city hospital at that place for three months.

FLETCHER M. DURBIN.

Second Lieutenant Fletcher M. Durbin, son of Colonel Durbin, is the youngest officer in the One Hundred and

Sixty-first Indiana Regiment. He was born at Anderson, Indiana, April 25, 1880. He attended the schools of Anderson, later took a two years' course at the Culver Military Academy, and spent two years in the school at Lawrenceville, New Jersey. Last spring he completed his examina-

SECOND LIEUTENANT FLETCHER M. DURBIN.

tions one month early in order that he might travel. He spent four months travelling in Europe. Mr. Durbin was commissioned as second lieutenant of Company A, November 30, 1898. He was appointed adjutant of the First Battalion, January 6, 1899.

COMPANY A HISTORY.

The Hammond company, like many other companies of this regiment, was formed at the first call for volunteers, and confidently expected to go out then. In this, however, they were disappointed, an event which was very de pressing upon the spirits of the loyal men, who were so anxious to fight for their country, but subsequent events have shown that this was the greatest blessing, however, that they could have received, for otherwise they would never have belonged to the " old One Hundred and Sixty-first."

It was at this stage of the history of the company that it met with one of its discouragements. Disappointed at not being included with those who were first to go into the service of the United States, many resigned and some others, dissatisfied, didn't even go through this formality but simply dropped out.

Interest in the company was at a very low ebb, drills and meetings were suspended on account of the lack of attendance.

A reorganization of the company was decided upon, however, by those who were still anxious to get into the service and a date set for an election of officers. Recruiting offices were opened in Hammond, Whiting, Crown Point and East Chicago, and upon the night of the election the recruits numbered one hundred and twenty-five. Lee Merritt Olds a graduate of the Michigan Military Academy, and also Northwestern University, was elected captain. George M. Silverthorn, a graduate of the same institution, was elected first lieutenant and August H. W. Johnson, of East Chicago, was elected second lieutenant. The election was none to soon, for their orders to hold themselves in readiness and proceed to Indianapolis to join the One

COMPANY A.

Hundred and Sixty-first Regiment Indiana Volunteer Infantry, forming there, were received from the Governor the next day.

The members of the company were duly notified of this fact and were all present with what scanty baggage they were to take with them at the appointed time; the Morton House in Hammond, which had been vacated, was reopened and occupied by them during the interval before leaving for Indianapolis. Transportation arrived on July 5th over the Monon and also an order to proceed at once to Indianapolis. The company were wildly enthusiastic when the orders were read to them, and at once got their belongings together preparatory to leaving; among the latter was the mascot, "Dewey," a large white sheep presented to the company by Chief James Fallon, of the Hammond Packing Company. An early dinner was had and at 12 o'clock they marched to the station led by the G. A. R. drum and fife corps, and greeted with cheers on all sides by the citizens of Hammond who turned out *en mass* to see the departure of the company which was to represent them in the Spanish-American war. Wives and sweethearts, "mostly sweethearts," were at the station to see the company off, and the scene there presented is one that will always be fresh in the mind of everyone present. Two special cars were attached to the regular train, and at 12:30 P. M., July 5th, we left for Indianapolis. We were joined by the company from Monticello on our way, and arrived at Camp Mount, Indianapolis, at about 5 o'clock in the afternoon. Immediately upon our arrival we were assigned to one of the vacant sheds in the fair grounds, which, during fair time, was occupied by the sheep exhibit. Stoves, dishes and blankets were issued to us, and those who enlisted as carpenters were called upon to show their skill in converting a sheep shed into a comfortable habita-

Non-Commissioned Officers, Company A.

tion. Thus at last our purpose was accomplished and we became a part of the One Hundred and Sixty-first Regiment, Indiana Volunteer Infantry.

COMPANY A ROSTER.

LEE M. OLDS, Captain—Promoted to Major Dec. 1, 1898.
GEORGE M. SILVERTHORNE, Captain—Promoted from 1st Lieut. Dec. 9. 1898.
AUGUST H. W. JOHNSON, 1st Lieutenant—Promoted from 2nd Lieut.
FLETCHER DURBIN, 2nd Lieutenant—Appointed Dec. 9, 1898.

SERGEANTS.

Meehan, James E., Franklin Pa., Steam Fitter.
Murray, Joseph E. D., Rochester N. Y. Reporter.
Carr, Stephen, Ashley, Ind., Railroad Employe.
Ripley, Stephen, Hammond, Ind., Clerk.
Schloen, Frank, Hammond, Ind., Clerk, appointed Serg't Dec. 3, 1898.
Main, William E., Chicago, Ill., Student, appointed Serg't Jan. 4, 1899.

CORPORALS.

Mason, Charles J., Hammond, Ind., Clerk.
Coates, John S., Chicago, Ill., Machinist.
Scheer, Robert, Milwaukee, Wis., Carpenter.
Green, George W., Hammond, Ind., Laborer.
Crandall, L. D., Chicago, Ill., Steam Fitter.
Ibsen, Frank, Chicago, Ill., Artist.
Hansen, Mike, Whiting, Ind., Machinist, appointed Corp. Aug. 27, 1898.
Eggers, Peter, Saginaw, Mich. Cooper, appointed Corp. Nov. 12, 1898.
Holzapfel, William, Chicago, Ills., Painter, appointed Corp. Jan. 4, 1899.

Crandall, Elbert, Chicago, Ills., Clerk, appointed Corp. Jan. 4, 1899.

ARTIFICER.

Cole, James, Waterloo, Ind., Blacksmith.

WAGONER.

Frenck, Fred, Hammond, Ind., Liveryman.

MUSICIAN.

Brown, Theodore, Chicago, Ill., Metal Polisher.

PRIVATES.

Adams, Elmer, East Chicago, Ind., Grocer.
Anderson, Fred, Chicago, Ill., Bricklayer.
Boyd, Dayton, La Grange, Ind., Hostler.
Brock, Joseph, Whiting, Ind., Fireman.
Baum, Edward, Cincinnati, Ohio, Laborer.
Ballog, Steve, East Chicago, Ind., Laborer.
Berry, Fred A., Vincennes, Ind., Clerk.
Bouchie, Louis, Vincennes, Ind., Laborer.
Cabice, Thomas, Bridgeport, N. Y., Driver.
Danielson, Daniel, East Chicago, Ind., Laborer.
Doran, Mathis, South Chicago, Ill., Laborer.
Driscoll, Charles J., Vincennes, Ind., Barber.
Eyerman, Max, San Francisco, Cal., Cook.
Fortune, Walter, Evansville, Ind., Farmer.
Faol, Edward, Hammond, Ind., Harnessmaker.
Finlayson, Daniel W., Hammond, Ind., Steamfitter.
Fleirman, Fred, Pullman, Ill., care of Soldiers' Home, Painter.
Fields, Alfred C., Kerney, N. J., Clerk.
Freel, John H., Whiting, Ind., Clerk.
Galloway, Joseph, East Chicago, Ind., Clerk.
Genter, Ernest, Chicago, Ill., Laborer.
Grohnert, Max, Ada, Mich., Painter.
Hanson, Louis, Chicago, Ill., Clerk and Nurse.
Hahlweg, Charles, Hammond, Ind., Law Student.
Hahlweg, Emil, Hammond, Ind., Gold Essayist.

Holtzkampf, August, Chicago, Ill., Pressman.
Hays, Frank J., Chicago, Ill., Teamster.
Hornack, George, Hammond, Ind., Machinist.
Howe, Charles, Hope, Ind., Farmer.
Handy, Algo, Terre Haute, Ind., Expert Bookkeeper.
Haas, Henry, Terre Haute, Ind., Cook.
Johnson, John, Brighton Park, Ind., Cook.
Jones, Patrick, Cleveland, Ohio, Iron Moulder.
Jones, Elmer, Garrett, Ind., Farmer.
Kroucell, John, Hammond, Ind., Gunsmith.
Koai, Frank, East Chicago, Ind., Laborer.
Keitzer, Peter, Hammond, Ind., Barber.
Kuchenberg, Fred, Jeance, Wis., Clerk.
Keller, Fred, Chicago, Ill., Electrician.
Kitchen, Joseph A., Harvey, Ill., Linguist.
Koutz, Charles, Beanville, Ind., Clerk.
Larson, Charles, Kane, Pa., Iron Worker.
Levy, Abraham, Danerorf, Germany, Rabbi.
Miller, Chris., Chicago, Ill., Farmer.
Miller, John, Oxford Furnace, N. J., Steel Worker.
Miller, Parley, Bloomington, Ind., Student.
Malic, Albert, Chicago, Ill., Ladies Tailor.
Mathis, John, East Chicago, Ind., Druggist.
McConnell, Fred, Clinton, Iowa, Law Student.
McGrath, Patrick, Hammond, Ind., Chef.
Nelson, William E., Chicago, Ill., Machinist.
Nichols, Robert, Oswego, N. Y., Engineer.
Nattress, Fred, Island Lake, N. D., Comm. Expert.
Neff, William E., Lowell, Ind., Inventor.
O'Connor, William, Put-in-Bay, Ohio, Malster.
Pondak, Joseph, East Chicago, Ind., Coal Dealer.
Peterson, John, Chicago, Ill., Medical Student.
Peto, Julis, East Chicago, Ind., Laborer.
Polgat, Steve, East Chicago, Ind., Iron Roller.
Poldar, John, East Chicago, Ind., Iron Puddler.
Parks, Albert, Stanley, Ind., Law Student.
Pope, Chode, Hammond, Ind., R. R. Foreman.

Ryan, Thomas, Hammond, Ind., Iron Worker.
Rogers, Jessie, St. Louis, Mo., Tailor.
Sabo, John, East Chicago, Ind., Miner.
Smith, Taylor, Lima, Pa., Butcher.
St. John, Louis, Victoria, B. C., Photographer.
Strabel, Henry, Crown Point, Ind., Cigarmaker.
Strom, Gus., Chicago, Ill., Silversmith.
Strecker, Henry, Chicago, Ill., Grocer.
Trahan, Ben., Valparaiso, Ind., Farmer.
Vacha, Joseph, Whiting, Ind., Grocer.
Vermetle, Carl A., Hammond, Ind., Artist.
Werner, John, Chicago, Ill., Designer.
Williams, John, Whiting, Ind., Fireman.
Woodward, Frank, Whiting, Ind., Physician.

TRANSFERRED.

Hay, George C., Whiting, Ind., Telegraph Operator, to Band Aug. 23, 1898.
Lunom, Martin, Effingham, Ill., Dealer in Spring Water, to Band Sept. 21, 1898.
Carr, Victor, Hartsville, Ind., Clerk, to Co. K Jan. 17, 1899.
Lucas, Horace, Alexander, Ind., Nurse and Student, to U. S. Hospital Sept. 10, 1898.
Kimball, Harry, Chicago, Ill., Nurse, to U. S. Hospital Aug. 20, 1898.
Byerley, Samuel, Bloomingdale, Ind., Railroader, to U. S. Hospital Sept. 10, 1898.
Larson, Andrew C., Chicago, Ill., Polisher, to U. S. Hospital Sept. 10, 1898.
Crandall, Eugene, Chicago, Ill., Student, to U. S. Hospital Aug. 20, 1898.

DISCHARGED.

Proulx, Louis, Hammond, Ind., Clerk, disability at Jacksonville, Fla., Sept. 29, 1898.
Wheeler, Burr O., Hammond, Ind., Printer, by order War Department, Feb. 18, 1899.
Rhodes, Peter, Athens, Ill., Clerk, by order Sec. of War,

Mar. 18, 1899.
Craick, William, Hammond, Ind., Clerk, by order Sec. of War, March 13, 1899.
Bowser, Corp. Emerson L., Valparaiso, Ind., Barber, by order War Department, March 13, 1899.
Butler, Edwin V., Van Wert, Ohio, Brakeman R. R, disability at Havana, Cuba, Dec. 22, 1898.
DeFrees, Fred B., Indianapolis, Ind., Civil Engineer, by order War Department, Dec. 1, 1898.
Larson, Carl A., Chicago. Ill., Painter, by order War Department. Jan. 16, 1899.
O'Connor, Thomas, Buffalo, N. Y., Butcher, by order War Department, Dec. 22, 1898.
Woods, William, New York, N. Y., Painter, disability at Ft. McPherson, Ga., Jan. 4, 1899.

DEATHS.

Puhlman, Ernest, Pittsburg, Pa., Clerk, broke neck diving off pier into Trout Creek, at Jacksonville, Sept. 4, 1899; buried at Pittsburg, Pa.
Schroeder, Fred, Hammond, Ind., Laborer, at Reg. Hospital, Jacksonville, Fla., Oct. 14, 1898; buried at Hammond, Ind.

COMPANY E.

JAMES W. FORTUNE.

Captain James W. Fortune was promoted from the rank of first lieutenant to that he now holds, to fill the vacancy occasioned by the resignation of Captain L. C. Baird. He was born at Lexington, Indiana, February 1, 1864. He attended Indiana University and graduated from the literary department in 1889, and from the department of law in 1894. Since that time he has been engaged in the practice of law at Jeffersonville, Indiana.

For two months previous to his promotion Captain For-

CAPTAIN JAMES W. FORTUNE.

tune was adjutant of the First Battalion. During a greater part of his service he has acted as regimental summary court officer and has officiated as judge advocate of several different court martials.

WILLIAM W. CROOKER.

First Lieutenant William W. Crooker is an old Indiana National Guard officer, having been in the service of the state for a number of years. He was second lieutenant of the command called out to quell the rioting during the coal miners' strike in Sullivan county.

Lieutenant Crooker was born, raised and educated at

First Lieutenant William W. Crooker.

Jeffersonville, Indiana. His business is that of an electrician. His great-grandfather served during the Revolutionary war, and his father was a captain during the Civil war. During the first two months' service of the One Hundred and Sixty-first Indiana Regiment Lieutenant Crooker acted as regimental commissary of subsistence. He entered the army as a second lieutenant.

EDWARD A. McCAULEY.

Second Lieutenant Edward A. McCauley was born at Jeffersonville, Indiana, August 2, 1873. He received his education in the public schools of this place. In 1893 he

SECOND LIEUTENANT EDWARD A. McCAULEY.

became a member of the Indiana National Guard, and was promoted to the rank of sergeant. At the breaking out of the Spanish-American war he was associated with his father, John S. McCauley, in the furniture and picture-framing business. On the president's second call for volunteers he assisted Captain L. C. Baird in raising a company, enlisted as first sergeant and was mustered in at Indianapolis with the company. On the resignation of Captain Baird Sergeant McCauley was promoted to second lieutenant and commissioned January 6, 1899, at Camp Columbia, Havana, Cuba.

HISTORY OF COMPANY E.

Jeffersonville, in common with all other Indiana towns of any importance, strove eagerly for the distinction of furnishing the state with a volunteer company on the first call for troops. Although unsuccessful in this she was destined to be one of the few Indiana cities whose organization saw service on foreign soil.

Enrollment for Company E began to be taken early in May at the office of attorney (now captain) James W. Fortune in the Spieth block, Jeffersonville. Considerable confusion was caused for a time by the presence of a rival organization, which also aspired to the honor of being selected by Governor Mount to represent the city in the makeup of the new regiment about to be furnished by Indiana. The confusion was largely due to the eagerness of a number of the recruits to get into the service. In order to make assurance doubly sure these young patriots had themselves enrolled with both companies. Another factor which contributed to the parlous state of affairs was the uncertainty as to whether or not the governor would allot a company to Jeffersonville. Many of the recruits—in fact the cream of those enrolled—sought relief from this state of uncertainty by enlisting in the regular service.

"All things come to him who waits," and the patience of Company E's promoters was finally rewarded by the welcome intelligence that the organization was one of the lucky twelve selected by the governor. This fact

COMPANY E.

being definitely assured, a mass meeting was held at the city hall on the evening of June 24, for the purpose of selecting the company officers and to enroll such additional recruits as might be necessary. The meeting was presided over by Colonel James Keigwin, of Louisville, Kentucky.

The officers were chosen with especial regard to their fitness, and at no time during their term of service did the members of the company, as a whole, have occasion to regret their choice. Lewis C. Baird was elected captain, James W. Fortune, first lieutenant, and W. W. Crooker, second lieutenant. Captain Baird and Lieutenant Crooker were both members of the State Guard previous to the disbanding of famous Company G, First Indiana National Guard. Captain Baird also brought to his duties the high military efficiency obtained during a course at the United Naval Academy at Ananapolis. Lieutenant Fortune had no previous training in military matters, but his record as first lieutenant and later as captain of the company proved him a born soldier and justified the confidence shown by the company in his selection.

Physical examinations of recruits were conducted daily at Jeffersonville and also at Scottsburg, Charlestown and Sellersburg, the last named three adjoining towns furnishing a number of recruits. These preliminary examinations were conducted by Dr. L. L. Williams, of Jeffersonville, and it is noteworthy that Company E had a smaller percentage of rejections, during the final tests at Indianapolis, than any company in the regiment.

On July 1, Company E went into camp at Indianapolis with one hundred and nine men. Although the examinations reduced this number slightly below the required maximum quota the gaps were speedily filled up. After the usual period of squad-drills, suspense and commisera-

SERGEANTS, COMPANY E.

tion for the unfortunate candidates the company was mustered into the service on July 12.

From this time on the history of the company is, with a few variations, the history of the regiment. When the fall of Santiago and the signing of the protocol occurred it had the dumps with its fellows. When the regiment was ordered to Jacksonville, Company E yelled with the loudest, for Cuba was drawing nearer. It had its share (perhaps more than its share) of the insidious Jacksonville malaria. When the regiment pitched camp at Savannah, Company E, for the first and only time in its history, was separated from the mother organization.

On November 9, the company was detached and sent to take charge of the Savannah Military Rifle Range, during its use for the largest practice of the Seventh Army Corps. The skill and good work of the company in manipulating the targets and conducting the corps target practice won unsparing commendation from the corps officers. The company remained at the range for a period of seventeen days and, while there, ate a Thanksgiving dinner, the menu of which would astonish the bean-fed veterans of the Civil war.

When Cuba was reached all settled contentedly down into the daily routine and began to look for mustering out orders. January 6 marked another epoch in the company's history. On this date notice was given of the acceptance of Captain Baird's resignation, previously tendered on account of business affairs at home which demanded his personal attention. He was succeeded in command by First Lieutenant Fortune. Second Lieutenant Crooker was thus advanced to second in command and First Sergeant Edward A. McCauley received the shoulder straps he so well deserved. The illness of Lieutenant Crooker was the only incident which marred the otherwise enjoyable

CORPORALS, COMPANY E.

stay in Cuba. The boys were sorry to leave him behind, even for the short time which elapsed between the regiment's departure and his return on the hospital ship. Arrived safely at home once more, the members of Company E can speak with justified pride of the showing they have made.

Not wholly unscathed did they come forth. By the death of Private Robert Angleton, Company E was deprived of one of her best and bravest. He died October 11, of typhoid fever, at his home in Jeffersonville while absent on sick furlough.

Company E was mustered out of the service with ninety-five men on the muster rolls. Eight were discharged, six were transferred and one died. As an offset to this five new men were either recruited or transferred to the company during its term of service.

Like many others, Company E had a company flag. On the night previous to the departure of the company for Camp Mount it was presented with a fine silk flag by the citizens of Jeffersonville. The presentation was made by Mayor Whitesides, who made a speech befitting the occasion. The flag remained with the company until Jacksonville was reached, from which place it was returned to its home, where it yet remains—a treasured reminder to the citizens of Clark county of the day when their boys strode away to do their country's bidding.

COMPANY E ROSTER.

L. C. BAIRD, Captain—Jeffersonville, Ind., Draftsman, resigned Jan. 5, 1899.

JAMES W. FORTUNE, Captain—Jeffersonville, Ind., Attorney, promoted from First Lieutenant Jan. 5, 1899.

W. W. CROOKER, First Lieutenant—Jeffersonville, Ind., Electrician, promoted from Second Lieutenant Jan. 5, 1899.

E. A. McCAULEY, Second Lieutenant—Jeffersonville, Ind., Merchant, promoted from First Sergeant Jan. 5, 1899.

SERGEANTS.

Van Liew John R., 1st Sergt., Jeffersonville, Ind., Clerk.
Timmonds, John W., Q. M. Sergeant, Jeffersonville, Ind., Engineer.
Meiboom, J. Henry, Jeffersonville, Ind., Packer.
Ferguson, Ross J., Jeffersonville, Ind., Clerk.
Stricker, Henry F., Charlestown, Ind., Farmer.
Samuels, Conway C., Jeffersonville, Ind., Clerk.

CORPORALS.

Biddle, Cal., Indianapolis, Ind., Farmer.
Biedenbach, John, Jeffersonville, Ind., Carpenter.
Bonnell, John H., Jeffersonville, Ind., Farmer.
Flora, Francis G., New Albany, Ind., Puddler.
Hyatt, Walter E., Sellersburg, Ind., Draftsman.
Keifer, Thomas F., New Albany, Ind., Painter.
Laidley, Willis J., Jeffersonville, Ind., Machinist.
LeClare, James N., Jeffersonville, Ind., Clerk.
Lee, John, Indianapolis, Ind., Brass Finisher.
Peckinpaugh, Thomas L., Jeffersonville, Ind., Farmer.
Pickering, John C., Indianapolis, Ind., Laborer.
Raines, Walter P., Utica, Ind., Brass Worker.

MUSICIANS.

White, Edwin, Northfield, Vt., Salesman, discharged Feb. 12, 1899.
Dumenil, Ellsworth, Indianapolis, Ind., Musician, transferred to Regt. Band Aug. 26, 1898.
Jones, Percy, Columbus, Ind., Farmer, transferred from Regt. Band.

ARTIFICER.

McClure, Julian C., Scottsburgh, Farmer.

WAGONER.

Kelly, Marion, Jeffersonville, Ind., Fireman.

PRIVATES.

Angleton, Robert, Jeffersonville, Ind., Blacksmith, died Oct. 11, 1898.
Applegate, Charles L., Woodsbury, Ind., Farmer.
Barnard, Charles O., Farmer.
Belknapp, William E., Jeffersonville, Ind., Laborer.
Bottorff, Harvey J., Sellersburgh, Ind., Farmer.
Bridgewater, Daniel, Scottsburgh, Ind., Painter.
Buckley, Benjamin C., Jeffersonville, Ind., Painter.
Carr, Charles F., Jeffersonville, Ind., Laborer.
Carr, Warren, Charlestown, Ind., Farmer.
Clemmons, Jesse, Jeffersonville, Ind., Stave Cutter.
Clemmons, Walter H., Jeffersonville, Ind., Farmer.
Davis, Charles S., Scottsburgh, Laborer.
Delanty, John, Jeffersonville, Ind., Moulder.
Dobson, Andrew, Jeffersonville, Ind., Laborer.
Dorsey, Walter A., Jeffersonville, Ind., Engineer, discharged Jan. 28, 1899.
Doane, Charles R., Washington, Ind., Laborer, transferred from 159th Ind. Vol.
Dunham, Jesse, Indianapolis, Ind., Farmer, transferred to Hospital Corps Aug. 20, 1898.
Edwards, Stephen, Sellersburg, Ind., Laborer.
Ellerman, William H., Louisville, Ky., Railroader.
Ervin, Howard L., Scottsburgh, Ind., Railroader.
Gilbert, William B., Jeffersonville, Ind., Clerk.
Griffiths, James C., Jeffersonville, Ind., Teamster.
Griffith, John A., Charleston, Ind., Horse Trainer, transferred to Hospital Corps, Sept. 15, 1898.
Harrell, A. Thomas, Scottsburg, Cooper.
Harris, James, Indianapolis, Ind., Painter.

Herberick, Jacob, Jeffersonville, Ind., Plumber.
Herman, John, Indianapolis, Ind., Laborer.
Harbin, Robert L., Charlestown, Ind., Farmer.
Hartley, Clarence, Jeffersonville, Ind., Farmer, discharged
    Feb. 18, 1898.
Howard, Frank L., Charlestown, Ind., Tinner.
Houghland, Rosco, Scottsburgh, Ind., Painter.
Jackson, Schuyler C., New Albany, Ind., Glass Worker.
Jacobs, James N., Jeffersonville, Ind., Painter.
Javens, Jackson E., Jeffersonville, Ind., Laborer.
Jones, David, Jeffersonville, Ind., Iron Worker.
Kelly, John E., Louisville, Ky., Bar Keeper.
Kelly, Albert E., Putnam, Putnam Co., Ind., Attorney, transferred from 159th Ind. Vol.
Kennedy, Hugh, Jeffersonville, Ind., Laborer.
Klosterman, Otto, Louisville, Ky., Farmer.
Knowland, William A., Charlestown, Ind., Cooper.
Koons, Walter I., Charlestown, Ind., Laborer.
Koons, Charles, Charlestown, Ind., Laborer.
Lewis, Horace I., Jeffersonville, Ind., Fireman, discharged
    Feb. 16, 1899.
Mayberry, Charles, Charlestown, Ind., Farmer.
Meadows, John R., Carrolton, Ky., Cook.
Meyer, John F., Jeffersonville. Ind., Farmer.
Meyer, John H., Jeffersonville, Ind., Farmer.
Miller, John I., Indianapolis, Ind., Painter.
Mitchell, Herbert, Jeffersonville, Ind., Laborer.
Mitchell, Berkie, Scottsburgh, Ind., Teamster.
McCafferty, William, Washington, Ind., Printer, transferred
    from 159th Ind. Vol.
Nelson, Fred., Detroit, Mich., Sailor.
O'Brien, Frank, New Albany, Ind., Glass Worker.
Ogden, Homer O., Jeffersonville, Ind., Railroader.
Oliver, James, Utica, Ind., Farmer.
Pearson, Theodore B., Jeffersonville, Ind., Student.
Perry, Archie C., Scottsburgh, Ind., Farmer.
Perry, Homer, Jeffersonville, Ind., Student.

Phillips, Orville G., Scottsburgh, Ind., Farmer, discharged Feb. 9, 1899.
Powers, Eugene, Jeffersonville, Ind., Clerk.
Powers, Claude B., Jeffersonville, Ind., Musician.
Rhodes, Fred P., Atlanta, Ind., Farmer, discharged Feb. 13, 1899.
Ryan, John E., New Albany, Ind., Laborer.
Rector, John A., Indianapolis, Ind., Varnisher.
Rogers, Charles T., Charlestown, Ind., Reporter.
Sauer, Elmer C., Jeffersonville, Ind., Machinist.
Stepp, Jesse, Sellersburgh, Ind., Laborer.
Smith, George, Indianapolis, Ind., Laborer.
Simms, Willis B., Utica, Ind., Farmer.
Taylor, George S., Jeffersonville, Ind., Railroader.
Tatum, William, Utica, Ind., Laborer.
Thomas, Wilmer H., Indianapolis, Ind., Moulder.
Tobin, James, Anderson, Ind., Laborer.
Tobin, Matthew, Anderson, Ind., Railroader, discharged Jan. 7, 1899.
Tomlin, Lafe W., Jeffersonville, Ind., Steamboatman.
Twomey, George W., Jeffersonville, Ind., Medical Student.
Thompson, James W., Indianapolis, Ind., Farmer.
Thompson, William M., Scottsburgh, Ind., Barber.
Tharp, Elmer, Jeffersonville, Ind., Carpenter, transferred to Signal Corps Dec. 10, 1898.
Vance, Arthur R., New Albany, Ind., Salesman.
Weaver, Howard, Jeffersonville, Ind., Blacksmith.
Webb, Frank F., Indianapolis, Ind., Paper Hanger.
Wright, Charles M., Jeffersonville, Ind., Railroader.
Wurlel, William, Jeffersonville, Ind., Plumber.
Worrell, Luther M., Jeffersonville, Ind., Electrician, transferred to Signal Corps Dec. 10, 1899.
Whittsett, Lemmel E., Duputy, Ind., Farmer, transferred to Signal Corp Dec. 10, 1899.
Youmans, Edward H., Jeffersonville, Ind., Laborer.

SECOND BATTALION

B, I, F, D.

Major Harold C. Megrew,

HAROLD C. MEGREW.

Major Harold C. Megrew prepared himself for the position he held in the regiment by his early choice of educational training and by his acquired experience in military affairs before he entered the service with the rank of major and appointment to the command of the Second Battalion. He was born in Indianapolis March 16, 1859, and after preparatory training was educated at the Howard Military Institute, in Maryland. He was a member of Company D, in the Washington (District of Columbia) Light Infantry, National Guard. He was a member of the National Guard in Ohio, serving by special appointment on the staff of Governors Foraker and Bushnell. He has been in the service of the government, filling positions of responsibility at home and in Europe. He was captain in the Ben Harrison Camp of the Sons of Veterans, and at the time of the president's call for troops was inspector-general of Indiana, and chief of staff of Governor Mount, with the rank of colonel. It was no small sacrifice of family and business interests that Major Megrew made on entering the volunteer service; but, with the hope of being actively engaged at the front, he accepted his commission and became major of the One Hundred and Sixty-first Indiana. He is a member of the Indiana commandery of the Loyal Legion, and one of its board of officers.

While at Camp Cuba Libre, Major Megrew was president of the general court martial of the Third Division, and was summary court officer from the regiment's organization until, by direction of the major-surgeon, he left for a thirty-days' leave of absence, January 16, 1899. He returned to the States, and, after a twenty days' extension, came back Monday, March 13. He was in every way an army official. He delighted in his work, was straightforward and impartial among his men. He returned to his professional duties at Indianapolis when mustered out.

COMPANY B.

WINSTON MENZIES.

Captain Winston Menzies is among the youngest of the captains of the regiment. He was born at Mt. Vernon, Indiana, November 22, 1875. His grandfather was a

CAPTAIN WINSTON MENZIES.

major-general in the Civil war and his father, G. V. Menzies, is a retired naval officer who held the rank of lieutenant-commander while in the service. After the usual preparatory training, which Captain Menzies received at Cornwall-on-the-Hudson, he entered the State University of Indiana in 1892, in which institution his collegiate education was finished in 1896. He took an active interest in athletics and was a member of various athletic teams of his college. .He engaged for a short time in the cotton business in Texas and returned to his native state in time to enlist for the war with Spain. When it became evident that the company organized in Mt. Vernon would not be accepted in the first call, Mr. Menzies enlisted as a private in Company H, One Hundred and Fifty-ninth Indiana, but upon the second call being issued obtained his discharge and came home to go out with the company of his choice as captain. During the sickness and absence of Major Megrew, Captain Menzies was in command of the Second Battalion.

ASA ELLWOOD WILLIAMS.

First Lieutenant Asa Ellwood Williams received his education at Purdue University and the State University of Indiana, in the former of which institution he was second lieutenant of Company A of the cadets. At the State University Mr. Williams made a specialty of the study of law and was admitted to the bar of Posey county shortly after graduation, where he practiced prior to his enlistment, and where he held the position of deputy prosecuting attorney. While in college he was a member of the college football team and manager of the baseball nine. On the 13th of June Lieutenant Williams was married to Miss

FIRST LIEUTENANT ASA ELLWOOD WILLIAMS.

Ethel Hinch; they were married under the beautiful silken flag of the company at 10 o'clock in the morning, and together came to Camp Mount, where Mr. Williams was mustered in as first lieutenant on the 11th of July.

PERCY WELCH.

Second Lieutenant Percy Welch was born at Shawneetown, Illinois, July 30, 1869. He received his early education in the common schools of southern Indiana, after which he took a course in Ewing College, Illinois. He taught school in Indiana for a period of eight years and was admitted to the Posey county bar in 1897. Mr. Welch was a member of the Indiana National Guard for three years, holding the position of first sergeant. He was married in 1894 to Miss Marguerite Jones, of New Harmony,

SECOND LIEUTENANT PERCY WELCH.

Indiana. In June he was elected to the second lieutenancy of Company B, and shared the fortunes of the company until detailed, January 10, for provost duty with the Tenth United States Infantry in Havana and Matanzas. He was relieved from this latter duty in time to join his regiment for muster out at Savannah. Mr. Welch will renew his legal studies in Indiana University and expects to engage in the practice of law in the county from which he came.

HISTORY OF COMPANY B.

During the month of April, while the dogs of war were growling and the motto "Remember the Maine" was uppermost in all men's minds, an attempt was made to organize a military company at Mt. Vernon. The first attempt was a failure as there was no possibility of acceptance on the first call. Winston Menzies, who was to have been captain of the company, fearing there would be no second call, enlisted as a private in Company H, One Hundred and Fifty-ninth Indiana. A. E. Williams and Percy Welch, two enthusiastic embryo warriors, held the organization awaiting the hoped-for second call. May 25 President McKinley issued his second call for volunteers, and Posey county responded nobly to the call. A recruiting office was opened in Asa E. Williams' law office and the new recruits were sent into camp at the base ball park at the fair grounds. Our first camp was named in honor of Governor Hovey. It consisted of three tents and the base ball amphitheater. The commissary department was presided over by Frank Jones, and it was a constant struggle to keep "the wolf from the door."

But the patriotic Women's Relief Corps and the charitable citizens of Mt. Vernon rallied to our support and a famine was happily averted in Camp Hovey. The city council of Mt. Vernon generously voted us a subsidy and we received a great bonanza from the proceeds of an ice cream festival held in the court house, by the Women's Relief Corps, for our benefit. In the last days of June the examinations of the recruits was held by Drs. Welch and

COMPANY B.

Hardwick at the Masonic hall. The examination was very thorough and many would-be warriors were disappointed by being rejected. Winston Menzies in the meantime had secured his discharge from the One Hundred and Fifty-ninth to come home as captain of the Mt. Vernon company. At the election of officers, Winston Menzies was chosen captain; Asa Williams, first lieutenant, and Percy Welch, second lieutenant. Drills were held daily at the fair grounds and nightly in the court house yard. The evening of June 29, while drilling in the court yard, we received a dispatch calling our company to Indianapolis. The glad news was received by the company with great rejoicing. At noon the next day, while in company front awaiting the captain's order to leave Camp Hovey, the company sustained the only defeat in its history, being suddenly charged upon by a blind cow, which caused an instantaneous stampede in our ranks. Captain Menzies, after rallying the company, marched us to the court house, where we were presented with a beautiful silken flag by Mrs. Charles Brenkman, on behalf of the Women's Relief Corps. Immediately after the flag presentation we marched to the Evansville & Terre Haute depot and departed for Indianapolis. Company B's first complement of arms was furnished by John Moeller, the patriotic cooper of Posey's capital; each man was armed with a mammoth Posey county hoop-pole and the company did valiant service with these arms on the guard line at Camp Mount. On the morning of July 1, Indianapolis was reached and we were quartered in barn "B." Company B has reason to be proud of its merited reputation in the regiment; always ready and cheerfully willing to perform its duty, always able to have out the largest number of men for drills or reviews; health record second to none, not a death while in the service.

Non-Commissioned Officers, Company B.

COMPANY B ROSTER.

WINSTON MINZIES, Captain—Mt. Vernon, Ind.
ASA E. WILLIAMS, First Lieutenant—Mt. Vernon, Ind.
PERCY WELCH, Second Lieutenant—Mt. Vernon, Ind.

SERGEANTS.

Lowenhaupt, Mike, 1st Serg't, Mt. Vernon. Ind., Merchant.
Jones, Frank, Q. M. Serg't, Springfield, Ind., Farmer.
Works, Edward, Mt. Vernon, Ind., Butcher.
Stephens, Harold, New Harmony, Ind., Student, discharged Feb. 1, 1899.
Fuhrer, William B., Mt. Vernon, Ind., Billposter.
Schultz, Oscar T., Mt. Vernon, Ind., Student, Serg't Maj. 2d Battalion.
Hovey, Randolph J., Mt. Vernon, Ind., Student, promoted Serg't from Corp. Feb. 16, 1899.

CORPORALS.

Bennett, Charles A., Mt. Vernon, Ind., Farmer, discharged Jan. 31, 1899.
Nash, Flairance W., Poseyville, Ind., Tinner.
Miller, Charles H., Mt. Vernon, Ind., Moulder.
Kreutzinger, James H., Mt. Vernon, Ind., Farmer.
Moore, Noble, Mt. Vernon, Ind., Clerk.
Tingle, George R., Princeton, Ind., Machinist.
Welsh, Michael, Richmond, Ind., Laborer, promoted to Corp. July 27, 1898.
Switzer, Harry T., Princeton, Ind., Machinist, promoted to Corp. Oct. 18, 1898.
Harris, John M., Princeton, Ind., Butcher.
Green, George, Jr., Mt. Vernon, Ind., Clerk, promoted to Corp. Dec. 1, 1898.
Stewart, William, Mt. Vernon, Ind., Pilot, promoted to Corp. Feb. 9, 1899.

Utley, James K., Mt. Vernon, Ind., Horse-shoer, promoted to Corp. Feb. 21, 1899.
Bays, Harold C., Sullivan, Ind., Electrician, promoted to Corp. Feb. 21, 1899.

ARTIFICER.

King, Samuel W., Mt. Vernon, Ind., Blacksmith.

WAGONER.

Kahn, Samuel, Mt. Vernon, Ind., Insurance Agent.

MUSICIANS.

Lord, Harry M., Mt. Vernon, Ind., Musician, transferred to Regimental Band Aug. 23, 1898.
Lance, Edward, New Harmony, Ind., Florist, transferred to Regimental Band Aug. 23, 1898.
Wehr, Otto, Mt. Vernon, Ind., Machinist.
Cravens, George W., Mt. Vernon, Ind., Printer.

PRIVATES.

Allen, James K., Mt. Vernon, Ind., Brickmason.
Alsop, Linwood Z., New Harmony, Ind., Plumber, discharged Feb. 4, 1899.
Bayer, George, Ft. Branch, Ind., Farmer.
Berlin, Charles T., New Harmony, Ind., Barber.
Bieker, Frank, Mt. Vernon, Ind., Farmer, discharged Feb. 2, 1899.
Boren, Ralph T., New Harmony, Ind., Clerk.
Brokaw, Arthur, Ft. Branch, Ind., Farmer.
Bruce, George M., Ft. Branch, Ind., Barber, discharged Mar 15, 1899.
Cantrell, James, West End, Ill., Farmer.
Casey, Benjamin F., Owensville, Ind., Farmer.
Cawthone, Arthur, New Harmony, Ind., Clerk, discharged Feb. 7, 1899.
Cooper, Levi, Ft. Branch, Ind., Farmer.
Cox, Charles F., Princeton, Ind., Laborer.

Cox, George, Carmi, Ill., Farmer.
Crilley, James, Ft. Branch, Ind., Farmer.
Cunningham, Isaac N., Hazelton, Ind., Farmer, discharged Sept. 27, 1898.
Drear, Thomas, Mt. Vernon, Ind., Carpenter.
Easmon, Jacob, Carmi, Ill., Laborer.
Frohman, Peter, Mt. Vernon, Ind., Farmer.
Grabert, Gustave W., Mt. Vernon, Ind., Miller.
Hanks, Charlie, Princeton, Ind., Laborer.
Harding, George F., Golden Gate, Ill., Farmer.
Hayes, William S., Mt. Vernon, Ind., Farmer.
Hill, Richard, Mt. Vernon, Ind., Farmer.
Holleman, Porter G., Mt. Vernon, Ind., Machinist.
Edwards, Calie, Scalesville, Ind., Farmer.
Estes, Samuel, New Harmony, Ind., Brickmason.
Houchin, Otta D., Pikeville, Ind., Farmer.
Jones, Lemuel P., Mt. Vernon, Ind., Grocerman.
Kaedel, Andrew, Mt. Vernon, Ind., Farmer.
Kennedy, John, Dekoven, Ky., Coalminer.
Koerner, Ferdinand, Mt. Vernon, Ind., Teacher.
Kuykendall, Noah, Bufkin, Ind., Farmer.
Lance, James, New Harmony, Ind., Farmer, discharged Jan. 25, 1899.
Lance, John, New Harmony, Ind., Farmer.
LeGrange, Oscar W., West Franklin, Ind., Carpenter.
Maus, Charles G., Mt. Vernon, Ind., Farmer.
Males, John W., Mt. Vernon, Ind., Moulder.
Marshall, David R., Mt. Vernon, Ind., Machinist.
McAtee, George, Oatsville, Ind., Farmer, discharged, Jan. 27, 1899.
Meadows, Floyd, Princeton, Ind., Farner, discharged Mar. 2, 1899.
Miller, Charles A., Mt. Vernon, Ind., Farmer.
Murphy, George A., Fitzgerald, Ga., Farmer.
Murphy Orval, Fitzgerald, Ga., Farmer.
Newell, Frank, Joplin, Mo., Farmer.
Nicholson, Arthur, Springerton, Ill., Farmer.

Nuthmann, Charles, Princeton, Ind., Railroad Caller.
Ott, Floyd, Princeton, Ind., Boilermaker.
Parke, James, Spurgeon, Ind., Farmer.
Parmer, Marion, Emma, Ill., Farmer.
Pearson, John F., Hazleton, Ind., Farmer.
Pfeifer, August, Mt. Vernon, Ind., Tailor.
Phifer, George B., Booneville, Ind., Engineer, dishonorably discharged Feb. 25, 1899.
Pirnat, Albert, Evansville, Ind., Druggist.
Powers, William M., Madisonville, Ky., Farmer.
Reavis, Fred G., Princeton, Ind., Stone Cutter.
Redenour, Frank, New Harmony, Ind., Hostler.
Reed, Robert R., Booneville, Ind., Shoemaker.
Rose, Henry, Owensville, Ind., Laborer.
Schaefer, August E., Mt. Vernon, Ind., Harnessmaker.
Singleton, Perry F., Pikeville, Ind., Farmer.
Sluder, Lafayette, Henderson, Ky., Farmer.
Smith, Jay J., Hazleton, Ind., Farmer.
Smith, Henry, Owensville, Ind., Lather.
Switzer, Lyman, Princeton, Ind., Carpenter.
Spencer, Samuel, Owensville, Ind., Farmer.
Summers, John, Evansville, Ind., Butcher.
Trapp, William, Carmi, Ill., Poultry Dresser.
Turner, Burl E., Owensville, Ind., Laborer, transferred to Hospital Corps Aug. 28, 1898.
Vint, Everett, Mt. Vernon, Ind., Farmer.
Wallace, Peter, Booneville, Ind., Farmer.
Walter, Edward, Mt. Vernon, Cook, transferred to Hospital Corps Aug. 20, 1898.
Ward, Clarence E., New Harmony, Ind., Farmer.
Weissinger, Jesse, Mt. Vernon, Ind., Carpenter.
Westfall, Thomas A., Hazleton, Ind., Farmer.
Williams, Harry, Mt. Vernon, Ind., Farmer.
Woerner, William, Evansville, Ind., Molder.
Yeager, Harvey, Owensville, Ind., Farmer.
Baldwin, Walter, Mt. Vernon, Ind., Carpenter, enlisted Aug. 5, 1898.

Corkin, William L., Indianapolis, Ind., Barber, enlisted Dec. 9, 1898.
Hoge, Smith, Delphi, Ind., Student, enlisted Aug. 10, 1898.
Norton, Nelson, Sullivan, Ind., Farmer, transferred from 159th Ind. Inf., Nov. 19, 1898.
Stalnaker, Morton, Terre Haute, Ind., Laborer, enlisted Dec. 10, 1898.

COMPANY I.

WILLIAM GUTHRIE.

Captain William Guthrie was one of the ablest men in the regiment; he is a lawyer by profession, and although he came into the service without any previous military training, he made out of his raw recruits a company of most excellent regimental standing. Captain Guthrie is a native of Ohio, being born in Hamilton in the year 1852. When a child his parents moved to Indiana, settling in the county of White. It was in the common schools of this county the young man began his early educational training; entering the high school of Monticello, the county seat, he studied in that institution until a few years later he went to Logansport and finished his course in the Academy of that place. For eleven years after graduation he was a teacher in the schools of his county and in 1880 was elected to the position of county superintendent of public instruction, when he was but twenty-eight years of age, which position he filled until the year 1884. While teaching he used his spare time in the study of law and was admitted to the bar of his adopted county in 1880, where he has since been practicing his profession in the law firm of Guthrie & Bushnell. He was a man of exemplary habits and took unusual interest in the morale of his company.

CAPTAIN WILLIAM GUTHRIE.

ANTHONY A. ANHEIRE.

First Lieutenant Anthony A. Anheire was born in the city Logansport, June 29, 1867, and received his early education in the German Catholic schools of that place, after which he entered Hall's Business College, also situated in Logansport. After completing his education he accepted a position with the Pittsburg, Cincinnati & St. Louis railroad, which position he retained for eight years. In 1886 Mr. Anheire moved to Monticello, where for several years he engaged successfully in the cigarmaking business and where he served for two years as city marshal, which position he occupied when he enlisted as first lieutenant of the company that came out from that place.

FIRST LIEUTENANT ANTHONY A. ANHEIRE.

Lieutenant Anheire was the first officer of the regiment to place his foot upon Cuban soil, being of a detail that preceded the regiment on the Roumania, that carried the greater portion of the regimental livestock. Mr. Anheire was on detached service while in Cuba with the Tenth Infantry at Havana and Mantanzas, leaving the regiment on December 10, and returning a few days before its departure for America.

JOHN R. WARD.

Second Lieutenant John R. Ward was born in White county, Indiana, on the first day of April, 1872. He was educated in the city schools of Monticello, after which he spent one year in the State Normal schools of Valparaiso,

SECOND LIEUTENANT JOHN R. WARD.

and then entered the State University at Bloomington in 1893, where he graduated in the school of law in 1893; in the same year he was admitted to the bar and was appointed to the position of deputy prosecuting attorney in his native city, Monticello, in which place he was engaged in the practice of his profession when he enlisted and came out as second lieutenant of Company I.

HISTORY OF COMPANY I.

"The Volunteers! the Volunteers!
God send us peace, through all our years;
But if the cloud of war appears
We'll see them once again."
WILLIAM HAINES LYTLE.

Yesterday shapes and colors to-day and history repeats itself. The example set by the fathers in 1861 was imitated by the sons in 1898. As soon as it was learned that war with Spain was imminent an enthusiastic public meeting, called by Tippecanoe Post, G. A. R., was held in the Court House at Monticello, April 21st, 1898, and after patriotic addresses and songs resolutions were read and adopted which concluded as follows:

"Being actuated by that patriotic spirit that has sustained our flag on land and sea and carried it to final victory on all occasions of the past, we hereby declare our full confidence in our National and State authorities. And we most respectfully represent to the Governor of the State of Indiana that we are now ready to perform in behalf of our Government and State such services in the present conflict with Spain as may be in our power and in his judgment required by the occasion."

A company was at once organized and the Governor of the State was notified that it was ready to be mustered into service at a moment's warning. This was before troops were called for, but the Governor assured Captain Guthrie and Lieutenants Anhier and Ward that the company would surely be needed, and said for them to drill it

and put it into condition for service, and on June 30th, 1898, he sent the following message:

"CAPTAIN WM. GUTHRIE: Your company will report at Indianapolis on next Monday, coming via "Monon." You will await further instructions from A. F. Houghton, Master of Transportation. JAMES A. MOUNT, Gov."

Upon receipt of this message the Captain wrote the Governor asking that the company be allowed to remain in camp at the Fair Grounds west of Monticello until Tuesday, July 5th, in order that the men might spend Sunday at home and celebrate "The Fourth" at Monticello. This request was granted and while some of the men spent Saturday and Sunday at home the parents of others visited them in camp. Monday, the Fourth, was spent at Monticello in celebrating and making final arrangements for departure. The ladies of the town served dinner to the company in the Court House.

Tuesday came and with it came friends from far and near to say good-bye and see the company take its departure. The G. A. R. and different civic organizations of the town turned out and escorted the company to the train and at 2:34 P. M., amid the boom of cannon, the waving of flags and handkerchiefs and tears of friends, the Company boarded the train for Indianapolis where on July 13th, 1898, it was mustered in as Company I, One Hundred and Sixty-first Regiment Indiana Volunteer Infantry.

The company was constantly with the regiment and participated in all its movements until January 8, 1899, when it was detailed on provost duty at Marianao, Cuba, where it remained until January 24th, returning to the regiment on that day.

The muster-out occurred on April 30, 1899, and on the same day the company took the train for home, returning

Non-Commissioned Officers, Company I.

by Washington, D. C., and Indianapolis, Indiana. Arrangements had been made for a review of the whole regiment at Washington by the President, but owing to the unexpected delay of trains this was not fully carried out. However, as this company and three others arrived on the first section of the train on Monday evening, May 1st, they were met by a committee of Indianians who escorted them to the White House where they were permitted to pass through the reception room. Each member of the company was presented with a silk badge bearing a cut of the Capitol building and these words: "Greeting: 161st Regiment Indiana Volunteers. By Indianians in Washington, D. C., May 1st, 1899."

Elaborate arrangements had been made for the reception of this and the Michigan City and Hammond companies on Tuesday evening, May 2, but the previous delay of the train made this impossible and in lieu of this an early breakfast was served on Wednesday morning. The generous and loyal hospitality of the ladies was greatly appreciated by the companies, and the greeting extended them by the Governor and his acceptance of the regimental flag and colors were most touching, eloquent and inspiring.

The company reached Monticello at 12 M., May 3rd, and were received with that joy that resides only in the hearts of those who have been anxiously waiting for the return of departed and long absent children. The home greeting will ever be remembered. Again the cannon boomed, flags waved, and bands discoursed music, while excited crowds surged along the streets, keeping pace with the boys and clasping their hands as they marched to the room where a home-coming feast had been prepared by the ladies of the town. The rapture of the delighted populace, the bounteous dinner, and address of welcome left an impress in the minds of the receiving as well as the returning never to be eradicated, and fully demonstrated the loyalty that resides in the hearts of the American people.

COMPANY I ROSTER.

WILLIAM GUTHRIE, Captain, Monticello, Lawyer.

ANTHONY A. ANHEIR, 1st Lieut., Monticello, Cigarmaker.

JOHN R. WARD, 2d Lieut., Monticello, Lawyer.

SERGEANTS.

Strubbe, Harry E., Goodland, Plumber, promoted 1st Sergt. Nov. 29, 1898, from corporal.

Imes, Fred. S., Q. M. Sergt., Monticello, Clerk, appointed Quartermaster Serg't from corporal Dec. 22, 1898.

Best, William D., Brookston, Laborer, mustered in as Serg't July 13, 1898.

Cromer, Robert H., Logansport, Clerk, mustered in as Serg't July 13, 1898.

Kassabaum, George W., Kentland, Lawyer, mustered in as Serg't July 13, 1898.

Hubbard, Charles E., Francesville, Farmer, mustered in as Serg't July 13, 1898.

CORPORALS.

Thompson, Clinton H., Monon, Student, mustered in as Corp. July, 13, 1898.

Hausman, William Earl, Rensselaer, Salesman, mustered in as Corp. July 13, 1898.

Holdridge, Leroy L., Wolcott, Farmer, mustered in as Corp. July 13, 1898.

Goodwin, Marion L., Battle Ground, Farmer, mustered in as Corp. July 13, 1898.

Wallace, Lew, Battle Ground, Carpenter, mustered in as Corp. July 18, 1898.
Burns, John, Logansport, Clerk, mustered in as Corp. July 18, 1898.
Garrigues, John U., Francesville, Carpenter, mustered in as Corp. July 18, 1898.
Gorman, Daniel V., Logansport, Express Agent, promoted Corp. from private Nov. 29, 1898.
Graham, John W., Kirkland, Laborer, promoted Corp. from private Nov. 29, 1898.
Gibson, Frank E., Remington, Telegrapher, promoted Corp. from private Nov. 29, 1898.
Coen, Newel M., Monticello, Clerk, promoted Corp. from Artificer Dec. 22, 1898.
Loughry, Howard, Monticello, Student, promoted to Corp. from private Dec. 21, 1898.

COOK.

Smock, Thomas W., Indianapolis, Cook, enlisted and enrolled as cook, Dec. 2, 1898.

MUSICIANS.

Conner, Charles A., Reynolds, Traveling Salesman.
Comer, William E., Reynolds, Carpenter.

PRIVATES.

Arrick, K. Guy, Monticello, Tanner.
Arnold, Charles E., Delphi, Machinist.
Ballard, Samuel P., Monon, Ditcher.
Bates, Wilbur F., Monticello, Harness Manufacturer.
Benica, Louis C., Logansport, Cook.
Best, Charles A., Brookston, Ditcher.
Bowman, George, Battle Ground, Farmer.
Boyles, Charles S., Battle Ground, Hunter.
Boyles, Benton A., Battle Ground, Barber.
Bugbee, George J., Remington, Teacher.
Burden, John W., Monticello, Laborer.

Brown, Arthur H., Monticello, Student.
Cooley, George, Brookston, Laborer.
Cowger, Raymond, Monticello, Farmer.
Crafton, Paul, Bedford, Ind., Farmer.
Crowell, Richard, Monticello, Clerk.
Coombs, Edward, Brownstown, Laborer, transferred from Co. G, 159th Ind. to 161st Ind., Dec. 1, 1898.
Dillman, William O., Battle Ground, Well Driller.
Downs, William A., Battle Ground, Carpenter.
Didlake, Roy P., Monticello, Student.
Diffy, John, Pickard, Laborer.
Evans, Albert, Wheatfield, Laborer.
Fehrle, John G., Goodland, Laborer.
Fox, Stuart T., Monticello, Student.
Garwood, Corydon, Monon, Farmer.
Goodrich, Guy, Wolcott, Carpenter.
Guest, Frank A., Monticello, Laborer.
Hager, Charles A, Logansport, Cigarmaker.
Hartz, John F., Logansport, Boilermaker.
Hart, Joseph, Monticello, Farmer.
Hawkina, William J., Rensselaer, Farmer.
Hayward, Lorenzo, Monon, Farmer.
Heglin, William, Monon, Cook.
Herron, Richard, Monticello, Cigarmaker.
Hurst, William A., Battle Ground, Barber.
Hollcraft, Charles H., Hammond, Laborer.
Horner, George W., Knox, Ind., Farmer.
Karp, George A., Monticello, Student.
Lee, Claude J., Logansport, Railroader.
Lefler, Israel J., Francesville, Hostler.
Leslie, Albert, E., Monon, Railroader.
Longwell, John, Francesville, Farmer.
Langner, Gustave A., Evansville, Laborer, transferred from Co. M, 159th Ind., to Co. I, 161st Ind., Dec. 4, 1898.
Mahoney, Daniel, Bessemer, Mich., Brakeman.
Mair, Albert, Monon, Baker.
Meyer, Henry Gustave, Remington, Painter.

Montrose, Jesse, Peru, Papermaker.
McCloud, Edward E., Sheldon, Ill., Clerk.
McChristy, Enos A., Round Grove, Farmer.
McNett, Walter, Wolcott, Farmer.
Murphy, Charles L., Remington, Farmer.
Myers, Oliver C., Brookston, Farmer.
Maxey, William, Booneville, Farmer, transferred to Co. I, 161st Ind., from Co. M, 159th Ind., Dec. 1, 1898.
McConnell, John F., Evansville, Clerk, transferred to Co. I, 161st Ind., from Co. M, 159th Ind., Dec. 1, 1898.
Miller, Reverdy J., Bloomington, Laborer, transferred to Co. I, 161st Ind., from Co. H, 159th Ind., Dec. 4, 1898.
Netzel, William, Medaryville, Laborer.
Pettit, William, Monticello, Laborer.
Reynolds, Elmer E., Monticello, Farmer.
Rogers, Alva J., Monon, Farmer.
Rinier, Edward L., Hopedale, Farmer.
Sheets, Samuel H., Monon, Farmer.
Shide, Frank, Remington, Farmer.
Simons, Walter A., Monticello, Student.
Smith, Bruce W., Goodland, Laborer.
Sorrel, Perry H., Rensselaer, Harnessmaker.
Stanley, Melvin, Monon, Farmer.
Strebe, Edward, Brookston, Blacksmith.
Tanguy, William E., Logansport, Printer.
Tharpe, Walter C., Rensselaer, Farmer.
Tharpe, Wilber, Rensselaer, Teacher.
Thompson, Wilber L., Monon, Railroader.
Tice, Stephen E., Goodland, Farmer.
Ward, James A., Monticello, Student.
Whitted, Elmer, Francisville, Painter.
Wood, Oliver H., Remington, Farmer.
Young, Harrison, Roachdale, Farmer.

DISCHARGED BY ORDER.

Shaull, Henry A., private, Lochiel, Farmer, discharged per

ONE HUNDRED AND SIXTY-FIRST INDIANA. 315

Special Order No. 6, War Department, Adjutant General's Office, Jan. 6, 1899.
Rourke, John P., private, Monon, Tailor, discharged per Special Order No. 16, War Department, Adjutant General's Office, Jan. 18, 1899, order dated Jan. 30, 1899.
Henry, Hiram, private, Monticello, Farmer, discharged Jan. 24, 1899, per Special Order 21, War Department, Adjutant General's Office.
McDaniels, George A., wagoner, Battle Ground, Farmer, discharged per Special Order No. 26, War Department, Adjutant General's Office, dated Feb. 1, 1899.
Newton, James B., private, LaFayette, Laborer, discharged Jan. 30, 1899, per Special Order dated Feb. 4, 1899.
Brooks, Edward E, private, Logansport, Laborer, discharged. per Special Order 29, War Department, Adjutant General's Office, Feb. 4, 1899.

TRANSFERRED.

Scott, Franklin G., Goodland, Carpenter, transferred to United States Volunteer Hospital Corps, per Special Order No. 10, dated August 20, 1898.
Dexter, Jacob W., Goodland, Carpenter, transferred to United States Volunteer Hospital Corps, per Special Order No. 10, dated August 20, 1898.
Tharpe, Walter A., musician, Remington, Teacher, transferred to United States Voluntser Signal Corps Dec. 10, per Special Order 282, Adjutant General's Office, dated Nov. 30, 1898.
Engle, Walter M., Francisville, Electrician, transferred to United States Volunteer Signal Corps Dec. 31, 1898, per Special Order 291, Adjutant General's Office, dated Dec. 10, 1898.

DIED OF DISEASE.

Kuns, Clarence D., Brookston, Barber, died Sept. 24, at Third Division Hospital o' typhoid fever, Camp Cuba Libre, Fla.

Stivers, Wallace D., Corp., Rensselaer, Farmer, died at Third Division Hospital, of typhoid fever, Camp Cuba Libre, Fla., Oct. 14, 1898.

Kepperling, George, Chalmers, Farmer, died Oct. 28, at Chalmers, Ind., while on furlough.

Weaver, William G., Monticello, Farmer, died in Second Division Hospital, Camp Onward, Ga., Nov. 7, 1898, of stomach trouble.

Turner, Joseph F., San Pierre, Blacksmith, died in Division Hospital, Camp Onward, Ga., Nov. 30, 1898, of pneumonia.

COMPANY F.

PAUL COMSTOCK.

Captain Paul Comstock is the son of Judge D. W. Comstock, of the Appellate Bench of Indiana. He was born at Richmond, Indiana, in the year 1873. After his early training he spent one year in the Oxford Military Naval Academy, at the close of which he entered the Richmond high school, graduating in 1891; his education was then finished in the Earlham College and the Ohio Wesleyan University. Mr. Comstock was then tendered a position in the general superintendent's office of the Pennsylvania Railroad Company at Columbus, and later in the engineering department at Indianapolis, in which position he continued until April, 1898, when he was appointed claim agent for the same road, in which service he was engaged when he enlisted for the war. Mr. Comstock was elected first lieutenant of his company and was for several months adjutant of the Second Battalion and upon the resignation of Captain Smith was promoted to the position of captain, April 1, 1899.

CAPTAIN PAUL COMSTOCK.

ELMER E. KIMMEL.

Second Lieutenant Elmer E. Kimmel, "Old Kim," as he was familiarly known, is the son of Charles F. and Catherine S. Kimmel, sturdy German stock. The father, a veteran of the Civil war, following the desires of his heart to give his first son a good name, remembered an illustrious officer who was among the first to give up his life for the union, Colonel E. Elmer Ellsworth, and called the son, born to him, August 3, 1874, Elmer Ellsworth Kimmel. Educated in the public schools of his native city, Dayton, Ohio, at the early age of thirteen, he began the struggle of life. The start was made as a cash boy at one dollar and a half per week, but not having a liking for mercantile

SECOND LIEUTENANT ELMER E. KIMMEL.

business finally drifted into book binding, at which trade he served a full apprenticeship. While following this trade he drifted into Richmond, Indiana, in June, 1894, adopting Hoosierdom as his chosen home; while here the desire came for a more complete education and having a favorable opportunity of working his way through Earlham, a Quaker college, he spent two years at that institution, from which place he enlisted as a member of the Richmond company and was commissioned second lieutenant, which office he filled until the resignation of Captain Will M. Smith, when promoted to the first lieutenancy. It is the intention of Lieutenant Kimmel to enter Ann Arbor University, taking up medicine as a special study.

WILLIAM H. DRAPIER.

Second Lieutenant Drapier's life has been spent in the city of Indianapolis, in which place he was born in 1869,

SECOND LIEUTENANT WILLIAM H. DRAPIER.

and in the public schools of which he received his education, graduating from the high school in 1887. After graduation Mr. Drapier embarked in the insurance business and there continued until the breaking out of the Spanish-American war. He enlisted with Company F as a private and was rapidly advanced through the line of promotion to the position of second lieutenant of the company. Mr. Drapier's promotion was due to his efficient and excellent military training, having served several years in various capacities in the Indiana National Guard.

HISTORY OF COMPANY F.

Richmond, the "Quaker City," is generally quiet, but when the news came of the blowing up of the Maine it woke up. Several enterprising young men, about four or five, who desired a captain's commission started a company, but as the city did not have a military company, she must wait for the second call before being represented in the army of the United States. Interest waned until the company organized by Will M. Smith was alone in the field. This company was at first intended to be an artillery company, and besides drilling in infantry drill quite a number of the men purchased old French bayonets, almost two feet long, and practiced the saber drill. We had free access to a large hall, and the gas company, with true patriotism, furnished the light gratis. The company met two nights each week, and after drilling a short time in the hall would drill around the court house square. In the meanwhile another company was organized, and for a time there was intense rivalry as to which company would be called upon after the second call came and it was known that Wayne county would have one company in the state quota.

Company F.

During the latter part of June it was daily expected that the call would come from the governor to come to Indianapolis. The signal agreed upon was for the large

CAPTAIN WILL M. SMITH.

manufacturing concerns to blow their whistles. Friday, June 24, the governor telegraphed who was to be the examining surgeon—Dr. Weist, a veteran of the Civil war, and at 4 P. M. the whistles gave the discordant alarm and the boys left their work benches, dropping their tools and hastened to the room in the Westcott hotel, where the news was read to them, telling them to be in readiness. Saturday and Sunday was spent in medical examinations, and Monday we expected to go to the state capitol; instead we were ordered to await further orders. Something must be done, as many had come in from the country and neighboring cities, expecting to leave Monday, and others having left their work would become impatient. Glen Mills, a natural park situated on the eastern side of Richmond, was decided would be a good place for a temporary camp, and

Sergeants, Company F.

procuring permission from the city to use it we went into camp Monday afternoon of the 24th of June. The dancing pavilion was used for sleeping and eating quarters. The first thing done was, each man carried an arm load of hay to sleep on, it being our first experience of the kind. The good people of Richmond subscribed liberally to procure food, and we did live in those days. We had guard mount every day, besides about four hours' drill every afternoon. We had free use of the boats on the lake, and were allowed the especial privilege of bathing in the lake. Great crowds came to see us drill, and here we lived and in each one's memory there will ever live the jolly times of those fond days at Camp Ostrander, our first camp. Friday we marched through the city to the depot, where we bid our relatives and friends a sad farewell, for little did we know whether we would ever meet again or not, and three of our number returned not.

At 10:40 Friday, July 1, we left for Camp Mount, being the fourth company to report for duty; from here our history became a part of the regimental history.

COMPANY F ROSTER.

WILL M. SMITH, Captain--Resigned March 31, 1899; Greensburg, Ind., Electrical Engineer.
PAUL COMSTOCK, Captain—Promoted from 1st Lieutenant. April 1, 1899; Richmond, Ind., Claim Agent.
ELMER E. KIMMEL, 1st Lieutenant—Promoted from 2d Lieutenant April 1, 1899; Richmond, Ind., Student.
WILLIAM H. DRAPIER, JR., 2d Lieutenant—Promoted from Sergeant, April 1, 1899; Indianapolis, Ind., Broker.

SERGEANTS.

Martin, William, 1st Serg't, Richmond, Ind., Laborer, discharged Feb. 18, 1899.

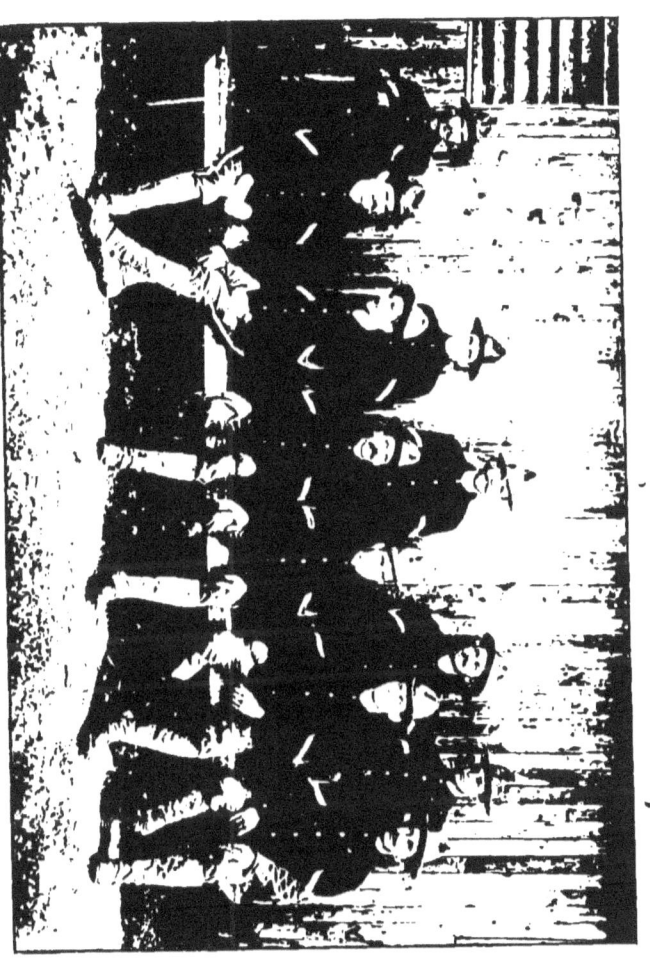

Corporals, Company F.

Moss, Abraham T., Eaton, Ohio, Machinist, discharged March 3, 1899.
Tawer, Oscar P., Jr., Richmond, Ind., Action Finisher, appointed Q. M. Serg't Jan. 17, 1899.
Edwards, Leroy, Richmond, Ind., Drayman.
Weissgerber, John C., New Castle, Ind., Salesman, discharged Jan. 16, 1899.
Keller, Frank, Richmond, Ind., Papermaker, appointed Corporal July 12, 1898; appointed Sergeant March 13, 1899.
Tawer, Paul O., Richmond, Ind., Florist, appointed Corporal July 12, 1898; appointed Sergeant March 13, 1899.
Sheppard, Henry W., Seymour, Ind., Florist, appointed Corporal July 12, 1898; appointed Sergeant March 13, 1899.

CORPORALS.

Bader, Charles O., Richmond, Ind., Student.
Kuhlman, Charles O., Richmond, Ind., Plumber.
Petry, Harvey C., Fountain City, Ind., Laborer.
Arnett, Willis W., Richmond, Ind., Laborer.
Steele, John J., Richmond, Ind., Printer, appointed Corp. Aug. 20, 1898.
Handley, Albert E., College Corner, Ohio, Painter, appointed Corp. Aug. 20, 1898.
Addleman, John F., Whitewater, Ind., Laborer, appointed Corp. Sept. 1, 1898.
Weissgerber, Frank H., New Castle, Ind., Florist, appointed Corp. Oct. 18, 1898.
Bode, Frederick, appointed Corp. March 13, 1898.
Stratton, Roy O.

MUSICIANS.

Foard, William G., Richmond, Ind., Clerk.
Muye, George, Richmond, Ind., Machinist.

WAGONER.

Hennigar, Gilbert S.. Richmond, Ind., Blacksmith, appointed Wagoner Jan. 18, 1899.

ARTIFICER.

Hennigar, Harry, Richmond, Ind., discharged March 11, 1899.

COOK.

Higgs, George, Richmond, Ind., Carpenter.

PRIVATES.

Addleman, Samuel C., White Water, Ind., Butcher.
Allen, Roy M., Liberty, Ind., Painter.
Allinder, William, Richmond, Ind., Machinist.
Bader, Robert S., Richmond, Ind.
Brown, Denver, W. Manchester, Ohio, Farmer, died in Jacksonville, Fla., Oct. 23, 1898.
Bucy, Charles E., Indianapolis, Ind., Polisher.
Caseley, John E., Richmond, Ind., Machinist, discharged Feb. 23, 1899.
Cassel, Walter H., Richmond, Ind., Machinist.
Clark, John W., Machinist.
Connaughton, John F., Machinist, discharged March 1, 1899.
Cook, Harry P., Richmond, Ind., Laborer.
Cook, Joseph R., Richmond, Ind., Operator.
Decker, Berttie E., Richmond, Ind., Painter.
DeVerse, Joseph E., Richmond, Ind., Papermaker, deserted Sept. 20, discharged without honors Nov. 3, 1898.
Dickerson, Benjamin F., Clymers, Ind., Laborer.
Dickey, Marshall D., Richmond, Ind., Painter.
Duke, James F., Richmond, Ind., Farmer.
Duke, William H., Richmond, Ind., Farmer.
Edwards, John, Richmond, Ind., Painter.
Elliott, Worley F., Richmond, Ind., Farmer.
Estep, William C., Richmond, Ind., Moulder.
Francis, John S., Metamora, Franklin Co., Ind., Printer.
Fudge, Rufus, Richmond, Ind., Printer.
Fossenkemper, Charles O., Glen Park, Richmond, Ind., Laborer.
Francis, George B., Indianapolis, Ind., Carpenter.
Granger, Herman E., DeMotte, Jasper Co., Ind., Carpenter.

Graham, Stephen R., Litchfield, Ky., Farmer.
Grice, Alonzo N., Richmond, Ind., Printer.
Haley, Jerry, Indianapolis, Ind., Lather.
Harmeyer, Harry, Richmond, Ind., Laborer.
Hassard, Richard B., Richmond, Ind., Polisher.
Henderson, Robert J., Lynn, Ind., Barber.
Hamilton, John, Indianapolis, Ind., discharged Feb. 7, 1899.
Hieger, William E., Richmond, Ind., Machinist, discharged Dec. 31, 1898.
Hites, John H., Richmond, Ind., Painter.
Hoar, John, Centerville, Ind., Farmer, transferred to Band Aug. 28, 1898.
Hollopeter, John, Richmond, Ind., Gr. Clerk.
Hollowell, Charles A., Danville, Ill., Actor.
Holtcamp, Charlie, Richmond, Ind., Boilermaker.
Horr, Argus O., Richmond, Ind., Machinist.
Hurst, Addison C., Richmond, Ind., Messenger.
Jarrett, Lilleton B., Cox Mills, Ind., Farmer.
Judy, Lista B., Laborer.
Kain, Harry F., Richmond, Ind., Laborer, died in Richmond, Indiana.
Kelly, Harry E., Richmond, Ind., Smith.
Lanius, Charles W., Richmond, Ind., Painter.
Loftus, Michael, Richmond, Ind., Coremaker.
Lovin, George E., Richmond, Ind., Weaver, discharged Feb. 24, 1899.
Morgan, Charles E., Buena Vista, Colo., Miner.
Mull, Albert, Carpenter.
Murray, Alden, Metamora, Ind., Printer.
Nolan, William, Richmond, Ind., Laborer, discharged Feb. 20, 1899.
Nye, Edward L., Prestonville, Ky., Clerk.
Pyle, John B. U., Mount Carmel, Ind., Saddler.
Reese, William, Hammond, Ind., Farmer, discharged Sept. 28, 1898.
Reckers, Henry J., Richmond, Ind., Laborer.
Rusche, Frank, Richmond, Ind., Carriage Trimmer

Ryder, Harry, Richmond, Ind., Machinist.
Stanley, Franklin B., Richmond, Ind., Gr. Clerk.
Snyder, William, Columbus, Ind., Laborer.
Sanders, John H., Richmond, Ind., Farmer.
Simpson, Walter, Richmond, Ind., Clerk.
Stegall, Everett E., Williamsburg, Ind., Blacksmith
Thomas, Harry J., Richmond, Ind., Teamster.
Thomas, Ira L., Richmond, Ind., Machinist.
Thompson, Joseph H., Richmond, Ind., Laborer.
Toler, George C., Richmond, Ind., Plumber.
Trakowski, Fred W., Richmond, Ind., Baker.
Trimble, Charles F., Richmond, Ind., Machinist, died at Camp Columbia, Cuba, Jan. 17, 1899.
Triplett, Harry N., Richmond, Ind., Farmer.
Vanzant, Charles E., Richmond, Ind., Laborer.
Weaver, Samuel J., Richmond, Ind., Teamster.
Woesner, William, Metamora, Ind., Farmer.
Wright, Silvester E., Lynn, Ind., School Teacher, transferred to Regimental Band, Aug. 28, 1898.
Yedding, Ferdinand, Richmond, Ind., Painter.
Zurwelle, George R., Cox Mills, Ind., Laborer.
Zurwelle, William S., Cox Mills, Ind., Gardener.

RECRUITED SINCE DAY OF MUSTER.

Burgan, Burton E., Terre Haute, Ind., Teamster, transferred from 159th I. V. I., Nov. 23, 1898.
Cline, Walter, Columbus, Ind., R. R. Fireman, appointed Corp. March 13, 1899.
Hill, John, Green Castle, Ind., Laborer, transferred from the 159th I. V. I., Nov. 23, 1898.
Lucas, Charles, Indianapolis, Ind., Masseuer, transferred from 159th I. V. I., Nov. 25, 1898.
Levy, Carl, Evansville, Ind., Moulder.
Metlin, Earl, Evansville, Ind., Bookkeeper, transferred from 159th I. V. I., Nov. 23, 1898.
Maxwell, Clifford C., Indianapolis, Ind., Clerk.
McCoy, Earl, Lawrence, Ind., Tile Moulder, appointed Corp.

March 13, 1899, transferred from 159th I. V. I., Nov. 28, 1898.

Shearer, Chester A., Terre Haute, Ind., Laundryman, transferred from 159th I. V. I.

Secrist, Leo, Terre Haute, Ind., Tinner, transferred from 159th I. V. I., Nov. 28, 1898.

Singler, George, Evansville, Ind., Baker, transferred from 159th I. V. I., Nov. 28, 1898.

COMPANY D.

RICHARD W. BUCHANAN.

Captain Richard W. Buchanan was one of the youngest officers of the regiment and was the youngest captain of the United States army in the recent Spanish war, born in Carrollton, Kentucky, June 28, 1879. His family moved to Madison, Indiana, when he was yet a child, where he was reared and where he received his early education, graduating from the Madison high school in 1896. At the close of his studies he became the city editor of the Madison Daily Democrat and afterwards associate editor of the Madison Daily Herald. He also corresponded for several metropolitan dailies and became well-known in newspaper circles. He so materially aided through his newspaper capacity in the organization of the Madison company that upon its acceptance he was elected to the position of second lieutenant. During the first days of camp life he acted as correspondent for the Indianapolis Journal, but finding it conflicting with his military duties he gave it up. Upon the resignation of Captain Cosby he was commisioned on the 8th of March as captain of his company.

Captain Richard W. Buchanan.

CYRUS A. JACKSON.

Prior to hostilities with Spain, Cyrus A. Jackson was the genial and obliging city superintendent of the Metropolitan Life Insurance Company, at Madison, Indiana. Mr. Jackson was elected first lieutenant of Company D, at the organization of that company. He assisted Chief McCullagh in the organization of the Metropolitan police force of the city of Havana, and distinguished himself by the capture of a burglar and desperado. Lieutenant Jackson

FIRST LIEUTENANT CYRUS A. JACKSON.

was born at Vincennes, Indiana, in 1865, educated in the public schools of his native city, and has spent the greater portion of his life in the far West.

LAYTON M. PARKHURST.

Second Lieutenant Layton M. Parkhurst entered Company D as a private, and was rapidly advanced through the line of promotion to first sergeant and was appointed second lieutenant of his company March 11, 1899. Mr. Parkhurst was born at Franklin, Indiana, October 14, 1876.

His parents dying when he was quite young, he made his home with his uncle at Lebanon, Indiana. After finishing

SECOND LIEUTENANT LAYTON M. PARKHURST.

the course of the schools of Lebanon Mr. Parkhurst engaged in the drug business at Lebanon until the outbreak of the war.

HISTORY OF COMPANY D.

Company D, of the One Hundred and Sixty-first Indiana, reported at Camp Mount for examination and muster in, on the 1st of July, 1898. But it must not be inferred that the Madison public nor the individual members of the

COMPANY D.

company, were so tardy in the offer of life and service for the nation as the mustering date of the regiment would indicate. Immediately upon the declaration of war a company was roughly organized in the "city neath the hills," but the claims of the rival leaders caused its partial disruption, a considerable number of the organizations combining with a similar faction from Roachdale to form a company in the One Hundred and Fifty-ninth. Upon the second call of the president for volunteers the disorganized and disheartened members came together, under the leadership of Captain Charles E. Cosby, and through the force

CAPTAIN CHARLES E. COSBY.

and persistency of patriotic fervor, secured from Governor Mount the approval which made their calling and election sure. The company moved to Indianapolis more than one

Sergeants, Company D

hundred strong. Not to be selfish, contingents were admitted to its ranks from Seymour, North Vernon and Bedford. Through the ordeal of examination, a high standard of physique and intelligence was maintained in the leadership of the body. Captain Cosby was sustained by Lieutenants Cyrus A. Jackson and Richard W. Buchanan. It fell to the lot of Company D to be quartered in one of the horse barns at the fair grounds; to the use of the commissioned officers was assigned the apartments once occupied by Star Pointer; the appointments, however, were too commodious for soldiers, so much so, that the boys were glad to be transferred to the canvas camp.

The thousand and one laughable incidents which marked the apprentice period of Company D, in common with other companies, lose their point in telling. Out of the confusion of this period, organization and soldierly discipline were gradually attained. At Jacksonville, the company suffered considerably from the climate; uncertainty to the future, dread lest it might be their lot to go home without having seen service, lowered the spirits of the men. In camp at Savannah, the town was more cheerful, the prospect was definite. No man in the company will ever cease to prize his experience in setting foot on Cuban soil, and no man in the company can fail to be thankful that old "D" had not quite entered San Lazarus street in the city of Havana at the supreme moment when our flag went up over Morro Castle, for each man was thus permitted to witness the transfer of empire. Reviewing all its experiences while on the island, Company D feels that it was very fortunate, favored in health, in pleasant camp site and in privileges to see and enjoy. Soon after the promotion of Lieutenant Richard W. Buchanan to captaincy, Company D became the color company and guide of the regiment.

CORPORALS, COMPANY D.

COMPANY D ROSTER.

CHARLES E. COSBY, Captain—Resignation tendered Feb. 8, 1899, accepted Feb. 25, 1899.
RICHARD W. BUCHANAN, Captain—Promoted from 2d Lieut. March 9, 1899.
CYRUS A. JACKSON. 1st Lieutenant.
LAYTON W. PARKHURST, 2d Lieutenant—Promoted from 1st Serg't March 10, 1899.

SERGEANTS.

Ferguson, W. Scott, 1st Serg't, Canaan, Ind., Engineer, appointed 1st Serg't March 15, 1899.
Taylor, John S., Q. M. Serg't, Hanover, Ind., Farmer, mustered as Q. M. Serg't.
Huckleberry, Silas D., North Vernon, Ind., Student, mustered as Serg't.
Carter, Everett, Seymour, Ind., Clerk, mustered as Serg't.
Griffith, Ulysses J., Vevay, Ind., Law Student, promoted to Corp Sept. 11, 1898, promoted to Serg't Dec. 9, 1898.
Stoner, Henry, Brightwood, Ind., Bookkeeper, promoted to Corp. Aug. 20, 1898, promoted to Serg't March 15, 1899.

CORPORALS.

Jeffries, John, Madison, Ind., Miller, mustered as Corp.
Rayborn, William E., Canaan, Ind., Farmer, mustered as Corp.
Vawter, Charles D., Madison, Ind., Traveling Salesman, promoted to Corp. Aug. 20, 1898.
Oliver, Samuel, Madison, Ind., Laborer, promoted to Corp. Aug. 20, 1898.
Sayers, Robert M., Madison, Ind., Stenographer, mustered as Corp.
Wheeler, Cale K., Evansville, Ind., Patternmaker, transferred to Co. D from Co. E, 159th Ind., Nov. 23, 1898, promoted to Corp. Dec. 9, 1898.

Burroughs, Elmer, Mt. Sterling, Ind., Farmer, promoted to Corp. Dec. 9, 1898.
Miles, Gus E., North Vernon, Ind., Carpenter, promoted to Corp. March 15, 1899.
Thorpe, Charles A., Cartersburg, Ind., Laborer, promoted to Corp. March 15, 1899.
Neal, DeCourcy, Brooksburg, Ind., Farmer, promoted to Corp. March 15, 1899.
Herring, William, Pleasant, Ind., Farmer, promoted to Corp. March 15, 1899.

MUSICIANS.

Harper, John E., Pleasant, Ind., Farmer, mustered as Musician.
Brownscombe, Chas. W., Bedford, Ind., Paper Hanger, transferred to Co. D, 161st Ind., from Co. H, 159th Ind., Nov. 28, 1898, appointed Musician Dec 7, 1898.

ARTIFICER.

Loyd, Joseph W., Versailles, Ind., Carpenter, mustered as Artificer.

WAGONER.

Riedel, Ronald H., Zion, Ind., Farmer, mustered as Wagoner,

COOK.

Ivor, Charles N., Canaan, Ind., Cook, mustered as Cook Dec. 2, 1898.

PRIVATES.

Abbott, Harrison, Madison, Ind., Laborer.
Adams, George W., Guthrie, Ind., Laborer.
Arnold, Edward, Vernon, Ind., Laborer.
Ballard, Martin, Madison, Ind., Laborer.
Bassett, Robert S., Versailles, Ind., Laborer.
Blue, Arther, Seymour, Ind., Tailor.
Bucy, Leander, Brightwood, Ind., Railroader.
Casey, Ashby, Madison, Ind., Cook.
Chambers, Clarence B., Kent, Ind., Farmer.
Clarkson, Andrew J., Madison, Ind., Laborer.

ONE HUNDRED AND SIXTY-FIRST INDIANA.   341

Coryell, Charles, Hayden, Ind., Farmer.
Crain, Gilbert D., Evansville, Ind., Student, transferred to Co. D, 161st Ind., from Co. E, 159th Ind., Nov. 23, 1898.
Davis, Chester, North Vernon, Ind., Student.
Dowlen, Henry, Bedford, Ind., Clerk.
Dugan, William M., Indianapolis, Ind., Tool Grinder.
Evans, Harry O., North Vernon, Ind., Laborer, transferred to Co. D, 161st Ind., from Co. G, 159th Ind., Nov. 23, 1898.
Foster, Charles, North Vernon, Ind., Laborer.
French, Emanuel, Indianapolis, Ind., Farmer.
Frooks, James, Madison, Ind., Riverman.
Gaussin, Clarence C., Bedford, Ind., Clerk.
Gilligan, Joseph, Faulkner, Ind., Farmer.
Griffin, Harvey, Canaan, Ind., Farmer.
Grubbs, Wilkerson E., Madison, Ind., Cabinetmaker.
Hagan, Robert E., Canaan, Ind., Salesman.
Haukins, James, Madison, Ind., Laborer.
Hargrove, Benjaman R., North Vernon, Ind., Clerk.
Harper, Charles E., Pleasant, Ind., Farmer.
Harrison, Thomas, Bee Camp, Ind., Farmer.
Hatcher, John H., Vincennes, Ind., Cutter, transferred to Co. D, 161st Ind., from Co. L, 159th Ind., Nov. 23, 1898.
Henderson, Arthur, Seymour, Ind., Farmer.
Henderson, Charles C., Seymour, Ind., Railroader.
Hill, William, Seymour, Ind., Clerk.
Hoskins, John W., Evansville, Ind., Clerk, transferred to Co. D, 161st Ind., from Co. E, 159th Ind., Nov. 23, 1898.
Hyatt, William, Madison, Ind., Steamboating.
Jackson, Hiram, China, Ind., Farmer.
Jenkins, William E., Madison, Ind., Ship Carpenter.
King, Otto, North Vernon, Ind., Laborer, transferred to Co. D, 161st Ind., from Co. G, 159th Ind., Nov. 23, 1898.
Lawler, Roy, North Vernon, Ind., Laborer.
Lostetter, George, Madison, Ind., Spoke Turner.
Lunger, Isaac, Madison, Ind., Laborer.

Mathew, James, North Vernon, Ind., Laborer.
Matthews, John H., Manville, Ind., Farmer.
Matthews, Aubrey E., McGregor, Ind., Farmer.
McGee, George, Madison, Ind., Laborer.
Metz, Fred, Versailles, Ind., Laborer.
Parsons, Elmore O., Madison, Ind., Laborer.
Prather, John K., Seymour, Ind., Egg Packer.
Ray, Wesley M., Bloomington, Ind., Farmer, transferred to Co. D, 161st Ind., from Co. H, 159th Ind., Nov. 23, 1898.
Rea, Harvey, Haney's Corner, Ind., Farmer.
Redman, Roland E., Bedford, Ind., Baker.
Reininga, William C., Ingelfield, Ind., Farmer, transferred to Co. D, 161st Ind., from Co. E, 159th Ind., Nov. 23, 1898.
Ricketts, Clarence, Vevay, Ind., Farmer.
Riley, David, Reddington, Ind., Farmer.
Robinson, Riley, Seymour, Ind., Clerk.
Ruth, Andy, Lawrenceville, Ill., Farmer, transferred to Co. D, 161st Ind, from Co. A, 159th Ind., Nov. 23, 1898.
Scanlan, Charles J., Seymour, Ind., Clerk.
Schwab, Frank, North Madison, Ind., Laborer.
Shepherd, Harry B., Dupont, Ind., Clerk.
Skinner, William A., Indianapolis, Ind., Clerk.
Spannagel, Joseph, North Vernon, Ind., Farmer.
Sthiar, Harry, Gosport, Ind., Laborer, transferred to Co. D, 161st Ind., from Co. H, 159th Ind., Nov. 23, 1898.
St. John, Joseph, Hayden, Ind., Farmer.
Strang, Morton O., North Vernon, Ind., Clerk.
Strickland, Lafe, North Vernon, Ind., Teamster.
Teepe, Ernest J., North Vernon, Ind., Student.
Thompson, William E., Bedford, Ind., Railroader.
Vandemore, Oris, North Vernon, Ind., Laborer.
Vawter, John S., Madison, Ind., Laborer.
Weed, Charles, Bedford, Ind., Laborer.
Welch, Homer M., Seymour, Ind., Laborer.
Whitaker, Albert L., Wilmore, Ky., Laborer.

Wilson, Charles S., Madison, Ind., Broommaker.
Whitaker, James K., Cloverdale, Ind., Cutter, transferred to Co. D, 161st Ind., from Co. H, 159th Ind., Nov. 23, 1898.
Wray, Millard, Clear Spring, Ind., Farmer.

DISCHARGED.

Gilbert, William B., Priv., Madison, Ind., Weaver, Aug. 21, 1898.
Euler, Nelson C. B., Priv., North Vernon, Ind., Painter, Sept. 13, 1898.
Groub, John C., Corp., Seymour, Ind., Clerk, Sept. 19, 1898.
Barnes, Walter, Priv., Anderson, Ind., Tinsmith, Jan. 3, 1899.
Boeglin, Louis, Corp., Bryantsburg, Ind., Farmer, Jan. 12, 1899.
Lostetter, Rudolph, Priv., Madison, Ind., Spoke Grader, Jan. 20, 1899.
Ferris, William, Corp., Lancaster, Ind., Miller, Jan. 31, 1899.
Hufford, Raymond H., Corp., Cartersburg, Ind., Farmer, March 15, 1899.
Jackson, Mathew, Priv., Seymour, Ind., Clerk, March 7, 1899.
Hawkins, John S., Priv., Ghent, Ky., Clerk, March 7, 1899.
Myres, William, Priv., Madison, Ind., Laborer, March 21, 1899.

DEATHS.

Sebree, John A., Priv., Ghent, Ky., Laborer, Oct. 14, 1898.
Green, Frank M., Priv., North Vernon, Ind., Steelworker, Nov. 3, 1898.
Graham, Alonzo N., Priv., Lancaster, Ind., Farmer, Jan. 24, 1899.

TRANSFERRED.

Logan, Michael M., Corp., Bryantsburg, Ind., Iron Roller, Aug. 20, 1898, Hospital Corps.
Renfroe, Marcus D., Corp., Canaan, Ind., Farmer, Aug. 20, 1898, Hospital Corps.

Dale, Wesley, Priv., North Vernon, Ind., Farmer, Aug. 20, 1898, Hospital Corps.
White, Harry K., 1st. Serg't, Dalton, N. Y., Traveling Salesman, Sept. 8, 1898, U. S. Vol. Signal Corps.

THIRD BATTALION

C, G, H, L.

MAJOR LEE M. OLDS.

LEE M. OLDS.

Major Lee M. Olds, one of the youngest majors in the volunteer service, is the son of Judge Olds, of Chicago, a former chief justice of the supreme court of the state of Indiana, and who was a Union soldier in the Civil war. Major Olds boasts a remarkable ancestry of volunteer soldiers who did good service in the colonial wars, in the war of Revolution and of 1812, as well as the late rebellion.

He was born at Columbia City, Indiana, October 21, 1874. He spent a few years at Wabash College, and then entered the Michigan Military Academy at Orchard Lake, from which institution he graduated in 1893. Immediately upon graduation he entered the Northwestern University, where he took a course in the classics, and later a thorough course in the law department of that university. He was president of the Chicago Law Students' Association, an organization of twenty-four hundred students of all law schools of the city. After completing his studies he practiced his profession simultaneously in Chicago and Hammond in the firm of Olds & Griffin, of which his father is senior partner.

Major Olds entered the service as captain of a company from Hammond, and by his military aptitude and hard practice brought his men to the enviable position of Company A. On September 9, 1898, Colonel Durbin commanding the brigade, Captain Olds was in command for months of the First Battalion, and upon the resignation of Major Peterson was appointed by Governor Mount to the majorship of the Third Battalion. His commission was presented by Colonel Durbin at regimental parade December 1, 1898, and on the evening of the same day the young officer was mustered as major by Major Longstreet.

Major Olds is a born soldier and commander; his appearance is commanding and his voice military to a finish. The young officer has borne his honors well.

COMPANY C.

THOMAS J. HUDGINS.

Captain Thomas J. Hudgins was born in Franklin county, Tennessee, October 22, 1859. His parents moved to Indiana in 1867. He attended school at Morristown Seminary, Morristown, Indiana; accepted a position with C., H. & D. R. R. in 1878, then to P., C., C. & St. L. R. R. in 1880, remaining with the Pennsylvania Company until 1884, then accepting a position with Big Four Railroad at Indianapolis; accepted position as general agent of the Big Four at Shelbyville, Indiana, November 14, 1888, and at the outbreak of the Spanish-American war organized a company at Shelbyville, Indiana, and tried to get the company accepted for first call for volunteers. The Big Four railroad granted Captain Hudgins two years' leave of absence and on his return his old position or a better one will be given him. Captain Hudgins, being the senior captain of the Third Battalion, was in command of the battalion the greater part of the time from August 14 to November 30, 1898. Captain Hudgins was married in 1882, and has one child, Leslie P. Hudgins.

The Captain's parents live at Morristown, Indiana, and his only brother, Robert H. Hudgins, Jr., was quartermaster sergeant for Company C.

Captain Thomas J. Hudgins.

GEORGE E. GOODRICH.

George E. Goodrich, first lieutenant, Company C, One Hundred and Sixty-first Indiana Volunteer Infantry, was born in Brandywine township, Shelby county, Indiana, at the old family homestead, April 6, 1872. He moved to Shelbyville with his parents in 1880. His forefathers originally came from Scotland, and knew the hardships of pioneer days in the states. His grandfather, George Goodrich, for whom he was named, was a veteran of the Mexican war. Three uncles also served in the Union army in the Civil war, one being killed in the battle of Peach Tree Creek. The surviving two are now residents of Shelbyville and Shelby county. On graduating from school,

FIRST LIEUTENANT GEORGE E. GOODRICH.

Lieutenant Goodrich assumed the management of Blessing's opera house, the only theater in Shelbyville, but resigned from the management near the close of his second successful season, in January, 1894, to accept a position on the reportorial staff of the Shelbyville Daily Democrat, edited by the late W. Scott Ray, one of the best known Indiana editors of his day. The position had been vacated by Edward A. Major, appointed postmaster of Shelbyville during President Cleveland's second tenure in office. During Lieutenant Goodrich's connection with the Democrat he served three years in the Indiana National Guard as first sergeant of Company K, Second Regiment, commanded by Colonel Ross. He continued with the Democrat until the second call for volunteers to serve in the Spanish-American war was made by President McKinley, in May, 1898, when he secured a leave of absence from his duties the following month to enlist in the company then being recruited at Shelbyville, and departed with the company for Camp Mount, July 2. Having been previously elected first lieutenant by the members of the company, he was mustered into the service as such on July 11, 1898, and commissioned by Governor Mount on July 20, 1898, and appointed adjutant of the Third Battalion by a regimental order a few days later. Lieutenant Goodrich is a member of Kiowa Tribe, No. 199, I. O. R. M., of Shelbyville.

IVY LESTER REYNOLDS.

Second Lieutenant Ivy Lester Reynolds was born in Franklin, Johnson county, Indiana, September 18, 1876, and in 1881 removed to Shelbyville, Indiana, with his parents He was educated in the public schools of Shelbyville, at the age of fourteen entered the employment of the Shelby Printing Company as carrier and collector, and later attached himself to C. Steinhauser, watchmaker and jeweler, at Shelbyville, to learn the art of watchmaking. Serving three and a half years there, he went to Indianapolis to complete his trade with Dyer & Matsumoto, manufacturing jewelers,.and later with Ikko Matsumoto, which position he filled much to the satisfaction of his employer, until in the fall of 1897, when he opened a shop at No. 49 Public Square, Shelbyville, and was favored with much success, closing up the business to enlist with the company under Captain Hudgins.

Under direction of Captain Clayton, Ivy Lester Rey-

SECOND LIEUTENANT IVY LESTER REYNOLDS.

nolds captained a company of boys brigade at the Christian church of Shelbyville, a few years later enlisted in Company K, of the Indiana National Guard, under Captain J. R. Clayton, serving two years of his enlistment, when, on going to Indianapolis, was transferred to Company A, Second Regiment Indiana National Guard, Captain H. C. Castor, in which company he rapidly received promotion from the rank of lance-corporal to second lieutenant in twenty-three months. During the service with Company A he participated in several prize drills at Indianapolis at the state fair gounds. Upon returning to Shelbyville, in 1897, he organized, drilled and uniformed the Rex Zouaves, a company which became very proficient in fancy military drills and was always a public favorite. He also commanded Company C a number of weeks at Jacksonville and Savannah during the time when Captain Hudgins commanded the Third Battalion in the absence of Major M. R. Peterson.

Upon arriving in Cuba Mr. Reynolds, with St. C. A. Jackson, was called to General Ludlow's staff and assigned to the police department as military instructor and inspector of police of the city of Havana, they receiving many high compliments as a result of diligent work.

HISTORY OF COMPANY C.

The trials, tribulations and vicissitudes attendant upon the organization and acceptance of Company C into the service were many and varied. To begin with, Captain Hudgins, an ardent supporter of the project then actively engaged in the political affairs of Shelbyville, was compelled to meet the accusation of a local newspaper of opposite political proclivities to the effect that the project was a political intrigue to induce certain voters to accompany him (Captain Hudgins) to some point not yet decided upon, and by keeping them out of the city until after election day, thus occasion them the loss of their votes. Nothing daunted by the assertion thus made, the captain persisted in his work of recruiting the company; an interesting feature of the final organization, being that one of his accusers, then on the reportorial staff of the paper in question, was not only won over to the captain's way of thinking but afterwards became one of the active supporters of the project and eventually a commissioned officer in the company. The first meeting relative to the proposed organization was held in the city council chamber.

Early in April, 1898, other meetings followed, with the result that when the first call for volunteers was made, later in the month, its services were offered in response. Not discouraged at its failure to be accepted, new quarters were sought in the armory of the old militia company, in the service of the Indiana National Guard, from April, 1894, to April, 1897, and drills vigorously continued. Not until after the second call for volunteers was made by direction of President McKinley, during the latter part of May, were the officers of the company formally elected by the members of the organization, although it was generally understood who they were to be. Renewed interest was now taken in the drills, which occurred nightly. Then came the crushing information that no new regiments would be mustered into the service, but that the additional volunteers, designated in the call for seventy-five thousand troops, would be used to recruit the regiments already in the field up to the full war strength, one hundred and six enlisted men. For a time the fate of the company wabbled in a balance, due to the "desertion" of a large number of recruits of the company to the organizations of the various branches of the service then in the field. This but served to strengthen the determination of those who "stuck to the old ship." To recruit the organization to its former strength with the result that when another regiment became an assured fact and the preliminary examination of the men was begun by Dr. J. W. Bowlby, designated by the governor to perform the duties, the influx of recruits was so great that for a few days it was necessary to provide

COMPANY C.

for their maintenance by going into camp at the fair grounds of the Shelby County Joint Stock Agricultural Association. To this project the citizens of Shelbyville responded most liberally in the donation of supplies, and a handsome cash balance was given the company, the net proceeds of a festival and bazar given under the supervision of about thirty of Shelbyville's best known young ladies. This was followed by a reception tendered the company by the Epworth League of the First Methodist Episcopal church, of Shelbyville, in the parlors of that edifice. A deplorable accident occurred just following the receipt of the information that the services of the company would be accepted. It having been agreed upon that Strong's Light Artillery, an organization within the Sons of Veteran's Encampment, of Shelbyville, should be the first to herald the information, on the day of its receipt they repaired to a spot just beyond the city limits, and while engaged in firing a specified number of volleys a premature discharge of their piece, an old cannon used in the Civil war, resulted in the loss of an arm to Warren Haehl and a mutilated hand to Wilber Smith, members of the battery. The departure of the company for Camp Mount, on July 2, was the occasion of a demonstration witnessed only in times of war, when home ties are broken and the pride of a household takes his departure from home and friends, probably never to return. The scene with its attendant incidents are best portrayed in the following clipping from the Shelbyville Republican, of that date:

"The company of which Thomas J. Hudgins is captain, George E. Goodrich, first lieutenant, and I. L. Reynolds, second lieutenant, finished its recruiting last evening and this morning marched in from the fair ground. Mechanic street was decorated from Vine to Harrison and as the boys marched along the people cheered them along. Harri-

Non-Commissioned Officers, Company C.

son street to the public square was decorated and the square and East Washington street to the station was almost a mass of flags. As the company neared the square they were met by the colored boys' "drum" corps. On the south side of the square the company was joined by the Grand Army of the Republic, the Strong Light Artillery and the Rex Zouaves, The column being formed with the Grand Army men at the post of honor, the Modern Woodman band in the lead, the march was taken up to the station. Washington street was simply a mass of people, the boys being given an ovation they will never forget. Warren Haehl, who lost his arm last week, was propped in bed and placed at the window so he could see the procession and as it passed it cheered and cheered and cheered. The recognition brought tears to the eyes of many. Two cars were on the side track in waiting, but the crush of people was so great that it was some minutes before the cars could be reached. When the doors were finally opened the soldier boys filed in and their friends after them. The jam was simply a crush. Women and strong men cried; mothers embraced their sons, sisters clung to their brothers and sweethearts made no attempt to check their tears. Hundreds and hundreds of people crowded along the cars to shake the hands of the boys and to give them a word of encouragement and advice. All this time the band was playing, the drums were beating and the Sons of Veterans were firing a salute.

"As the train that was to carry the boys away entered the city, the factory whistles that had been blowing a perfect salvo during the morning, greeted the train with a welcome blast that was continued until the train was out of the city. After the usual stop at the station it required but a few minutes for the train to back down and take on the two extra cars. In another minute, the air being filled

ONE HUNDRED AND SIXTY-FIRST INDIANA. 359

with cheers, the waving of flags, handkerchiefs, the blasts of the whistles and the sound of musketry "Shelbyville's first company in the war against Spain started for the front —a brave, gallant set of boys."

The company, together with its friend, Hon. Sidney Conger, arrived at Camp Mount shortly after ten o'clock, having been tendered an ovation at all the villages along the route, and were immediately quartered in barn H. In the physical examination that followed over one hundred and twenty men met the requirements, a sufficient number were retained to recruit the company to its full war strength, one hundred and six enlisted men; the remainder were transferred to other companies not having the required number of men. The company was mustered into the service on the eveniug of July 11, being among the first to be thus administered the oath of allegiance. A few days later the company was presented with a handsome flag by a delegation of ladies and gentlemen of the Ladies Relief Corps, an auxiliary of Dumont Post No. —, G. A. R., of Shelbyville, representing the citizens of that city. The presentation speech was made in the presence of the company by Mr. John Byers, a veteran of the Civil war, and was feelingly responded to by Captain Hudgins. The corp itself gave to each member of the company a comb, whisk broom, towels, etc. This was followed a few days later by the presentation of a copy of the New Testament to each of the officers and men by Rev. L. A. Gould, of the First Baptist church, representing the churches of Shelbyville. The company's departure for Jacksonville, Florida, on August 11, was made the occasion of a monster demonstration in Shelbyville by reason of the fact that the special trains conveying the regiment passed through the city *via* the Big Four route.

It is safe to assert that three-fourths of the citizens of

Shelbyville, blocked the streets for squares in all directions, bands played, salutes were fired and other tokens of the high esteem in which the company is held were manifest. During the stay of the regiment at Camp Cuba Libre, Company C suffered considerably from the prevailing maladies, and many of the sick men were compelled to succumb and go to the hospital, a great many never to rejoin their command. Being left behind at the time of the removal of the regiment to Savannah, Georgia, they were scattered in the various hospitals throughout the country and recovering from their illness were mustered out of the service after the regiment was sent to Cuba. During the interval when the sickness at Camp Cuba Libre was most marked, the relatives and friends of the boys at home forwarded by express a large amount of palatable delicacies and nutritious food best suited for the use of the ailing. The removal of the troops to Camp Onward marked a gradual improvement in the health of the company. This was also true of the period spent at Camp Columbia, Havana, when the general health was excellent. During its career in the service not a single death occurred in Company C, and during their entire stay in Cuba, with the exception of four or five days following their arrival, the company was on detached service as a special guard at General Lee's corps headquarters, and rejoined the regiment on its march to the docks to embark on the United States transport "Logan," homeward bound.

COMPANY C ROSTER.

THOMAS J. HUDGINS, Captain, Shelbyville, Ind.
GEORGE E. GOODRICH, 1st Lieut., Shelbyville, Ind.
IVY L. REYNOLDS, 2d Lieut., Shelbyville, Ind.

SERGEANTS.

Maddox, Robert C., 1st. Serg't, Shelbyville, Ind., Drug Clerk, discharged Nov. 19, 1898.
Parkison, Moses A., Shelbyville, Ind., Cabinetmaker, promoted to 1st Serg't Nov. 19, 1898.
Hudgins. Robt. H., Jr., Q. M. Serg't, Shelbyville, Ind., Telegrapher.
Hopkins, John S., Hariford, Maryland, Painter.
Ballard, Walter B., Shelbyville, Ind., Clerk.
Miles, Con L., Shelbyville, Ind., Furnisher, discharged March 31, 1899.
Dickman, Joseph, Shelbyville, Ind., Upholsterer, promoted from Corp. to Serg't Dec. 3, 1898, discharged January 27, 1899.
Alexander, Earl, Indianapolis, Ind., Pressman, promoted Serg't from Corp. Feb. 7, 1899.
Wilson, Major, Shelbyville, Ind., Clerk, promoted Serg't from Corp. April 5, 1899.

CORPORALS.

Kuntz, Mathias, Shelbyville, Ind., Harnessmaker.
Vanarsdall, Elmer, Shelbyville, Ind., Farmer, promoted to Corp. Jan. 25, 1899.
Davis, Edwin F., Workland, Ind., Stationary Engineer.
Ray, John T., Hope, Ind., Farmer.
Matthews, James G., Shelbyville, Ind., Farmer, discharged Dec. 22, 1899.
Vanpelt, Downey, Shelbyville, Ind., Clerk.
Dale, George H., Jamestown, Ind., School Teacher, promoted to corporal Feb. 7, 1899.
Goodrich, Charles, Shelbyville, Ind., Painter, promoted to Corporal Feb. 12, 1899.
King, William F., Shelbyville, Ind., Cabinetmaker, appointed Corporal October 31, 1898.
Law, Eugene E., Shelbyville, Ind., Welldriller, promoted to Corp. Aug. 1, 1898.

Leffler, Fay, Shelbyville, Ind., Upfitter, appointed Corp. Dec. 8, 1898.
Oaks, Bert, Edinburg, Ind., Finisher, appointed Corp. Dec. 8, 1898.
Roemerman, Chris., Shelbyville, Ind., Factory Hand, promoted to Corp. Aug. 8, 1898, Jan. 14, 1899.
Wiles, Miller, Shelbyville, Ind., Varnisher, promoted to Corp. April 5, 1899.

MUSICIANS.

Michelsen, William A., Shelbyville, Ind., Barber.

ARTIFICER.

Moore, Wiley F., Shelbyville, Ind., Blacksmith, transferred from Artificer to Musician, Aug. 8, 1898.

WAGONER.

Cummins, Walter, Indianapolis, Ind., Fireman, discharged Nov. 4, 1898.

PRIVATES.

Beard, Otto, Shelbyville, Ind., Farmer, discharged Feb. 6, 1899.
Bounsall, William H., Unionville, N. Y., Painter, discharged Jan. 30, 1899.
Byers, John, Shelbyville, Ind., Polisher.
Carson, Arthur, Shelbyville, Ind., Painter, assigned company cook Feb. 21; 1899, relieved as cook April 10, 1899.
Chesser, Marshall, Winterowd, Ind., Carpenter, made artificer Aug. 8, 1898.
Chueden, Albert, Shelbyville, Ind., Painter, reduced to ranks Aug. 8, 1898.
Clark, Harry, Indianapolis, Ind., Barber.
Collins, William, Shelbyville, Ind., Machinist, discharged Jan. 26, 1899.
Comstock, John, Shelbyville, Ind., Plasterer.
Cooper, John, Shelbyville, Ind., Metalworker, assigned company cook April 10, 1899.

Cosler, Curtis, Shelbyville, Ind., Bicycle Polisher, discharged Feb. 6, 1899.
Cutsinger, Henry, Shelbyville, Ind., Engineer.
Dale, August M., Jamestown, Ind., Farmer.
Davis, Larue, Shelbyville, Ind., Cabinetmaker.
Dickman, John, Shelbyville, Ind., Clerk.
Didlein, Herman A., Indianapolis, Ind., Bookkeeper.
Ditsch, Frank, Indianapolis, Ind., Textile Worker.
Ebner, Edward, Indianapolis, Ind., Varnishmaker.
Ellis, Fred, Anderson, Ind., Lather, appointed Wagoner Oct. 31, 1898.
Evans, John, Shelbyville, Ind., Painter, discharged Feb. 15, 1899.
Feaster, Ora, Shelbyville, Ind., Bandsawyer.
Feaster, Wilber, Shelbyville, Ind., Machine hand.
George, Horace, Indianapolis, Ind., Plumber.
Gregg, Charles E., Indianapolis, Ind., Waiter, deserted Sept. 10, 1898, discharged without honor Nov. 4, 1898.
Hietand, John F., Shelbyville, Ind., Farmer.
Hendrickson, True, Shelbyville, Ind., Farmer, discharged Feb. 27, 1899.
Hilt, Henry, Shelbyville, Ind., Farmer.
Itce, John, Shelbyville, Ind., Gardener.
Johnson, Camden A., Oakland, Ind., Farmer, discharged Jan. 11, 1899.
Johnson, George S., Shelbyville, Ind., Farmer.
Jolliff, Finley, Flatrock, Ind., Farmer.
Kelly, Austin U., Indianapolis, Ind., Waiter.
Lane, Harry, Shelbyville, Ind., Finisher.
Law, George, Shelbyville, Ind., Farmer, discharged Jan. 14, 1899.
Louden, Charles A., Shelbyville, Ind., Clerk.
Ludwig, John M., Indianapolis, Ind., Laborer.
Madden, Charles H., Indianapolis, Ind., Bookkeeper, discharged March 21, 1899.
Mitchell, Charles, Shelbyville, Ind., Farmer.

Mott, Charles G., Shelbyville, Ind., Laborer, deserted Oct. 16, 1898.
Morris, Leroy, Shelbyville, Ind., Painter, discharged Jan. 25, 1899.
Omsted, Edward, Edinburg, Ind., Laborer.
Osborn, William, Mount Vernon, Ind., Wood Turner.
Parrish, George W., Shelbyville, Ind., Hardwood Finisher.
Perkins, Omer E., Rushville, Ind., Farmer.
Perry, Andrew J., Shelbyville, Ind., Farmer, discharged Feb. 2, 1899.
Perry, Howard, Lawrence, Ind., Teamster.
Palmer, Marshall, Fairland, Ind., Farmer, discharged March 20, 1899.
Prosser, Ora, Indianapolis, Ind., Laborer.
Price, Ira J., Shelbyville, Ind., Farmer.
Roberts, William, Shelbyville, Ind., Clerk, discharged May 4, 1899.
Roth, Robert, Shelbyville, Ind., Clerk.
Runyon, James, Shelbyville, Ind., Laborer.
Rupert, Frank, Shelbyville, Ind., Farmer.
Stittsworth, Ora, Louisville, Ind., Farmer.
Schacherer, Louis, Shelbyville, Ind., Factory Hand.
Schumaker, William, Sunman, Ind., Merchant.
Shipley, George, Indianapolis, Ind., Painter.
Simms, Thomas, Shelbyville, Ind., Teamster.
Sieg, John, Flatrock, Ind., Farmer, deesrted Dec. 10, 1898.
Sims, Everet, Indianapolis, Ind., Tinner.
Smith, John A., Shelbyville, Ind., Laborer.
Spice, Arthur, Huntington, Ind., Glassworker.
Southern, Harry J., Indianapolis, Ind., Moulder, deserted Sept. 8, 1898, discharged without honor Nov. 21, 1898.
Steely, John, Indianapolis, Ind., Machinist, discharged Aug. 19, 1898.
Titus, Joseph R., Winterowd, Ind., Carpenter, discharged at Winterowd, Ind., March 1, 1899.
Towns, Arthur, Shelbyville, Ind., Mechanic.

Vaught, Fred, Shelbyville, Ind., Mechanic, discharged Sept. 29, 1898.
Wheeler, Jerry, Shelbyville, Ind., Farmer.
Westerfield, Commodore, Manilla, Ind., Engineer.
Wiles, Robert, Jr., Shelbyville, Ind., Finisher.
Wilson, William W., Shelbyville, Ind., Cabinetmaker, discharged Feb. 17, 1899.
Williams, James A., Shelbyville, Ind., Farmer, discharged March 16, 1899.
Winterowd, Floyd, Indianapolis, Ind., Laborer.
Woods, George, Smithland, Ind., Farmer.
Worland, Frank, Shelbyville, Ind., Gardener.
Worland, Maurice, Shelbyville, Ind., Plumber.
Wycoff, Oscar, Edinburg, Ind., Laborer.
Youngman, Leon E., Shelbyville, Ind., Carpenter.

LATER ENLISTMENTS.

Molder, William, Shelbyville, Ind., Furnituremaker, enlisted Aug. 9, 1898.
Vanpelt, George W., Shelbyville, Ind., Clerk, enlisted Aug. 10, 1898.
Kloer, Arthur, Terre Haute, Ind., Clerk, enlisted Dec. 9, 1898.

TRANSFERRED.

Hamm, Michael, Vincennes, Ind., Butcher, transferred from Co. A, 159th Ind. Vol. Inf., Dec. 1, 1898.
Kopp, John G., Evansville, Ind., Barber, transferred from Co. E, 159th Ind. Vol. Inf., Dec. 1, 1898.
Burke, John, Vincennes, Ind., Student, transferred from Co. L, 159th Ind. Vol. Inf., Dec. 1, 1898.
McCrisaken, James, Vincennes, Ind., Butcher, transferred from Co. L, 159th Ind. Vol. Inf., Dec. 1, 1898.
Soden, Charles, Vincennes, Ind., Laborer, transferred from Co. L, 159th Ind. Vol. Inf., Dec. 1, 1898.
Coats, William T., Shelbyville, Ind., Student, transferred from Co. K, 161st Ind. Vol. Inf., Jan. 26, 1899.

COMPANY G.

ALBERT D. OGBORN.

Captain Albert D. Ogborn was born on a farm in Wayne county, Indiana, in 1864, and spent the first eighteen years of his life there. He was educated in the common schools, graduating therefrom at thirteen. In January, 1883, he removed to Newcastle and worked for a firm

CAPTAIN ALBERT D. OGBORN.

dealing in farm implements and later for a dealer in shoes. During this time he educated himself as a stenographer. In November, 1887, he was appointed storekeeper of the Northern Indiana Hospital for Insane at Logansport. He gave up this position in April, 1889, to accept that of official shorthand reporter for the judicial circuit in which he resides. While a court reporter he found time to study law. He was admitted to the bar in 1894, and is now practicing law in connection with court reporting. He has been deeply interested in military affairs from boyhood, and for ten years before entering the army was an enthusiastic worker in the Uniform Rank Knights of Pythias. He is colonel of the Third Indiana Regiment in this organization, having been granted an unlimited leave of absence to enter the army. Captain Ogborn is unmarried.

JAMES I. MEYERS.

First Lieutenant James I. Meyers first saw light in Wells county, Indiana, in September, 1864. He was educated at the schools of the city of Bluffton. He learned the baker's trade and followed it for several years. In 1887 he removed to Newcastle and was engaged in the restaurant business there when he entered the army. He received the practical knowledge of things military possessed by him when he enlisted, in the Uniform Rank, Knights of Pythias; and resigned the captaincy of Newcastle company in that organization when he became a soldier. He is married and has a fine family of three children.

First Lieutenant James I. Meyers.

CHARLES M. PITTMAN.

Second Lieutenant Charles M. Pittman was born in Newcastle, in 1874, and was educated in the schools of that city, graduating from the high school in 1892. While in school he was agent for a city newspaper, the daily edition of which he delivered to his patrons. For a time after leaving school he was engaged with his father in the farm machinery business. Later he began the study of civil engineering and was engaged in the practice of that profession when he entered the army. He lives with his parents and is unmarried.

SECOND LIEUTENANT CHARLES M. PITTMAN.

HISTORY OF COMPANY G.

In the Civil war Henry county sent as many soldiers to the front as any county in Indiana in proportion to its population; and one of them, the venerable, William Grose, came back a major-general. The bravery and patriotism of these men, proven on a hundred battlefields, descended to their sons. When the Spanish students tore down the American flag in Barcelona in 1895, Captain Ogborn sent the following message to Governor Matthews: "If Spain insists upon being whipped, I desire a commission to raise

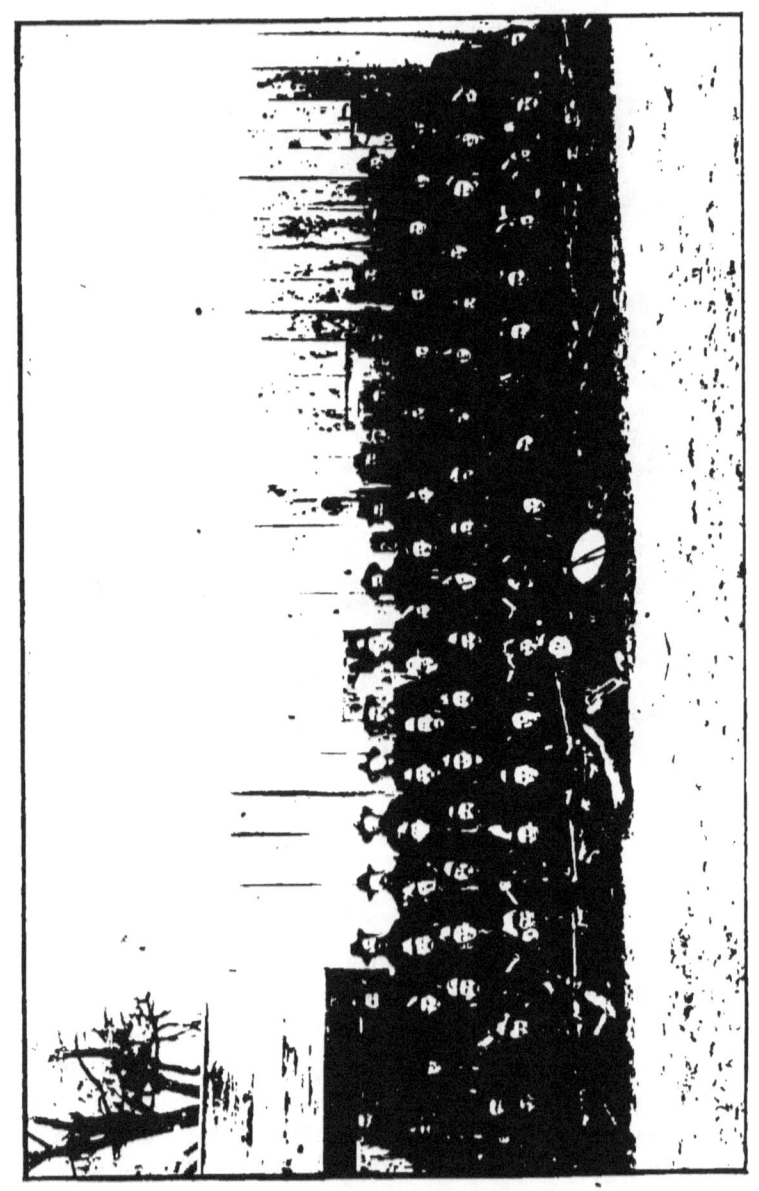

Company G.

a company in Henry county to help to do it." When the Maine was destroyed he again tendered his services to Indiana's governor, believing that war was inevitable. Before the formal declaration of war and afterwards he begged the governor to accept his services in any capacity in which they might be thought useful.

When the first call for volunteers was made many young men of Henry county went to Indianapolis and tried to get in the service, some of them succeeding; among them was Lieutenant Charles W. Pittman. Believing that a second call would be made, and that if it were, a company could get in from Henry county, Captain Ogborn and Lieutenant Myers began to organize a company in anticipation thereof, and were afterward joined by Lieutenant Pittman. One hundred and thirty names were enrolled, a majority from Newcastle, the remainder all from Henry county; drilling was kept up in the face of long delay, and the quiet opposition of the "Peace at any price" element. Young men who drilled faithfully were sneered at by apron string slaves, too lazy and too cowardly to enlist or drill. The turning point was reached one night in June, when the ears of a small band of the faithful who were drilling in the street were greeted by the "Rogues March" whistled by some one in a barber shop; the squad was wheeled and lined up along the sidewalk, and a demand made for the offender. He finally admitted his identity; and was warned that it would not be safe for him or any other person to ridicule any one who had enlisted in the company. From that hour the tide was with the volunteers.

When the company was finally ordered to appear for their preliminary examination, to their shame be it said, over thirty of the men enlisted showed the white feather; ten of the remainder, including some of the best fellows

SERGEANTS, COMPANY G.

alive, were rejected, some other good men yielded to the entreaties of their families and withdrew. In this emergency the captain turned to Muncie, from where an eloquent appeal for opportunity to enlist had come from First Sergeant Fred W. Puckett. He and about thirty other Delaware county men, including as good soldiers as ever wore the blue, were finally accepted and have done much to make the fine record of the company what it is. When the examinations begun, committees of patriotic citizens arranged for the entertainment of the men, and during the four days which elapsed before the company started for Indianapolis did everything possible to make them comfortable. The examinations began at 10 o'clock A. M. on June 27th, and ended at 1 P. M. on the 29th. The captain telephoned the governor that he had one hundred and nine men accepted by the local surgeon.

On the morning of July 1st, every business house in the city was closed and a great crowd gathered in the public square where patriotic speeches were made by leading citizens and some of the orators in the company. Each man was given a slight token of the friendship of the citizens of New Castle. A great procession, headed by a band and composed of the G. A. R. Post, Uniform Rank Knights of Pythias and hundreds of citizens, escorted the company to the station, and the train bearing it left the city followed by the cheers of five thousand people who had assembled there.

The sincere goodwill of the citizens of New Castle toward the company was further shown by their presentation to each of the three officers of a handsome sword.

The company was the fourth to arrive at Indianapolis and the first one ready to be mustered. It was mustered in on July 12, 1898.

CORPORALS, COMPANY G.

COMPANY G ROSTER.

ALBERT D. OGBORN, Captain, New Castle.
JAMES I. MEYERS, 1st Lieutenant, New Castle.
CHARLES M. PITMAN, 2nd Lieutenant, New Castle.

SERGEANTS.

Puckett, Fred W., 1st Serg't., Muncie, Ind., Medical Student, mustered as private July 27, 1898, appointed 1st Serg't Aug. 1, 1898.
Owens, Charles B., Franklin, Ind., Grocer.
Engle, T. William, Indianapolis, Ind., Printer, transferred to Hospital Corps U. S. A, Aug. 20, 1898.
Welsbacher, John, Meadville, Pa., Glass Blower.
Martin, Albert O., Muncie, Ind., Dental Student, mustered as Corp. July 12, 1898, appointed Serg't Mar. 20, 1899.
Eilar, Benjamin W., Newcastle, Ind., Bridge Builder, appointed Corp. Dec. 20, 1898, appointed Serg't Feb. 17, 1899.
Luther, E. Murray, Q. M. Serg't., Blountsville. Ind., Clerk, mustered as Corp. July 13, 1898, appointed Q. M. Serg't Dec. 22, 1899.

CORPORALS.

Keesling, Ray, Mechanicsberg, Ind., Clerk.
McKimmey, Linley W., Muncie, Ind., Engineer.
Elliott, George H., Mechanicsburg. Ind., Well Driller.
Fadely, Joseph H., Honey Creek, Ind., Farmer.
Gontner, Charles R., Muncie, Ind., Salesman.
Baldwin, Ellwood L., Spiceland, Ind., Farmer.
Nugent, Harry S., Kennard, Ind., Editor.
Allen, Alonzo, Muncie, Ind., Bartender, transferred to Hospital Corps, U. S. Army, Aug. 20, 1898.
Goddard, Joseph, Middletown, Ind., Glass Blower, appointed Corp. Dec. 20, 1898.
Gaddis, Max P., New Castle, Ind., Cook, appointed Corp. Dec. 29, 1898.

Shellenbarger, Charles, Muncie, Ind., Laborer, appointed Corp. Feb. 17, 1899.
Robinson, Elmer, Franklin, Ind., Laborer, appointed Corp. Mar. 20, 1899.
Baxley, Robert F., Princeton, Ind., Laborer, transferred from 159th I. V. I., Dec. 1, 1898, and appointed Corp. Dec. 29, 1898.

MUSICIANS.

VanDyke, Henry W., Lewisville, Ind., Blacksmith, discharged Mar. 17, 1899.
Beeson, Edward, Dalton, Ind., Farmer.

ARTIFICER.

Hutchens, Huston, New Castle, Ind., Mechanic.

WAGONER.

Livezey, Oscar, Newcastle, Ind., Farmer.

COOK.

Snider, Daniel Vorhees, Muncie, Ind., appointed Company Cook Oct. 10, 1898.

PRIVATES.

Akers, Joseph, Middletown, Ind., Glassblower, discharged Feb. 6, 1899.
Barnett, Guy, Newcastle, Ind., Plasterer.
Barnes, Henry, Muncie, Ind., Finisher.
Bock, Claud, Newcastle, Ind., Laborer.
Brown, Roy W., Newcastle, Ind., Drum Major, transferred to band Aug. 27, 1898.
Buckley, Guy, Newcastle, Ind., Laborer.
Canaday, James, Newcastle, Ind., Laborer.
Cecil, Fred P., Muncie, Ind., Student.
Darling, Alva, Spiceland, Ind., Farmer.
Darnell, Harry C., Indianapolis, Ind., Student.
Davenport, Frank N., Newcastle, Ind., Painter.

Detrich, George Carlos, Muncie, Ind., Bottler, discharged Sept. 28, 1898.
Dolan, John, Cambridge City, Ind., Fireman, transferred to Hospital Corps, U. S. Army, Aug. 20. 1898.
Faulkner, Henry, Muncie, Ind., Laborer, discharged Jan. 13, 1899.
Filson, James Leroy, New Lisbon, Ind., Sawyer.
Fisher, Frank W., Newcastle, Ind., Ball Player.
Frazee, Walker, Byers, Ohio, School Teacher.
Freeman, Perry, Muncie, Ind., Laborer.
Freeland, Thomas, New Lisbon, Ind., Farmer.
Foster, Frank, Spiceland, Ind., Farmer.
Goodman, Bud, Muncie, Ind., Laborer.
Hale, Frank, Springport, Ind., Farmer.
Hale, Thomas T., Dublin, Ind., Farmer.
Halfaker, Edgar B., Franklin, Ind., Blacksmith, discharged Aug. 22, 1898.
Hamilton, Frank M., Newcastle, Ind., Dentist.
Hamilton, Benton F., Greensboro, Ind., Clerk.
Hanna, John W., Ft. Worth, Texas, Laborer.
Harper, Charles, Indianapolis, Ind., Ironworker.
Hickman, Herbert H., Springport, Ind., Farmer, discharged Mar. 13, 1899.
Holton, Hoyt A., Indianapolis, Ind., Printer, discharged Jan. 12, 1899.
Huddleston, Arthur A., Dublin, Ind., Tinner.
Irwin, George, New York City, N. Y., Broommaker.
Israel, William G., Franklin, Ind., Farmer.
Jackson, Solomon, Franklin, Ind., Laborer.
Lamb, Oltie F., Dalton, Ind., Blacksmith.
Lane, Fred, Mooreland, Ind., Farmer.
Leech, J. Morris, F., Muncie. Ind., Decorator, transferred to Hosp. Corps Aug. 20, 1898.
Leonard, John M., Muncie, Ind., Wheelworker.
Leonard, Arthur, Muncie, Ind., Rougher.
Lykens, Sebastian, Spiceland, Ind., Laborer.
McCoy, Charles, Muncie. Ind., Bricklayer.

McCoy, Clarence, Muncie, Ind., Laborer, discharged Sept. 27, 1898.
Martin, Henry C., Jr., Muncie, Ind., Laborer, discharged Feb. 17, 1899.
Martindale, George, Hagerstown, Ind., Photographer.
Miller, James W., New Castle, Ind., Clerk.
Mitchell, Lemuel, Middletown, Tinplateworker.
Morgan, Cliff, Greensburg, Ind., Farmer.
Netz, Charles, Ashland., Ind., Farmer.
Newby, Otis, Greensboro, Ind., Miller.
Newby, George W., Greensboro, Ind., Farmer.
Nichols, Noah A., Honey Creek, Ind., Jockey.
Paul, John J., Muncie, Ind., Glassworker.
Pierson, Joseph M., Muncie, Ind., Laborer, discharged Dec. 22, 1898.
Prager, James M., Seattle, Wash., Prospector, transferred to Hosp. Corps, U. S. A., January 9, 1899.
Rawlins, Winfield, Byers, Ohio, Mining.
Reece, Benjamin F., Muncie, Ind., Wheelworker.
Rogers, Paul, Muncie, Ind., Hatter, mustered as 1st Serg't July 12, 1898, by his own request was reduced to ranks July 31, 1898.
Rothbaust, Jesse, Franklin, Ind., Laborer, discharged Feb. 8, 1899.
Sears, Walton D., Spiceland, Ind., Laborer.
Sherer, Albert, Muncie, Ind., Laborer.
Shuee, Edward C., Muncie, Ind., Laborer.
Swaim, Clarence T., Dublin, Ind., Clerk.
Sweezy, John, Franklin, Ind., Laborer.
Wahl, John, Indianapolis, Ind., Laborer.
Walden, Edgar Otis, Muncie, Ind., Glassworker.
Wilmuth, Arthur, Kennard, Ind., Laborer.
Wilson, John W., Muncie, Ind., Glassworker.
Winnings, Mark, Ashland, Ind., Laborer.
Winnings, Walter A., Ashland, Ind., Laborer.
Wintersteen, Minor, New Castle, Ind., Farmer.

Wolfe, Edwin, Mooreland, Ind., Laborer, discharged Feb. 10, 1899.
Woods, Harry, Dublin, Ind., Farmer.
Yates, Ira O., Middletown, Ind., Laborer, discharged March 17, 1899.

LATER ENLISTMENTS.

Green, Oscar, Muncie, Ind., Machinist, mustered Aug. 8, 1898.
King, Fred C., Muncie, Ind., Carpenter, mustered Aug. 8, 1898.
Reynolds, Clyde B., Hagerstown, Ind., Farmer, mustered Aug. 8, 1898, discharged Jan. 19, 1899.
Sheller, Charles, Muncie, Ind., Carpenter, mustered Aug. 8, 1898.
Sherman, William A., Middletown, Ind., Laborer, mustered Aug. 8, 1898.
Armstrong, John L., Princeton, Ind., Farmer, transferred from 159th I. V. I., Dec. 1, 1898.
Hogue, Edward H., Princeton, Ind., Laborer, transferred from 159th I. V. I., Dec. 1, 1898.
Malone, Clarence A., Princeton, Ind., Butcher, transferred from 159th I. V. I., Dec. 1, 1898.
Robinson, Floyd W., Larwell, Ind., Machinist, transferred from 159th I. V. I., Dec. 1, 1898.
Newsum, Fred B., Patoka, Ind., Miner, transferred from 159th I. V. I. Dec. 1, 1898.
Turnage, George W., Princeton, Ind., Laborer, transferred from 159th I. V. I., Dec. 1, 1898; discharged Feb. 8, 1899.
Warren, Benjamin F., Evansville, Ind., Farmer, transferred from 159th I. V. I. Dec. 1, 1898.
Wolfe, Walter G., Evansville, Ind., Blacksmith, transferred from 159th I. V. I. Dec. 1, 1898.
Taylor, Eugene B., Carmi, Ill., Mechanic, transferred from Regimental Band Dec. 22, 1898.

COMPANY H.

JAMES M. GWINN.

Captain James M. Gwinn was born at Burlington, Carroll county, Indiana, in 1847. He gave up completing his education to enter the Civil war, enlisting in July, 1863,

CAPTAIN JAMES M. GWINN.

as a private in the One Hundred and Sixteenth Indiana, from which he was discharged the March following. In December, 1864, he re-enlisted in the Forty-sixth Indiana, and was mustered out September 4, 1865. He participated in five engagements during his term of service, the principal ones of which were Bull's Gap, Tazewell and Walker's Ford. After the war he farmed for a time, but for the last twenty years has been engaged in the livery business at Rushville.

HENRY B. PATTON.

Henry B. Patton, first lieutenant Company H, was born near Spring Hill, Decatur county, Indiana. His youth was spent on the farm. At an early age he removed with his parents to Rush county, where he has since

First Lieutenant Henry B. Patton.

resided. He attended the common schools near his home and afterward attended DePauw University, graduating with the class of '94. He served as deputy clerk of the Rush circuit court for three years, resigning his position to accept a commission as second lieutenant. When the regiment went to Camp Cuba Libre he was appointed aide-de-camp to General L. F. Hubbard, commanding Third Division, Seventh Army Corps, serving in that capacity until the division was abolished, pending General Hubbard's retirement, when he was returned to his company. He was commissioned first lieutenant August 28, 1898, vice John F. Joyce, resigned.

GEORGE H. CALDWELL.

George H. Caldwell, second lieutenant Company H, One Hundred and Sixty-first Indiana Volunteer Infantry, is a native of Rushville, Indiana. His boyhood and early manhood were spent on a farm near that city. He was educated in the common schools and at the age of seventeen was licensed as a teacher, which pursuit he followed for two years. At the expiration of that time and for ten years following he was employed as a clerk in a dry goods store at Rushville. For a number of years since that time he has acted as a traveling salesman in the same line. He enlisted in Company H as a private, but was appointed first sergeant at the final organization at Indianapolis. On August 28th he was commissioned second lieutenant by the governor of Indiana to fill a vacancy caused by the resignation of Lieutenant Joyce. He is a Republican in politics and a member of Ivy Lodge No. 27, Knights of Pythias.

Second Lieutenant, George H. Caldwell.

COMPANY H HISTORY.

Company H was organized at Rushville by Captain Gwinn and Lieutenant Joyce, who had each previously raised companies and tried to secure recognition on the first call for volunteers. Realizing that it would be necessary to combine their forces in order to secure recognition, the companies were united, Lieutenant Joyce agreeing to accept second place in consideration of Captain Gwinn's previous service.

The company at once began drilling, and having been

COMPANY H.

assured of a place in the new regiment to be organized, it went into camp at the fair grounds on June 20th, remaining there ten days until ordered to Camp Mount, being the first one to arrive there. It was mustered into the service on July 12, 1898. It is composed principally of Rush county men, although quite a number of other counties throughout the state are represented, the principal one being Fayette.

COMPANY H ROSTER.

GWINN, JAMES M., Captain—Rushville, Ind., Liveryman.
JOYCE, JOHN F., 1st Lieutenant—Rushville, Ind., Lawyer; resigned; resignation accepted Aug. 30, 1898, at Jacksonville, Fla., ill health.
PATTON, HENRY B., 1st Lieutenant—Richland, Ind., Clerk, promoted from 2d Lieutenant Sept. 8, 1898.
CALDWELL, GEORGE H., 2d Lieutenant, Rushville, Ind., Farmer, promoted from 1st Sergeant Sept. 10, 1898.

SERGEANTS.

Caldwell, Joseph J., Rushville, Ind., Watchman.
Comstock, Charles E., Lyons, Iowa, Druggist.
Hunt, Geston P., Orange P. O., Clerk.
Wolfe, Charles E., Rushville, Ind., Musician.
Stiers, Edgar, Richland, Ind., School Teacher.
Ailes, Jesse W., Stipps Hill, Ind., Farmer, promoted to Corp. Aug. 28, 1898, promoted to Serg't Dec. 31, 1898.
Beale, Fred R., Rushville, Ind., Tailor, promoted to Corp. Dec. 27, 1898, promoted to Serg't Jan. 4, 1899.

CORPORALS.

Felts, Jacob D., Rushville, Ind., Cabinetmaker.
Gross, Fred, Manilla, Ind., Clerk.
Wertz, Harrison E., Arlington, Ind., Farmer.
Johnson, Riley, Richland, Ind., Farmer.

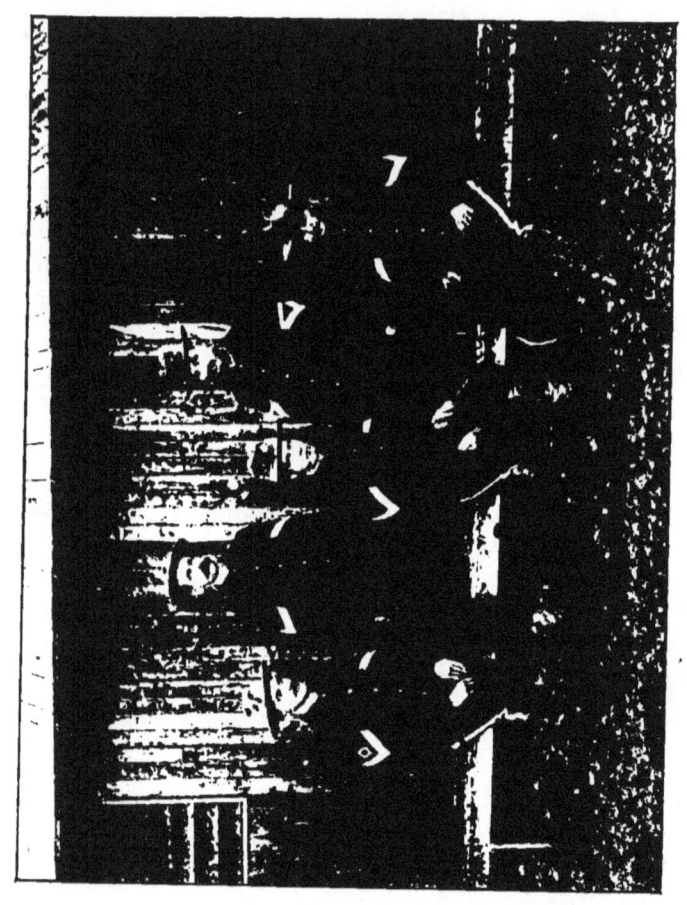

SERGEANTS, COMPANY H.

Innis, John W., Rushville, Ind., Aeronaut, transferred to U. S. Vol. Signal Corps Dec. 1, 1898, per order Adjutant General's office
Alexander, Fred., Rushville, Ind., Telegrapher, promoted to Corp. Dec. 27, 1898.
Caldwell, Robert G., Rushville, Ind., Student, promoted to Corp. Jan. 26, 1899.
Gardner, William E., Rushville, Ind., Farmer, promoted to Corp. Aug. 16, 1898.
Gilson, James, Rushville, Ind., Laborer, promoted to Corp. Jan. 26, 1899.
Hall, Harry H., Connersville, Ind., Clothing Clerk, promoted to Corp. Oct. 1, 1898.
Harry, Vernie, Richland, Ind., Farmer, promoted to Corp. Aug. 23, 1898.
McCoy, Michael P., Rushville, Ind., Turner, promoted to Corp. Dec. 27, 1898.
Pearsey, Chase, Rushville, Ind., Heading Worker, promoted to Corp. Dec. 27, 1898.
Vieke, Edward C., Corporal, Vincennes, Ind., Cigarmaker, promoted to Corp. Dec. 27, 1898, transferrrd from 159th Ind. Vol. Inf., Nov. 23, 1898.

MUSICIANS.

Huffman, Edward, Rushville, Ind., Musician, transferred to to 161st Reg. Band Aug. 23, 1898.
Middleton, Basil, Connersville, Ind., Cabinetmaker.
Jameson, Jesse K., Rushville, Ind., Blacksmith.

WAGONER.

Miller, Charles, Rushville, Ind., Laborer.

PRIVATES.

Adams, James F., Rushville, Ind., Cook.
Allenthorp, Ira, Arlington, Ind., Student, transferred to 161st Reg. Band Aug. 23, 1898, transferred back to Co. Dec. 22, 1898.

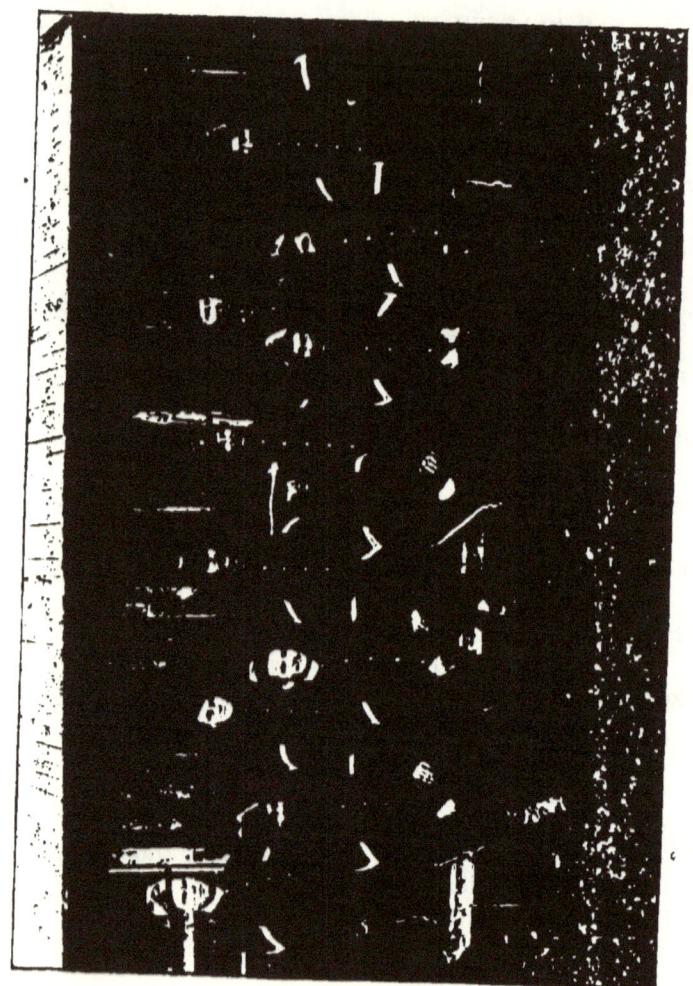

Corporals, Company H.

Armstrong, John H., Rushville, Ind., Artist.
Armstrong, Joseph A., Jr., Rushville, Ind., Telegrapher, transferred to U. S. Vol. Signal Corps Sept. 8, 1898, per order Adjutant General's office.
Baylor. Frank C., Rushville, Ind., Clerk.
Baker, Arthur, Rushville, Ind., Laborer,
Ball, William H., Rushville, Ind., Machinist.
Bartlett, Orville, Rushville, Ind., Tinner.
Boling, George W., Rushville, Ind., Printer.
Bowne, Owen O., Rushville, Ind., Table Waiter, discharged by order Maj.-Gen. Lee, Sept. 27, 1898, for disability.
Brown, Leslie B., Richland, Ind., Farmer.
Burdock, Harry, 76 Clarkson St., New York City, N. Y., Mechanic.
Cassady, Rue, Rushville, Ind., Laborer.
Cauley, Anthony B., Rushville, Ind., Machinist.
Davis, Harry W., Rushville, Ind., Laborer.
Devers, Bert L., Rushville, Ind., Farmer.
Emmons. Harrie E., Rushville, Ind., Horseman.
Fox, Bert, Arlington, Ind., Painter, discharged by order Maj.-Gen. Lee Feb. 10, 1899, for disability.
Francis, Fred. C., 68 Blaine ave., West Indianapolis, Ind., Tinner.
Gable, Clyde C., Ind'anapolis, Ind., Bedmaker, died in Ft. McPherson, Ga., Hospital, Nov. 3, 1898, of typhoid fever, body interred at Union City, Ind.
Geiger, Ira E., Rushville, Ind., Printer.
Glass, John, Rushville, Ind., Farmer.
Glisson, Will, Connersville, Ind., Painter.
Graves, Fred, Thorntown, Ind., Student.
Greenlee, Earl, Rushville, Ind.
Guire, Jesse W., Rushville, Ind., Drayman.
Hambrock, Charles E., Manilla, Ind., Farmer.
Hatfield, John W., Rushville, Ind., Laborer.
Heaton, Clarence, Muncie, Ind., Laborer, transferred to 3rd Div. Hospital Corp, Aug. 20, 1898.
Hilligoss, Oscar R., Rushville, Ind., Farmer.

Hoffner, Charles S., Connersville, Ind., Painter.
Holder, George, Connersville, Ind., Woodcarver.
Jester, Cheniah F., Rushville, Ind., Sawyer.
Jones, George B., Rushville, Ind., Physician, appointed Hospital Steward Sept. 10, 1898.
Kenner, Ralph H., Rushville, Ind., Farmer.
Klingworth, William, Rushville, Ind., Painter.
Lindsay, Charles F., Price Hill, 3789 Warsaw ave., Cincinnati, Ohio, Painter.
Lohrman, Walter, Indianapolis, Ind., Cabinetmaker.
Levi, Harry C., Rushville, Ind., Laborer.
McClain, Clinton, Rushville, Ind., Laborer.
McCrory, Fred, Rushville, Ind., Farmer.
Marvin, Buford, Rushville, Ind., Farmer.
Mathews, Charles M., Rushville, Ind., Laborer.
Miller, Clint M., Arlington, Ind., Barber.
Mitchell, William T., Rushville, Ind., Drop-forger.
Moore, Thomas C., Rushville, Ind., Veneer Layer.
Mootz, Fredric, 1517 S. Reisner St., West Indianapolis, Ind., Baker.
Morford, Irwin, Anderson, Ind., Farmer.
Myers, Will, Connersville, Ind., Machinist.
Newbor, Charles A., Clarksburg, Ind., Horseman.
Newman, William G., Rushville, Ind., Poultry Dresser.
Norris, Frank, Rushville, Ind., Farmer.
O'Day, James, Rushville, Ind., Painter.
Owsley, Carl W., Thorntown, Ind., Student.
Palmes, Ira H., Rushville, Ind., Electrician.
Parker, Ralph C., 880 Broadway, Indianapolis, Ind., Student, discharged Sept. 21, 1898, for disability, by order Secretary of War.
Perkins, Greely, Rushville, Ind., Tinner.
Perkins, Jesse F., Rushville, Ind., Laborer, discharged April 21, 1899.
Phillips, Joseph, Rushville, Ind., Machinist.
Plummer, George A., Connersville, Ind., Carriage Trimmer.
Pollett, Edward, Arlington, Ind., Laborer.

Ragan, Ernest L., Connersville, Ind., Painter, discharged Sept. 27, 1898, for disability by order of Major-General Lee.
Robertson, William H., Rushville, Ind., Farmer.
Rucker, Henry V., Arlington, Ind., Farmer, transferred to Regimental Band Sept. 8, 1898.
Runk, Jacob J., Rushville, Ind., Stone Cutter.
Seibel, Henry, Hamburg, Ind., Farmer.
Shields, Robert H., Rushville, Ind., Farmer.
Smith, Chinonie R., New Salem, Laborer.
Smith, Lewis, Williston, O., Miner.
Stiers, William M., Richland, Ind., Farmer.
Stratton, Lemon M., Rushville, Ind., Timber Dealer.
Vest, Charles, Rushville, Ind., Laborer.
Wallace, Leven E., Rushville, Ind., Printer, transferred to 3rd Div. Hosp. Corps, Aug. 20, 1898, discharged Dec. 22, 1898, per order Adjutant General's office, at Josiah Simpson Gen'l Hospital.
Wells, Dudley, Indianapolis, Ind., Machinist.
Whalen, William T., Rushville, Ind., Teamster.
Wilson, Harold E., Rushville, Ind., Student.
Young, Monroe E., Richland, Ind., Farmer.

TRANSFERRED FROM 159TH IND. VOL. INF., NOV. 23, 1898.

Cassell, Don H., Private, Indianapolis, Ind., Clerk.
Dodd, Edward L., Private, Rusellville, Ill., Farmer.
Fedder, John H., Private, Bloomington, Ind., Filler.
Lee, Harry, Private, Washington, Ind., Baker.
Maher, William, Private, Washington, Ind., Hostler.
McGahan, Claude, Private, Terre Haute, Ind., Cook, discharged April 22, 1899.
Thompson, Charles K., Private, Terre Haute, Ind, Laborer.
Trimble, John W., Private, Evansville, Ind., Potter.
Talbott, Gerald, Private, Gosport, Ind., Laborer.
Vaughn, William H., Private, Vincennes, Ind., Student.
Vance, Arlyn T., Private, Irvington, Ind., Student, mustered in Dec. 22, 1898.

Westfall, Walter, Private, Iona, Ind., Farmer.
Harris, Isaac, Private, Washington, Ind., Farmer.

LATER ENLISTMENTS—AUGUST 9, 1898.

Kendall, Robert, Private, Lewis Creek, Ind., Farmer.
Bask, William, Private, New Castle, Ind., Laborer.

COMPANY L.

JAMES L. ANDERSON.

James L. Anderson, captain of Company L, was born near Selma, Clark county, Ohio, July 2, 1850. He came with his parents to Warren county, Indiana, in 1853, where he resided until 1874. He took a business course in the Commercial College at Oberlin, Ohio, and a course in the School of Pharmacy at the University of Michigan, leaving there in 1877. He engaged in school teaching for several terms after returning to Indiana, and in 1879 went into the drug business in Montgomery county, Indiana. In November, 1880, he was united in marriage to Miss Florence M. McClure, at Wingate, Indiana. They have one child, Carl R. Anderson. In 1885 he sold out and went to Frankfort, Indiana, and went on the road for a commercial firm for a year, but returned to the drug business in 1887. In 1890 he sold out his business to accept a position as traveling salesman, and in 1895 was appointed as guard at the Indiana State Prison North, where he was employed when war was declared with Spain, and resigned his position to enter the service as captain of Company L. Captain Anderson is of English descent, his father's family settling in eastern Maryland and his mother's in old Virginia, and

CAPTAIN JAMES L. ANDERSON.

though of Quaker descent had five brothers in the Union army during the war of the Rebellion, and is a distant relative of Major Anderson, of Fort Sumter fame.

ELI W. PETERSON.

First Lieutenant Eli W. Peterson was born near Decatur, Indiana, in 1873. His parents moved to Decatur while he was an infant, and as he grew up he was educated there. In 1885 he emigrated with them to Mead Center,

Kansas, residing there three years. From there he went to Colorado, returning to Decatur in 1890. He entered the regular army in 1891, receiving an honorable discharge

FIRST LIEUTENANT ELI W. PETERSON.

three years later. Again returning to Decatur, he went into the printing business, which he gave up after two years to accept a position as guard at the Indiana State Prison North, and which he resigned in order to accept his commission as lieutenant.

CHARLES E. DORITY.

Second Lieutenant Charles E. Dority was born in Waterville, New York, in 1874, removing from there to Three Oaks, Michigan, in 1889. In 1896 he removed to

SECOND LIEUTENANT, CHARLES E. DORITY.

Michigan City, Indiana, and entered the employ of Ford, Johnson & Co., wholesale furniture manufacturers, remaining with them until he enlisted.

On the trip to Jacksonville he was appointed provost marshal of the Third Battalion. His work proving satisfactory, he was at once detailed as assistant to Major Harrison, provost marshal of the Seventh Army Corps, which position he very creditably filled.

HISTORY OF COMPANY L.

Company L was organized at Michigan City, Indiana, at the beginning of hostilities between Spain and the United States. On May 1st, 1898, a meeting was held at which time the present officers were elected. Owing to its failure to be accepted on the first call many changes took place; many feeling that there would be but one call, left to join other organizations that had been accepted and had still many vacant places.

This, however, did not have a demoralizing effect as the company had many on its lists in excess of the required number. When it became apparent that the second call would be made, much enthusiasm was evinced and the organization gained many new members from all parts of Laporte county, and also a few from southern Michigan.

On June 24th word was received by Captain Anderson of the acceptance of the company and also to prepare it for service.

Immediately preparations were begun. Each member was subjected to a rigid examination which resulted in turning out a company of men who were perfect specimens of physical manhood. On July 1st the company was ordered to report at Indianapolis, which it did, leaving Michigan City, at 8 o'clock on the morning of July 2nd and arriving at Indianapolis about 2:30 o'clock of the same day. The company was taken to Camp Mount and quartered in one of the numerous buildings there. Preparations were immediately begun for the final examination and muster. While at Camp Mount a few more members were taken

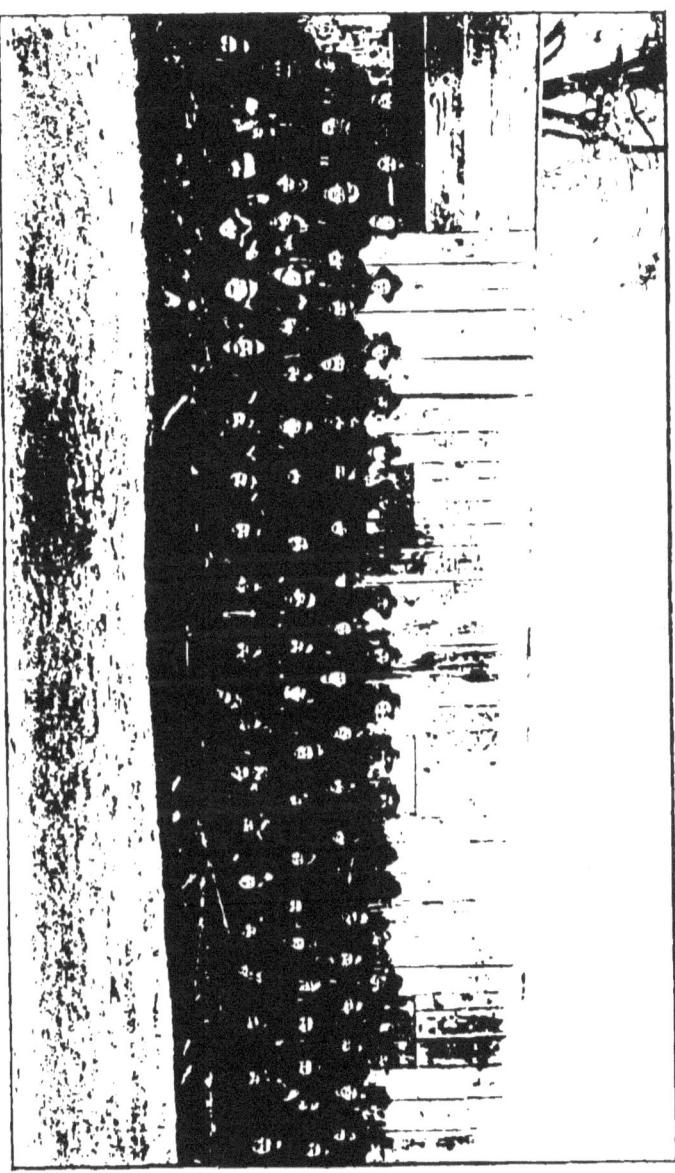

Company L.

into the company from Indianapolis and Bedford, Indiana. The final examination took place on Friday, July 8th and was followed on July 13th by being mustered into the service of the United States as full pledged soldiers.

COMPANY L ROSTER.

JAMES L. ANDERSON, Captain, Frankfort, Ind.
ELI W. PETERSON, 1st Lieutenant, Decature, Ind.
CHARLES L. DORITY, 2d Lieutenant, Michigan City, Ind.

SERGEANTS,

Cissel, Ernest W., Laporte, Ind., Printer.
Ansley, Robert, Westville, Ind., Medical Student.
Southard, William E., Michigan City, Ind., Plasterer.
Brown, Arthur R., Lebanon, Ind., Clerk.
McDonald, Joseph, Michigan City, Ind., Laborer.

CORPORALS.

Ongman, Carl, Michigan City, Ind., Carpenter.
Dilworth, Leslie, Michigan City, Ind., Laborer.
Kinnel, Howard M., Michigan City, Ind., Mechanic.
Dodds, William L., Zelina, Ind., Railroad employe.
Jackson, Henry B., Laporte, Ind., Printer, promoted from ranks Aug. 20, 1898.
Birjinski, Frank, Michigan City, Ind., Woodpolisher, promoted from ranks, Aug. 20, 1898.
Kalies, Charles T., Westville, Ind., Clerk, promoted from ranks Aug. 20, 1898.
Walton, Edward V., Wanatah, Ind., Painter, promoted from ranks Aug. 20, 1898.
Davidson, Reynolds, Michigan City, Ind., Tailor, promoted from ranks Aug. 20, 1898.
Hall, Henry M., Michigan City, Ind., Painter, promoted from ranks Aug. 20, 1898.

SERGEANTS, COMPANY L.

Simpson, Washington W., Laporte, Ind., Laborer, promoted from ranks Dec. 21, 1898.
Fiffer, Fred., New York City, Shoemaker, promoted from ranks April 10, 1899.

MUSICIANS.

Gorden, Albert, Michigan City, Ind., Laborer, appointed from ranks Aug. 1, 1898.
Thomas Edward, Brookville, Ind., Editor, transferred from 159th Ind., Nov. 28, 1898.

COOK.

Schott, John P., Buffalo, N. Y., Jeweler, enlisted as cook Dec. 6, 1898, at Savannah, Ga.

ARTIFICER.

Renfro, Lorenzo D., Three Oaks, Mich., Brickmason, appointed from ranks Aug. 27, 1898.

WAGONER.

Chronister, Benjamin F., Laporte, Ind., Farmer, enlisted as wagoner.

PRIVATES.

Akers, William H., Paoli, Ind., Laborer.
Babcock, Virgil P., Porter, Ind., Farmer.
Babcock, Daniel D., Babcock, Ind., Farmer.
Baldwin, Charles F., Michigan City, Ind., Blacksmith.
Bays, George R., Three Oaks, Mich., Laborer.
Bauman, Irvin, Michigan City, Ind., Laborer,
Bello, Antonio, Michigan City, Ind., Marble cutter.
Bottume, Gurdon, Laporte, Ind., Laborer.
Campbell, Herbert, Indianapolis, Ind., Laborer.
Closser, Paul M., Laporte, Ind., Farmer.
Cole, Frank L., Westville, Ind., Laborer.
Creider, Oliver P., Bedford, Ind., Quarryman.
Cromey, Henry A., Valparaiso, Ind., Farmer.
Cronin, Andrew, Westville, Ind., Farmer.

Corporals, Company L.

Culbertson, Sant, Westville, Ind., Printer.
Denny, William S., Michigan City, Iud., Painter.
Dreblow, Louis H., San Pierre, Ind., Painter.
Drewer, Winfred F., Laporte, Ind., Fireman.
Feistel, Gustave W., Michigan City, Ind , Cabinetmaker
Flewellen, Fred., Battle Creek, Mich., Farmer.
Gassow, Charles, Michigan City, Ind., Laborer.
Graves, Edward, Winamac, Ind., Laborer.
Harness, Jason, Stillwell, Ind., Farmer.
Harris, Allen C., Westville, Ind., Farmer.
Haskins, Ernest, Niles, Mich., Laborer.
Hawkins, George F., Westville, Ind., Farmer.
Hixon, Warren H., Westville, Ind., Farmer.
Hoff, Horace, Bedford, Ind., Mechanic.
Hopkins, William, Michigan City, Ind., Fireman.
Johnson, Edwin R., Bedford, Ind., Laborer.
Kennedy, Joseph J., Michigan City, Ind., Laborer.
Kernoodle, William, Michigan City, Ind., Laborer.
Klingler, Emanuel G., Three Oaks, Mich., Farmer.
Larson, August, Chesterton, Ind., Farmer.
Lederer, Alexander, Evansville, Ind., Dentist.
Lotridge, Henry G., Bloomington, Ind., Railroader.
Low, Henry J., Three Oaks, Mich., Laborer.
Lyons, Elza, Westville, Ind., Farmer.
Mojensky, Joseph, Michigan City, Ind., Laborer.
Mutch, Hubert, Michigan City, Ind., Laborer.
McGinnis, Robert C., Westville, Ind., Laborer.
Noakes, Willard L., Michigan City, Ind., Painter.
Osborn, Gaylord, Wanatah, Ind., Farmer.
Owens, Robert E., Bedford, Ind., Farmer.
Pace, Frank, Bedford, Ind., Engineer.
Palmateer, Wilber, Michigan City, Ind., Moulder.
Rapp, Frank H., Otis, Ind., Laborer.
Reynolds, Ray, Westville, Ind., Carpenter.
Rittenour, William L., Union Mills, Ind., Farmer.
Romepagle, Albert C., Laporte, Ind., Painter.
Shaw, Charles F., Westville, Ind., Laborer.
Sheffer, Charles E., Laporte, Ind., Laborer.

Smith, Clarence, Seafield, Ind., Farmer.
Smith, William F., Seafield, Ind., Farmer.
Swan, Benjamin, Lake Station, Ind., Plasterer.
Waggoner, George, Laporte, Ind., Laborer.
Watkins, Edward W., Crawfordsville, Ind., Laborer.
Will, Ernest, Michigan City, Ind., Barber.
Wirth, Herman T., Waterford, Ind., Laborer.
Youngblooth, Edmund, Pittsburgh, Pa., Laborer.
Zuelke, August, Michigan City, Ind., Laborer.

LATER ENLISTMENTS.

Browne, Roy W., New Castle, Ind., Drum Major, transferred from band Jan. 1, 1899.
Carter, Howard, Epsom, Ind., Student, transferred from 159th Ind., Nov. 23, 1899.
Duree, William C., Br gton, Ind., Paper hanger, transferred from 159th Ind., Nov. 23, 1898.
Murphy, George H , Evansville, Ind., Potter, transferred from 159th Ind., Nov. 23, 1898.
McClintock, Harrie C., Buffalo, N. Y., Locomotive fireman, enlisted Dec. 6, 1898, at Savannah, Ga.
Schwaner, Robert T., Evansville, Ind., Clerk, transferred from 159th Ind., Nov. 28, 1898.
Willis, William G., Terre Haute, Ind., Paper Hanger, enlisted Dec. 10, 1898, at Savannah, Ga.

DISCHARGED FOR DISABILITY AND OTHER CAUSES.

Bloomhuff, John L., Union Mills, Ind., Carpenter, Aug. 22, 1898.
Bonadore, Martin, Three Oaks, Mich., Farmer, January 3, 1899.
Bowen, George, Stillwell, Ind., Farmer, March 20, 1899.
Clark, Guy O., Union Mills, Ind., Tinner, March 10, 1899.
Durbin, Sheldon M., Michigan City, Ind., Laborer, Nov. 21, 1898.
Faris, William A., Fariston, Ky., Quarryman, Jan. 30, 1899.
Felio, James E., Michigan City, Ind., Sailor, Nov. 3, 1898.
Hamilton, Leroy, Westville, Ind., Laborer, April 4, 1899.

Hittle, Benjamin F., Indianapolis, Ind., Decorator, Dec. 22, 1898.
Hunt, James E., Rolling Prairie, Ind., Farmer, March 6, 1899.
Lettan, Edward C., Michigan City, Ind., Laborer, Feb. 14, 1899.
Long, William, Hobbyville, Ind., Quarryman, March 25, 1899.
Maddox, John A., Bedford, Ind., Stonemason, Jan. 30, 1899.
Massengill, James, Bedford, Ind., Laborer, Jan. 25, 1899.
McMillan, George W., Union Mills, Ind., Farmer, March 6, 1899.
Parkhurst, Curtis, Hamilton, Mich., Farmer, Feb. 27, 1899.
Robe, Daniel, Galien, Mich., Laborer, Jan. 31, 1899.
Spitzmesser, Nicholas B., Greensburg, Ind., Bookkeeper, Sept. 23, 1898.
Young, Jacob W., Bedford, Ind., Quarryman, Jan. 13, 1899.

TRANSFERRED.

Leland, Charles M., Serg't, Michigan City, Ind., Painter, to Regimental band as band sergeant Jan. 9, 1899.
Johanm, Frank, Corp., Union Center, Ind., Farmer, to Hospital Corps, Aug. 23, 1898.
Jones, John G. B., Laporte, Ind., Student, to Hospital Corps, Aug. 23, 1898.
Meissner, August, Laporte, Ind., Druggist, to Regimental Band, Aug. 23, 1898.
Paxton, George, Jr., Michigan City, Ind., Clerk, to Regimental Band, Aug. 23, 1898.
Reinhart, Walter W., Laporte, Ind., Laborer, to Regimental Band, Aug. 23, 1898.

DIED

Leiter, Charles E., Gilboa, Ohio, Blacksmith, Oct. 17, 1898, in hospital at Jacksonville, Fla.

DESERTED.

Jones, William D., Three Oaks, Mich., Laborer, Oct. 16, 1898, at Jacksonville, Fla.

MEDICAL DEPARTMENT

Major Wickliff Smith.

WICKLIFF SMITH

Major Wickliff Smith is a self-made man; the fine reputation he has sustained as a physician and surgeon has been acquired by the greatest perseverance, under most adverse circumstances. He was born November 24, 1851, in Marion county, among the hills of West Virginia. His parents were well-to-do farmers and the young man began life's struggle with the grain of his makeup straightened and tempered by that training so peculiar to such environment. His early education was received in the country schools and later, in Jefferson College, Waynesburg, Pennsylvania. After his literary course he returned once more to the farm and here in the midst of his work spent his spare time in the study of medicine. His father's estate had been lost during the war, sickness laid hold upon them and the young man was facing the future with an extra heavy burden to bear. He succeeded in entering the Cincinnati Medical College in 1871, graduating three years later. After a very brief practice in Calida, Ohio, he went to Delphi, Indiana, where he has since resided, with a practice that has steadily grown until the demand upon his time was greater than he could meet. He is held in high esteem by the people of his place, and considered an authority in medical science the state over. To his careful attention to details of camp cleanliness and other sanitary conditions is due much of the healthfulness which has attended the regiment in which he served as surgeon. No man was more popular in the regiment than Major Smith, and his brave deportment in the threatened smallpox plague gained for him the admiration of every soldier that knew him. He will return to Delphi when mustered out.

MILLARD F. GERRISH.

First Lieutenant and Assistant Surgeon Millard F. Gerrish was born at Paris, Jennings county, Indiana, February 27, 1856. His father was a surgeon in the Sixty-

First Lieutenant Millard F. Gerrish.

seventh Indiana during the Civil war. After finishing his preparatory studies, he entered the medical department of the University of Pennsylvania, where he graduated in and began the practice of his profession.

He sacrificed a large practice to enter the volunteer service, and was commissioned first lieutenant and assistant surgeon, in June. Twice during the absence of the major-surgeon, October 5–15, he became acting surgeon in charge, and was found at all times faithful to his important commission, and to his untiring service must be credited much of the excellent health of his regiment.

Lieutanents Gerrish and Wilson were appointed as medical examiners for the Fourth Virginia and Forty-ninth Iowa, on occasion of their preperation for muster out.

JAMES WILSON.

James Wilson, first lieutenant and assistant surgeon, was born at Wabash, Indiana, in 1865, November 15. He was educated in Greencastle, Indiana, at DePauw University, after which he entered the University of Michigan, at Ann Arbor, from which institution he graduated in 1888. He repaired at once to New York city and entered Belleview Medical College, graduation from medical course in 1890. His professional studies being finished he engaged in practice of medicine in the city of his birth. Upon the second call for troops, he offered himself to the governor for service in the One Hundred and Sixty-first Indiana Volunteer Infantry, and was mustered in as assistant surgeon with the rank of first lieutenant in June. On August 26, he was detached from regiment and placed in charge of one of the wards of the Third Division hospital, at Jacksonville, from which position he was reluctantly released on October 24, to rejoin his regiment, which was then starting for Savannah, Georgia.

FIRST LIEUTENANT JAMES WILSON.

HISTORY OF THE MEDICAL DEPARTMENT.

This department of the One Hundred and Sixty-first Indiana as organized in the beginning consisted of Surgeon-Major Wickliff Smith, of Delphi, Assistant Surgeon Lieutenants Millard F. Gerrish, of Seymour, and James Wilson, of Wabash, all eminent physicians of the state who were selected by the governor on account of their high professional standing, and Hospital Stewards William H. Rathert, druggist and medical student of Indianapolis; Jas. G. Espey, druggist and medical student of Rising Sun, Indiana, and John I. Lewis, recent graduate physician of Bedford. A regiment could hardly have had a better equipment of men in the medical department. When the regiment was first mustered in at the state fair grounds it was thought unnecessary to organize a field hospital for the large healthy men then in camp and all cases were treated at their quarters for the first few weeks. But the surgeons had not much more than gotten through with their duties of finishing the mustering papers when they found a sick call of sufficient magnitude to preclude much idleness on their part and on the 6th of August a hospital was started in the upper story of the administration building. The quarters were very pleasant, being commodious and airy. Private Horace Lucas, of Company A, an experienced nurse, and Doctor Jones, then a private of Company H, were detailed to nurse and prepare the diet. Some cots, an old cook stove, tables and some other useful articles, property of the state militia, were pressed into service, and these, with some cooking utensils purchased out of a fund placed at our disposal by Colonel Durbin and Major Smith, made up our first equipments. Out of this same fund a few delicacies and a daily supply of milk were purchased, but when once started the good ladies of Indianapolis made donations of good things to eat and bed linen that had the regiment remained at this camp very much longer the hospital would have had a stock of provisions sufficient to supply a dozen such institutions.

Three patients were received on the afternoon of the 6th. Other cases soon followed until the records would show from ten to fifteen in the hospital each day. The morning reports would show about an average of forty or fifty answering sick call. This did not include many who were taking medicine for minor causes and not going on the sick book. The sickness was due principally to malarial infection, being fever, diarrhea, etc., predisposed by the changes always incident to camp life.

While camp life was new to the men, they failed to realize to any great extent that it was necessary to exercise some precautions in the care of their health; that a few mild chills in Indiana might be the cause for protracted malarial fever in the tropical country, or that a disordered stomach predisposed to a prolonged attack of camp diarrhoea. Thus it was that when we left Camp Mount, although considered a healthy regiment, the men really had not the physical stamina they had when they came into camp six weeks before. On breaking camp about half of the patients in the hospital were furloughed home, the balance taken along, as they were so desirous of staying with the regiment, that it was almost impossible to refuse to take them. Just before starting the first discharge in the regiment was granted to Corporal William Gilbert on the ground of disability. Not being of strong constitution, the six weeks of camp life had been too rough for him and the surgeons decided he was unfitted for further military service. On arrival at Panama Park, Florida, on the bright Sunday morning of August 14th, only three men were willing to be admitted to the hospital, the others being so benefited and buoyed up by the trip and changes manifest everywhere about them that, although some had fever, they were desirous of keeping out of the hospital. Each case had received close attention during the trip, there being a surgeon aboard each section of the train. When the regiment first went into camp here it was the order from corps headquarters to have a regimental hospital to hold the patients for not longer than three days to determine the gravity of the ailment, after which the patient was to be sent to the division hospital or returned to quarters as the seriousness of the case would indicate. This was not a very practical rule, to say the least, and was not followed closely by any of the regiments in the corps, possibly on account of the lack of the facilities at the division hospital at the time for the care of the sick. As for our own regiment, Major Smith insisted that he preferred keeping the sick under the direct observation of himself and the assistant surgeons. However, a close supervision was kept of the cases and any one that bid fair to be protracted for a length of time was transferred to the Division hospital.

According to general order No. 58, of the war department, a limited number of enlisted men of the volunteer service were given an opportunity to be transferred to the hospital corps of the United States Army. The Third Division hospital at the time of arrival of the regiment at Panama Park had just been started, and the demands on the accommodations of the same by reason of a heavy per cent. of sickness in some of the other regiments, made it necessary for us to furnish our quota of men to act as nurses within a few days after our arrival. At their own request the following men were transferred: Company A, Horace Lucas, Jean Crandall, Andrew Larson, S. Byerly, Harry C. Kimball; Company B, Burle Turner and Edward Walter; Company D, Wesley Dall, Michael Logan, Marcus Renfrow; Company E, John Griffith, Jesse Dunhan; Company F, Granville Williams, William Prifogle, Sylvester Wright; Company G, J. Morris Leech, John Dolan, William T. Engel, Alonzo Allen; Company H, Leven Wallace, Clarence Heaton; Company I, Jacob W. Dexter, Franklin G. Scott; Company K, John Romain, James Keith, Harry McCoy, Fred Rowell; Company L, J. G. B. Jones, T.

Johanna; Company M, John Cox, Ernest Bales. These men when transferred would draw the increased pay of $21.60 per month. Lucas was soon made acting steward. Walters and Griffith were immediately detailed back to the regiment, Walters as orderly to Major Smith, and Griffith as hostler, which positions they held until exchanged, April 30, 1899. Not many good things can be said of the hospital at Camp Cuba Libre, nor are many pleasant memories stored away by those connected with it during the long dreadful siege of malaria that followed. The first hospital was erected on the second day after arrival, and consisted of a tent, 14 x 16, furnished with two bales of hay for beds, and for four weeks of rainy weather was without a floor, due (is it to be presumed) to the scarcity of lumber in that region of pine forests? No provisions were made for feeding the sick, other than from their regular rations, which had already become repulsive to their weak stomachs. Milk was hard to get in that barren country, as well as ice, another very desirable article for the sick; but it was not long until the Red Cross Society came to our assistance with ice each day. A short time afterward the society presented the hospital with a large chest, which proved very useful. Getting the floor seemed to be a good starter, for in a few days Colonel Durbin ordered a lot of matresses dropped at the door; the hay was discarded and the patients put on real beds. Eighteen cots were next secured from the medical supply house. About this time a nice lot of bed linens, night shirts and towels were received from the ladies of Monticello, Indiana, and also jellies, canned fruit and fruit juices were received from the Woman's Relief Corps, of Indianapolis, which had been collected from different parts throughout the state. Soon after a very large box, containing new sheets, feather pillows, pillow cases and towels, was sent direct from the

Pettis Dry Goods Company, of Indianapolis, by these same Woman's Relief Corps ladies. These articles and the foods were doubly appreciated, on account of coming in a time when so sorely needed. The culinary department also began to receive some attention. A stove was found and a few dishes and the mess and food chest, drawn from the medical supply depot, fitted up a very respectable kitchen. On the 14th of September, Louis C. Benica was detailed as cook, and remained with the kitchen as long as the hospital existed. For the first ten days after our arrival at Camp Cuba Libre the sick call was somewhat lighter than at Camp Mount, but the frequent showers and hot sun soon got in their work, and the line that filed up to the dispensary behind the sergeant in charge each morning became a little longer. The happy, enthusiastic boys of a fortnight before were becoming a listless and forlorn-looking crowd, their systems loaded down with malarial poison. It would be impossible for pen to describe the suffering these men passed through in getting acclimated to the sunny south.

On September 4th the regiment was shocked by the first death, that of Earnest R. Pullman, of Company A, who dove off of a railroad trestle into the shallow water of Trout Creek striking his head on the bottom. After being rescued by his comrades and brought to camp it was found that he had broken his spine just below the shoulders. He lived only thirty hours after receiving the injury. Steward Lewis was admitted to the hospital the latter part of August with a temperature of 103°. It was thought his illness was only temporary, but in a few days complications arose and he was sent to the division hospital, where it was hoped that better care and food would cause him to rally but he failed to improve and died the 8th of September. His loss was deeply regretted by his host of friends in the regiment and those at home. Dr. George B. Jones was chosen steward in his place. Just about this time Steward Espey was taken sick and Geo. W. Twomey, of Company E, a medical student, was detailed to the hospital, where he remained until the regiment landed in Cuba. In September Ralph H. Kenner, of Company H, was detailed as drug clerk and with the exception of nine days that he was sick you would have found him at his post day and night. Kenner was a most faithful clerk and was kept very busy filling, while at Cuba Libre, two and three hundred prescriptions per day. Not all the boys had implicit faith in the remedies prescribed, partly perhaps because the drugs did not have the same effect they would have had under different surroundings and in another climate, consequently quite an amount of malarial specific was disposed of in a way not intended by the prescriber. In one instance pills and powders enough to fill a quart cup were found under the bunk of a young man who had been furloughed home. He had been answering sick call for quite a while and had disposed of his medicine in this way instead of swallowing it.

In the latter part of September, the service of a lady nurse, Miss Mollie Ward, was secured, which was a great advantage to the hospital and an improved appearance was most apparent after a few days in care of Miss Ward. She was a sister of Lieutenant Ward, of Company I, and a graduate of the Chicago Training School. About this time a new bath house was built and it was at this time that an effort was being put forth to secure the allowance of sixty cents per day granted by the government to each patient in the hospital. This was not secured, however, until a month later and the hospital had to depend on money secured from friends for means to pay the laundry bills and buy milk for the patients, there being ten gallons used daily. On October 1st, Hospital Steward Espey started for his home in Indiana, more dead than alive, where after a lingering illness he recovered, but applied for his discharge, which was granted without returning to the regiment. On October 18th, Major Smith was taken sick and removed to

JAMES G. ESPEY.

a hotel in Jacksonville, and three days later started for his home in Indiana on a thirty days' sick leave. Lieutenant Gerrish was now placed in charge of the medical department and Lieutenant Wilson, who had been detailed to the Third Division hospital, was returned to the regiment. It had required a detail of two men from the regiment all the time as nurses and although inexperienced these men were always faithful and did their duty as best they could; they received no extra pay but they will be most gratefully remembered by those who were recipients of their kindness. Those who were regularly detailed and remained for a length of time were: Marshall D. Dickey, Company F; Charles Best, Company I; Samuel J. Weaver, Company F, at Jacksonville, Savannah and in Cuba; John Myers, Company E; John W. Wilson, Company G; Charles Nash,

Company G; Henry Spencer, Company M. On the night of October 1st, began a rain which ended in a wind storm lasting all next day that will always be remembered. The hospital was only saved by being tied down and even as it was the bedding got soaked and a large quantity of the drugs destroyed. After this storm jaundice seemed to increase and the men began to look more like a race of Mongolians than Americans.

Up to this time only one death had occurred in the regimental hospital, Fred Shrœder, of Company A, who died very suddenly on October 14 of a hemorrhage of the bowels during an attack of typhoid fever. On October 22 the patients remaining in the regimental hospital, some fifty or sixty in number, were removed to the Third Division hospital preparatory to our leaving for Savannah the next day. Some of these poor fellows never lived to join the regiment. Others were furloughed home and granted discharges. Few came back. Sixty-four was the highest number in the regimental hospital at one time, and when the regiment left for Savannah there was hardly a person who had not suffered from some form of malaria. On October 16 a large wooden building that would accommodate fifty or more patients was completed and ready for use. This came too late to be of much service.

SAVANNAH.

The camp at Savannah was quite a contrast to the one we had just left and the hospital was very poorly patronized. Some thirty cases of measles broke out, but these were sent to the division hospital, and deaths occurred as follows: William G. Weaver, Company I, fever; Joseph F. Turner, Company I, measles. Just before leaving for Cuba the following privates from the hospital corps, United States Army, were transferred to this regiment for duty at regimental hospital: Morris F. Leech, Jacob W. Dexter, Franklin Scott and John Cox, who were among those originally transferred from this regiment to United States hospital corps. These having had six months experience in the division hospital, and the hospital funds now being granted made the hospital able to take care of the sick much better than ever before.

CUBA.

When we arrived in Cuba there was but one ambulance load of sick. These were mostly measles and all able to sit up. The eight-mile march to Marianao, although hot and dusty, had no bad effect on the men, but rather served as a means of relief after having been penned up on board the transport for four days. After shifting the tents around from place to place for a few days, a location was at last found on a nice grassy spot about one, quarter of a mile from the regiment. The nurses had just gotten rid of all the cases of measles and were preparing to have an easy time when a worse woe overtook them. A case of smallpox broke out in the hospital, December 27, Fred Imes, of Company I, being the patient. None of the corps had ever had this disease and none were foolhardy enough to run into it; but since it was their duty to take care of this case, and having been already exposed, no one even intimated that he was unwilling to do his duty. The hospital was immediately put under quarantine. It was necessary for some one to take the patient to an isolated tent, two hundred yards away, and live there the life of a hermit until the case terminated. Franklin Scott, a personal friend of Imes, volunteered to go and nurse him, as brave an act as a soldier ever did. The Imes case not being a bad one, he was back in his company at the end of nine weeks. The next two cases were Jacob Dexter, of

THE MEDICAL OFFICERS AND HELPERS.

Company I,' a night nurse, and Andrew Graham, of Company D, who was just convalescing from measles when Imes was brought in. Dexter took on the hemorrhagic form and died in less than a week. Graham, on whom the eruption appeared almost solid, lived a week longer.

Every thing was favorable to good health as could be anywhere, and, aside from the sore arms, not many men were excused from duty. A pleasant northeaster almost incessantly blowing across the isle. To the hospital corps and attaches the time is one long to be remembered. To Major Smith they are indebted for many pleasures that the hospital corps of other regiments did not have. It was due to his kindness that they were permitted to have an ambulance to go to the sea-shore twice a week as well as to take an occasional trip to the surrounding country. Marshall Dickey, of Company " F," was the third case to be admitted. His proved to be a mild attack of veriloid, however, and he soon recovered. He was then utilized to assist in nursing the others. John Werner, of Company "A," who had the small-pox some years before, volunteered his services as nurse also, which were gladly accepted. Scott had a very severe attack of the disease; for a time his life was despaired of but he finally recovered at the end of two months. Everything that could be procured for the comfort of these patients was ordered by Major Smith, such as milk at twenty-five cents per quart, butter at fifty cents per pound, eggs at forty cents per dozen and canned delicacies regardless of cost. The major was equally as careful of his patients in every way, visiting them two or three times a day and seeing to their burial. The major had had some experience with this disease and he was very successful in preventing its spread through the regiment. Vaccination was begun immediately on the appearance of the first case, but the virus proved to be inert. Good virus was procured as soon as possible; and the whole regiment vaccinated. Some arms that were produced were a sight to behold. For some reason the vaccine and small pox seemed to be of especial virulent type. While the hospital was under quarantine Chas. Trimble, of Company " F," died at the Second Division hospital of malarial cacxia. The boy had never recovered from a long siege of malarial fever at Jacksonville and had not the constitution to withstand further hardships. The quarantine was raised and the hospital moved up by the camp on February 3rd. The hospital was in its new location but a few days when Andrew Gould, of Company M, was admitted for malarial fever; shortly symptoms of small pox began to appear and he was immediately placed in a detention tent. In two more days the disease was fully manifest and he was removed to the Second Division hospital. In ten days more we heard the sad news of his death. The loss of all these cases was felt much heavier on account of their being young men somewhat above the average in morals and intelligence. It was sad indeed to see those brave boys so full of vigor, stricken in a foreign land so far from home and loved ones. Comrades have sodded their graves with green and placed a carved stone at the head of each. And in after years when all their comrades have passed away we know that a grateful country will protect that lonely spot, hallowed by their dust and keep those graves forever green.

The day before leaving for America the patients in the regimental hospital were returned to quarters and on the next day all were able to go aboard the transport; six men who were in the division hospital were all that were left behind. On arrival at Savannah, Georgia, the hospital was broken up; all cases requiring more care than could be afforded them in quarters were sent to the military hospital in the city of Savannah. Some four or five cases were all that required removal. The cases in the Second Division hospital were brought over from Cuba just before the regiment was mustered out, all convalescent. On looking back over the eight months of hospital experience in the field, one of the striking features is the lack of the variety of diseases, the overwhelming majority of cases being due to malarial infection; few cases of typhoid fever are recorded and but one case of pneumonia, that one a complication of measles. The twenty deaths that occurred is not a great mortality but the effects of the poisonous miasma of Florida will be in greater evidence in the broken constitution of many a survivor in after years.

REGIMENTAL BAND

ERNEST S. WILLIAMS.

Mr. Ernest S. Williams, chief musician, was appointed to his position December 3, 1898. He is the son of S. E. Williams, one of the foremost musicians of the state, and was born at Fountain City, Indiana, on the 27th

ERNEST S. WILLIAMS.

day of September, 1881. He received his education in the schools of Winchester, Indiana, but at a very early age it became apparent that he was, by his natural gifts, fitted above everything else for the musical profession. At the early age of seven, under the direction of his father, he began the study of the rudiments and the practice of the cornet. Mr. Williams has had connection with the leading bands of the state, and since his appointment as chief

musician in the One Hundred and Sixty-first Indiana he has proven efficient and acceptable in every particular, bringing the band to a recognized position as one of the very best of the Seventh Army Corps. One of Mr. Williams' latest and best compositions is the "March of the One Hundred and Sixty-first," which he has just published and dedicated to the members of that regiment.

MEMBERS.

Warren, Bronson, baritone.
Byers, John, snare drum.
Braselton, E. K., solo alto.
Coffey, Albert, fourth alto.
Darnell, Charles, slide trombone.
Dumenil, Ellsworth, slide trombone.
Hammock, John, first B-flat cornet.
Harris, W. S., first clarinet.
Hoar, John, bass drum.
Hay, G. C., solo cornet.
Huffman, Ed., tenor trombone.
Jakes, David, second clarinet.
Lance, Ed., third alto.
Lunow, Martin, slide trombone.
McCloud, John, E-flat clarinet.
Meissner, A. C., E-flat bass.
Reinhart, Walter, second B-flat cornet.
Paxton, George, piccolo.
Rucker, H. V., E-flat bass.
Walker, Fred, baritone.
Williams, E. S., solo cornet.
Webb, M. S., second alto.
Leland, Charles, drum-major.
Cocker, Joe, cook.

ORGANIZATION.

Shortly after the formation of the regiment at Camp Mount, the proper steps were taken preparatory to the regimental musical organization. A careful search through the different companies brought forth several fair musicians and they at once secured instruments, some owning their own, and some using instruments rented by the officers from dealers in the city; during the remainder of the month of July and up to August 12 the boys lent their efforts toward furnishing band music for the regiment and visitors. Upon leaving Indianapolis for Jacksonville, the rented instruments were returned, and those who owned them shipped theirs home. After Mr. Beck, of Columbus, Indiana, after several other conclusions, concluded that the sand of Florida would certainly destroy his already failing eyesight, Mr. Antonio Montani, of Indianapolis, was appointed chief musician (band master) and Mr. H. M. Lord, of Mt. Vernon, Indiana, as one of the principal musicians.

Arriving at Jacksonville it was several days before a new set of band instruments was received, and when they did arrive they were of a very inferior grade; however some progress was made under Mr. Montani's direction.

The Second Mississippi Regiment had been furnished by their state with a fine set of Boston musical instruments, valued at three thousand five hundred dollars, and prior to leaving for home on September 12, the instruments had been turned to account with the government, and late in the night of September 11, Major Megrew returned from a conference with Chief Quartermaster Pond bearing an order for the Second Mississippi instruments to be turned over to the quartermaster of the One Hundred and Sixty-first Indiana, and on the morning of the 12th they were in the possession of the One Hundred and Sixty-first Regimental Band.

About this time Mr. Montani's health began to fail, and on this account, and also on account of sickness in the band, no progress was made, although the organization was sufficient for the needs at this time.

On October 21st, the regiment was ordered to Savannah, and after arrival there Mr. Montani secured his discharge. The position of director fell to Principal Musician Harry M. Lord, and under him the band took a fresh start and accomplished much. Mr. Lord was taken sick two weeks later, however, and was sent to the division hospital. At this juncture it was evident the One Hundred and Sixty-first Indiana would go to Cuba, and Captain Stott started for Indiana, the result being that several good musicians were secured. Mr. E. S. Williams, of Winchester, solo cornetist, being appointed chief musician, and Frederick Walker, from Shelbyville, as principal musician; much needed music was secured and the band made great strides. Arriving in Cuba, Mr. G. A. Hay, cornetist, was appointed principal musician to succeed Mr. Lord, who had been furloughed and discharged. Although handicapped by some sickness the band never lost a member. They withstood the climate of Cuba admirably, and returned to Savannah March 29, 1899, with the regiment. The band was scheduled for one concert each week at division headquarters, the majority of which were given. Several concerts were played at St. James Park in Jacksonville, and one at the Windsor hotel; two were given at the De Sota in Savannah, and one at General Lee's residence in Marianao, Cuba. Music was also furnished for the One Hundred and Sixty-first reception at Marianao on the evening of March the 20th, besides several concerts furnished after the return of the regiment to America. As a band this ranked second to none in the Seventh Army Corps. All are as proud of their record as the men are of the record of the regiment during the Spanish-American war.

BUGLE AND DRUM CORPS.

The organization of the Bugle Corps was effected early in the history of the regiment and was made by the selection of two men from each company, but until sufficient practice enabled them to sound a call that could be recognized for what it was meant, John Strauss, of Company M, did the bugle work for the regiment, and was thereafter chief bugler, under whose directions the men became quite proficient in their art, and many a time when "Dutch," of Torrey's calvary, would startle the stillness of the night with his fine expression of Retreat, the response that went back from camp the One Hundred and Sixty-first was like it.

The drum corps came into existence just before going to Cuba, and have aided materially in the department of music to which they belong, especially in the morning, "Can't get 'em up."

There have been changes in both these bodies, but at mustering-out time they were composed as follows:

BUGLE CORPS.

Company A, Parley Miller.
Company B, Otto Ware.
Company C, Will Mickelson and Wiley Moore.
Company D, Charles W. Brownscome and John E. Harper.
Company E, Percy Jones.
Company F, Will G. Ford and George Muye.

BUGLE AND DRUM CORPS.

Company G, Henry Vandyke and Edward Beeson.
Company H, John Fedder and B. Middleton.
Company I, Charles E. Conner and William E. Comer.
Company K, Horace Israel and Alexander Clarke.
Company L, A. E. Gordon and A. E. Thomas.
Company M, Charles L. Kelsey.

DRUMMERS.

Company A, William Fortune.
Company B, George W. Cravens.
Company D, John K. Prather.
Company E, Edward White.
Company F, Fred. B. Stanley.
Company G, Eugene Taylor.
Company I, Walter Simons.
Company K, William Fuller.

ROLL OF HONOR

ROLL OF HONOR.

This is the saddest part of the writer's task, to chronicle the death of his comrades, who came out with glad enthusiasm for the cause they espoused and with patriotic devotion to the flag they loved. With a heart for any fate they made the great sacrifice and laid down their lives for the flag they had sworn to defend; not on the battle field, in the midst of the smoke and flame and leaden hail, falling by some comrade's side—that had been better; but in the miasmic atmosphere of the army hospital, with fevered cheek and glistening eye they tossed upon their cot, dragging the long days and weary hours through, hoping still, till touched by the silence of death. They all died bravely, uncomplaining, as soldiers ought to die. Those who paid the great price on native soil were sent home for burial. In many cases escorts from their companies went to the city and gathered round the flag-draped coffin in which their comrade lay and after a brief service by the chaplain the remains were escorted to the depot for shipment. Those who died on foreign soil are resting to-day beneath the palms of Cuba. There are four of them whose graves are No.'s 16, 17, 19, and 26 in that soldier row that lies just up from Playa's coast.

On Friday, March 12, 1899, Lieutenant-Colonel Backus and the chaplain with a detail of men from the companies to which these dead comrades belonged sodded the graves and placed at their heads l rge blocks of limestone, each containing a marble slab upon which is chiseled the name and other appropriate facts concerning the departed soldier. These stones were prepared at the instance of Colonel Durbin by Antonio Bello, of Company L, a practical worker in marble, and are of such a substantial character as to last as

long as time, if not disturbed, and thus our comrades are sleeping in their silent graves of glory where their devotion to the stars and stripes has laid them to rest. No. 16 is Jacob W. Dexter's grave, the first of the three low stones on your left if you look at them from the foot of the graves; the next No. 17, is Charles Trimble's, and No. 19, nearest to the high stone is Alonzo M. Graham's, while No. 26 is seen to the extreme right being the grave of Andrew Gould. We knew when we left that destiny with its silent tread would touch perhaps the threshold of many a heart to bid it prepare for the unseen world. These comrades of ours, brave and strong on that day, were the ones to hear the call and when the hour was ready they made the sacrifice that placed their names on the Honor Roll and made for themselves a glory as undying as the memory of a grateful people. Whether they are resting to-day side by side with dear ones in the Holy fields at home where loving hands have laid them away or whether their sleeping forms sanctify the red soil of that land they went to save, their companionship and their sacrifice will be an evergreen spot in the memory of us all. "Under the sod and the dew waiting the judgment day;" they did their duty; we honor them for it and leave the rest with God.

ERNEST R. PUHLMAN.

Private Ernest R. Puhlman, Company A, was born in Berlin, Germany, in 1877. The first death in the regiment occurred by accident; Ernest R. Puhlman with some of his comrades were bathing in Trout creek September 3; Puhlman, misjudging the water's depth, dove from a railroad trestle and striking bottom dislocated his third spinal vertebra; he was unconscious up to the moment of his death,

ERNEST R. PUHLMAN.

and died at 6:30 P. M., September 4, 1898, in the Third Division hospital, Camp Cuba Libre.

JOHN J. LEWIS.

Hospital Steward John J. Lewis was born near Mitchell, Lawrence county, Indiana, May 2, 1878. He received his early education in Germany, and his medical training in the medical department of the University of Indianapolis, graduating with honor March 27, 1898. He was appointed chief hospital steward of the One Hundred and Sixty-first Indiana Volunteer Infantry upon the unanimous recommendation of his college faculty. He discharged all his duties faithfully and acceptably; he was courteous and reserved, and especially kind to his associates. His illness began about September 1, and was not thought to be serious; patient in suffering, he always replied, "I'm all

JOHN J. LEWIS.

right," but his illness suddenly became serious, and heart failure ensued, from which he died at 9:40 P. M. on Thursday, September 8, 1898, in the Third Division hospital at Camp Cuba Libre.

CLARENCE D. KUNS, COMPANY I.

Private Clarence D. Kuns, Company I, was born at Dayton, Ohio, in 1874; died of typhoid at 12:30 A. M.,

CLARENCE D. KUNS, COMPANY I.

September 24, 1898, at Camp Cuba Libre; buried at Brookston, Indiana.

* ROBERT ANGLETON, COMPANY E.

Private Robert Angleton was born at Jeffersonville, Indiana, in 1878, and died October 11, 1898, of typhoid fever at the same place while on a sick furlough.

* JOHN A. SEBREE, COMPANY D.

Private John A. Sebree, age 22, died of typhoid fever October 14, 1898, at Camp Cuba Libre; he was born in Ghent, New York, to which place his remains were shipped for burial.

WALLACE D. STIVERS, COMPANY I.

Corporal Wallace D. Stivers, age 21, died of typhoid fever October 14, 1898, at Camp Cuba Libre; his remains were sent to Rensselaer for burial.

WALLACE D. STIVERS, COMPANY I.

* FRED SHROEDER.

Private Fred Schroeder, age 22, died in the regimental hospital, at Camp Cuba Libre, of typhoid fever, October 14, 1898; buried at Hammond, Indiana.

* CHARLES E. LEITER, COMPANY L.

Private Charles E. Leiter, age 28, died of typhoid fever October 17, 1898, at Camp Cuba Libre. He was born at Gilboa, Ohio, to which place the remains were sent.

HENRY STILLE, COMPANY M.

Private Henry Stille, born in July, 1878, at New Point, Indiana, died of typhoid fever October 17, 1898, at Camp Cuba Libre.

HENRY STILLE, COMPANY M.

GEORGE KEPPERLING, COMPANY I.

GEORGE KEPPERLING, COMPANY I.

Private George Kepperling, age 21, died of typhoid fever October 23, 1898, at Chalmers, Indiana, where he was at that time on sick furlough.

DENVER BROWN, COMPANY F.

Private Denver Brown, age 30, the color bearer, died of typhoid fever October 23, 1898, at Camp Cuba Libre.

DENVER BROWN, COMPANY F.

He was born in West Manchester, Ohio, at which place the remains were buried.

* CLYDE C. GABLE, COMPANY H.

Private Clyde C. Gable, age 21, died of typhoid fever at Fort McPherson, November 3, 1898.

* FRANK M. GREEN, COMPANY D.

Private Frank M. Green, age 24, died of typhoid fever November 3, 1898, in the Third Division hospital at Camp Cuba Libre, after the regiment had left for Savannah. His remains were sent to North Vernon, Indiana.

WILLIAM G. WEAVER, COMPANY I.

Private William G. Weaver, age 31, died of typhoid fever at Camp Onward, Savannah, November 7, 1898. He

WILLIAM G. WEAVER, COMPANY I.

was born near Monticello, Indiana, and was buried in the cemetery near his home, Chaplain Biederwolf, who was at that time home, having charge of the funeral services.

JOSEPH F. TURNER, COMPANY I.

Private Joseph F. Turner, age 25, died of pneumonia November 30, 1898, at Camp Onward. His remains were interred at Wheatfield, Indiana.

JOSEPH F. TURNER, COMPANY I.
(TAKEN THREE DAYS BEFORE DEATH.)

JACOB W. DEXTER, COMPANY I.

Private Jacob W. Dexter, age twenty-two, enlisted at Monticello, June 28, 1898. He was transferred to the hospital corps August 20, 1898, and by testimony of the chief surgeon was one of the most obedient and best nurses in the corps. Exposed to the smallpox while on duty, he stood at his post and cared for his comrades until the dread disease fastened upon him, and he died on January 17. He was buried in the United States military cemetery, side by side with his dead comrades. His grave is No. 16.

ONE HUNDRED AND SIXTY-FIRST INDIANA. 447

JACOB W. DEXTER, COMPANY I.

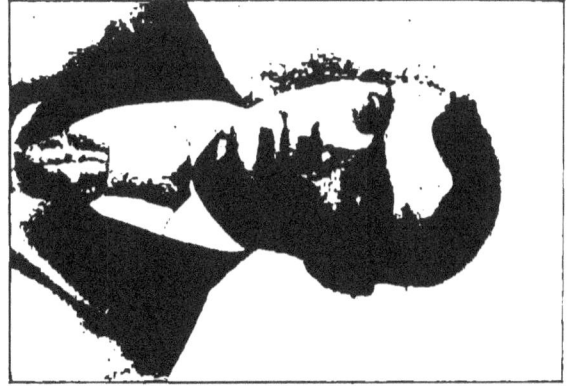

CHARLES EVERSON, COMPANY K.

448 HISTORY OF THE

CHARLES EVERSON, COMPANY K.

Private Charles Everson, age twenty-nine, died of typhoid fever December 2, 1898, at Camp Onward, and his remains were sent to his home at Columbus, Indiana.

CHARLES TRIMBLE, COMPANY F.

Private Charles Trimble, age nineteen, died of typhoid fever at Camp Columbia, Cuba, January 18, 1899, and was

CHARLES TRIMBLE, COMPANY F.

buried in the United States military cemetery, near Playa de Marianao, Cuba. His grave is No. 17.

ALONZO M. GRAHAM, COMPANY D.

Private Alonzo M. Graham, age twenty-six, born at Lancaster, Indiana, and died of smallpox January 24, 1899,

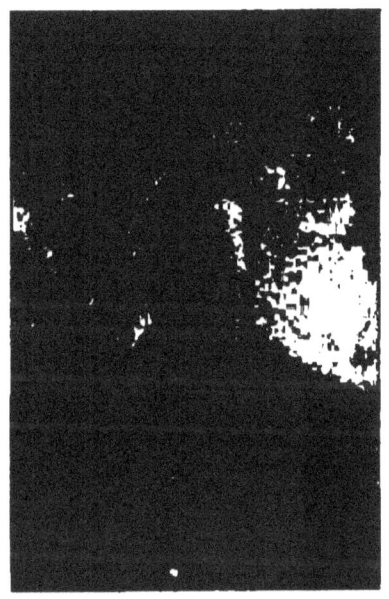

ALONZO M. GRAHAM, COMPANY D.

at Camp Columbia. His grave is No. 19 in the United States military cemetery, near Playa de Marianao.

ANDREW GOULD, COMPANY M.

Private Andrew Gould, born at Lawrenceburg, Indiana, and died of smallpox February 17, 1899, at Camp Columbia, Cuba. His grave is No. 26 in the United States military cemetery, near Playa de Marianao.

ANDREW GOULD, COMPANY M.

* Photographs not obtainable.

www.ingramcontent.com/pod-product-compliance
Lightning Source LLC
Chambersburg PA
CBHW022143300426
44115CB00006B/325